Environment, Economy, and Christian Ethics

Environment, Economy, and Christian Ethics

Alternative Views on Christians and Markets

Alistair Young

Fortress Press
Minneapolis

ENVIRONMENT, ECONOMY, AND CHRISTIAN ETHICS

Alternative Views on Christians and Markets

Cover image: © Thinkstock: Sea Waves/CPD-Labs/iStock/Thinkstock

Cover design: Alisha Lofgren

Library of Congress Cataloging-in-Publication Data

Print ISBN: 978-1-4514-7964-5

eBook ISBN: 978-1-4514-9418-1

The paper used in this publication meets the minimum requirements of American National Standard for Information Sciences — Permanence of Paper for Printed Library Materials, ANSI Z329.48-1984.

Manufactured in the U.S.A.

This book was produced using PressBooks.com, and PDF rendering was done by PrinceXML.

Contents

Acknowledgements

I was fortunate in my first academic post. I was taken on as a research assistant at the University of Glasgow to work on a plan for the recreational and touristic development of Lochlomondside, an area of Scotland renowned for its great natural beauty. I was fortunate not least to work under Dr Derek Nicholls, a most patient and helpful supervisor, to whom I shall always be grateful. That early experience started me thinking about the relationship between economics and the environment, which has continued to interest me ever since. Subsequently, I benefitted from the opportunity to develop my ideas on the subject when teaching postgraduates at the Centre for Environment and Waste Management in what is now the University of the West of Scotland, and also when tutoring for the Open University.

My interest in the implications for economic policy of the Christian faith is also of long standing. I was helped in my reflections on this through an association in the 1980s and 1990s with the Scottish Churches Industrial Mission. In particular, I benefited greatly from discussions with the Industrial Mission Director, the Rev. Dr. Hugh Ormiston, and with others in the Forth Valley Area.

It is only fair to add that none of my contacts in any of the organizations mentioned above will necessarily be in sympathy with the views expressed in this book, and some will almost certainly disagree with a number of them.

I am grateful to Will Bergkamp, of Fortress Press, for his willingness to proceed with this project, and also to his colleagues; in particular, Michael Gibson, the Theology Acquisitions editor, and Lisa Gruenisen, the Development Editor, who have seen it through with exemplary helpfulness and patience.

Finally, I am deeply indebted to the Rev. Evie Young for more than four decades of unfailing support and encouragement.

1

———

Introduction

The impact of human economic activity on the natural environment and what, if anything, governments should do about it have become matters of frequently bitter controversy among advocacy groups. Many Christians have joined in the controversy with enthusiasm. But they have not spoken with one voice; rather, their contributions have covered nearly the full range of ideological positions and (sometimes regrettably) debating styles.

Alternative Views on the Environment

In the United States, the diversity of opinion among Christians was clearly demonstrated by a Pew Research Center survey published in 2009.[1] The survey focused on "global warming," currently perhaps the most controversial environmental issue (though by no means the

1. Pew Research, Religion & Public Life Project, "Religious Groups' Views on Global Warming," April 16 2009, http://www.pewforum.org/2009/04/16/religious-groups-views-on-global-warming/. The sample covered 1,502 American adults.

only important one). It sought opinion on two questions. First, was there "solid evidence" that the earth had been getting warmer in recent decades? Those replying yes were asked a further question: had such warming been mostly caused by "human activity" rather than "natural patterns in the environment"? For the sample as a whole, almost half—47 percent—agreed that there had indeed been sustained global warming and that human activity was the cause. Another 18 percent thought the earth was getting warmer but natural, nonhuman environmental factors were causing the change. And only 21 percent of the total thought the earth had not been getting warmer.

These figures were almost identical to those for the subsample of white mainline Protestants. But other groups split very differently. Among those with no Christian affiliation, as many as 58 percent thought that human activity was causing global warming. By contrast, only 34 percent of white evangelical Protestants believed this, while as many as 31 percent of them denied that the earth was warming at all.

Differences in opinion among Christians about the human impact on the environment are compounded by differences over what is to be done about it. Clearly, those who do not think there is an environmental crisis do not consider that any significant action needs to be taken. But among those who agree that the word *crisis* is not too strong, there are still differences about appropriate policies.

The purpose of this book is threefold. It will examine the evidential basis for the different positions taken by Christians on the problems of the environment, not simply on the global warming question but on a range of other important issues. I hope this exercise will be helpful to those whose minds are not already made up. There will also be an examination of the policy alternatives offered by those of different theological persuasions. Here we will be considering in particular the *economic* implications of recommendations based on theological arguments. In part, the object of this examination will be to clarify the relative costs or advantages of implementing the policies arising from the different approaches. At the same time, the exercise will allow us to pursue a third objective: to see how far the value judgments underlying the developing discipline of *ecological economics* are in harmony or conflict with those of some theologians. Christians do not only differ about the environment; they also differ about economics. Some of those who are most convinced about the need to protect the environment from the depredations of modern industry are also most hostile to the use of economic analysis to help us do this.

Chapter 2, then, examines the main alternative positions taken up by Christian writers and activists who have considered the question of the human impact on the environment. At the opposite extreme from conservative evangelicals are more radical theologians, including some who blame Christianity itself for environmental damage. Some ecofeminist theologians attribute this damage to the patriarchal attitudes they claim underpin all three Abrahamic faiths. Other theologians focus on the instrumentalist view of nature characteristic of Western Christianity, in particular, and passed on to the more secular industrial civilization that emerged first in the West. Both these groups are highly critical of economists, whom they see as apologists for the system of market capitalism within which industrialization developed.

Alternative Views on the Economy

When theologians criticize the economics profession for its attitude toward environmental issues, they have not always fully appreciated the range of attitudes on the environment to be found among economists themselves. Chapter 3 tries to describe the basic model of the relationship between economy and environment, in as nontechnical a manner as possible, and to clarify the ethical questions underlying the analysis.

Neoliberal or Neoclassical Economics?

In their reluctance to countenance economic intervention by government, conservative commentators espouse, consciously or otherwise, a neoliberal model of the economy, which argues for a minimalist role for the state. Those who attack this model sometimes confuse it with the neoclassical economic model, perhaps lumping them both together in the portmanteau category "market economics" (or, as some prefer, "discredited market economics"). True, neoclassicists use the same analytical methods as neoliberals to study the operations of free markets, but they give more emphasis to the various causes of market failure. The branch of the subject known as "neoclassical welfare economics" contains a well-elaborated theory of how governments should intervene to correct market failure in the interests of economic efficiency. Among the failures the theory considers, and to which it offers policy solutions, are those that involve environmental pollution. Neoliberals, of course, are aware of these arguments but counter them by claiming either that the problems have been greatly exaggerated or that the failures of the market have to be compared with the failures of governments, whose actions, they believe, may very well make matters worse rather than better.

The neoclassical model serves as a very convenient starting point from which to develop a framework for environmental policy analysis. It is therefore presented briefly at the beginning of chapter 3, in which we turn to economists' views of the problem of environmental pollution in a market economy. To summarize the argument even more briefly here, for the neoclassical economist the key environmental problem is not the malign influence of patriarchal religion, nor the rapid growth of global industrialization through the application of science and technology to business, nor the expansion of the rule of the market. On the contrary, the problem is the limitations of the market's domain—more precisely, the absence of well-defined property rights in certain important environmental resources. Because of this, businesses can treat these scarce resources as if they were free. By so doing, they unload costs on the rest of society that the individual business itself does not have to pay; these are known as "external costs" in the jargon of economists.

Environmental or Ecological Economics?

Although the techniques of neoclassical environmental economics can take us a long way from the more complacent neoliberal approach, some economists feel that it does not always go far enough. To these economists, the interaction between the economy and the environment (or better, perhaps, "ecosystem") should be central to economists' concerns, rather than an optional extra as it is often presented in standard textbooks or university courses. They also want to see more integration of politics and ethics in the economic analysis of environmental (and other) issues. In chapter 3 we also consider how far the concerns of these ecological economists overlap with those of the theologians and ethicists whose arguments are reviewed in chapter 2.

As we shall see, economists have been trained in a tradition which emphasizes that individual preferences are to count in social decision making. They also tend to use the language of utilitarianism in defining social objectives. Theologians, even those from a Protestant tradition, worry about the emphasis on individualism rather than community, and they are often suspicious of utilitarianism. For their part, ecological economists do not neglect the importance of individual preferences but do stress the interaction between individual preferences and community norms in decision making, and they try to take altruistic behavior into account. As far as utilitarianism is concerned, ecological economics does not dispense with the concept of utility maximization. But this is not seen as the sole goal of policy, and it is hedged about with ethical constraints—not least on the distribution of utility as well as its total sum.[2] Economists of this school also stress the importance not merely of the outcomes of policy but also of the processes through which the outcomes are reached.[3]

An important difference between at least some theologians and some ecological economists concerns the linked issues of economic growth and globalization. They are linked because trade and the international transfer of technology through foreign investment have been seen by many economists as major engines of growth. To orthodox mainstream economists, economic growth is seen as desirable because it rescues people from poverty; globalization is on balance a positive factor because it allows the benefits of growth to be diffused around the world. By contrast, as was noted earlier, the global spread of market capitalism has been identified by some theologians and other antiglobalization activists as a major force in causing our environmental woes. The benefits of growth, if any, are considered to be outweighed not only by the laying waste of forests, damage to wetlands, and pollution of the oceans but also

2. Michael Common and Sigrid Stagl, *Ecological Economics: An Introduction* (Cambridge: Cambridge University Press, 2005), 11.
3. For a summary of the differences between neoclassical welfare economics and ecological economics, see John Gowdy and Jon D. Erickson, "The Approach of Ecological Economics," *Cambridge Journal of Economics* 29, no. 2 (2005): 207–22.

by the destruction of traditional ways of life, the creation of huge unsanitary slums around urban centers, and the transformation of subsistence farmers living (supposedly) in harmony with nature into sweated labor engaged in alienating and exploitative work in unsafe and unhealthy factories. Similarly, trade and foreign investment may be seen principally as ways of extracting natural resources from poor countries for the benefit of shareholders in rich countries and their corrupt accomplices in the governments of the poor ones.

Ecological economists, like other economists, have a range of views but are perhaps most likely to be found in an intermediate position between those who take a positive view of economic growth and globalization and those of more pessimistic inclination. As economists, they are aware of the beneficial impact of economic growth in increasing life expectancy, reducing malnutrition, and expanding educational and other opportunities. But their ecological concerns lead them to doubt that current rates of global resource consumption are in fact sustainable. So while they want to see growth for those countries still in serious poverty, they are eager to call a halt to further growth for those already industrialized.[4] And they are skeptical of the usefulness of traditional measures of economic growth, such as changes in gross domestic product.

On the question of globalization, ecological economists would certainly be concerned about the effects of trade intensification and hence international transportation on the environment, as well as about the destruction, through overexploitation, of the world's natural resources and fragile environments. Yet they would acknowledge that trade and technology transfer can help lift nations out of poverty as long as the gains from trade are fairly distributed, and they would urge the adoption, by the institutions that manage

---

4. Common and Stagl, *Ecological Economics*, 194.

international economic relations, of rules for sustainable trade and clean technology transfer.[5]

What about the hostility expressed by some theologians toward what they consider the *commodification* of the environment—the buying and selling of environmental assets? Ecological economists, too, are concerned with setting appropriate boundaries for the territory over which the market is to hold sway. But this does not mean they would necessarily agree with theologians about where to erect the fences. True, for reasons that will be explained in later chapters, it is not always feasible to create marketable property rights in environmental goods. However, where it is feasible, it could be a potentially useful instrument for reducing harmful emissions, and it would be a pity if policymakers were denied the use of it. The suggestion that the sale of permits to pollute is equivalent to the medieval practice of selling indulgences obscures more than it clarifies, and is arguably a category error.[6]

All these issues are addressed in chapter 3. But to grasp fully the practical significance of the ideological distinctions being made, the different approaches must be applied to actual environmental problems. This is the task of chapters 4 through 6 of this book. Finally, chapter 7 explores some implications for Christian environmental activism.

---

5. Ibid., 468–71.
6. This issue will be considered at length in chapter 6.

2

Alternative Discourses

Beginners in the study of economics are often introduced to a list of questions all societies must answer. These might include some or all of the following: What should we produce with our scarce resources? How should these goods be produced—using which methods of production, or "technologies"? Where should these goods be produced—in which locations within a particular country and in which regions of the world? Who benefits from the outcomes of these economic processes—that is, how should the output be distributed among members of society? Soon the novices come to understand that there is another, overarching question: Who says? Who has the power to decide such matters?

The ways in which societies answer these questions have a profound influence on the environment: on the local and global ecosystems that ultimately support life. The theologians and ethicists whose views we shall be considering in this chapter are all concerned, to varying degrees, with the impact of modern economic systems on the environment. They see environmental damage as arising from the ways in which these systems try to solve the problems listed above: the what, how, where, for whom, and who says questions. But they differ in the ways in which they arrive at their particular environmental concerns. Furthermore, they often explore the ideological roots of the economic choices made.

In this chapter we will be considering a range of theological commentary on environmental topics. Although the range is wide, the scope of this review is limited in two ways. First, the views to be considered all reflect the Western Christian tradition in a broad sense. That is to say, their authors include some who have reacted against Christianity in favor of neo-paganism, or who have come to see spiritual significance in nature without reference to a divinity; others who are comfortably within the broad sweep of mainstream Christian orthodoxy; and others again who claim a Bible-based evangelical faith. The second limitation is that the review is not intended to cover all issues raised by environmental theology but only those aspects that relate to economic analysis or policy.

In the first part of this chapter, I will try to classify the different views in terms of the particular economic issues on which each writer or group focuses and the environmental implications that follow. In this process I hope to present the material in ways the authors themselves would recognize as an accurate summary of their own ideas. In the later part of the chapter, I shall briefly outline my disagreements with at least some of the views and indicate my own position on these issues. Much of the remainder of the book will be taken up defending this position in depth.

A Spectrum of Viewpoints and Critiques

A useful starting point for any discussion of these different viewpoints is an influential article, "The Historical Roots of our Ecologic Crisis," published in 1967 by Lynn White Jr., to which many of the contending parties refer, either in support of White's views or in criticism of them.

Lynn White's Critique of Christian Attitudes to Nature

In this article, published in *Science*, Lynn White accuses the authors of the biblical creation account of fostering an anthropocentric and exploitative attitude to nature.[1] This account, of course, has traditionally been accepted (often literally, but at least metaphorically) by Jews, Christians, and (with amendments) Muslims; White, however, stresses its influence as mediated in particular through Western Christianity, and he considers that this influence has continued to be powerful even among those who would regard themselves as nonbelievers.[2]

White is not making these criticisms from an atheistic or anti–Christian perspective; in an aside, he describes himself as a "churchman," albeit a "troubled" one, and he concludes by recommending St. Francis of Assisi as a "patron saint for ecologists."[3] His target is the particular belief, which he ascribes to mainstream Christians, that nonhuman nature exists only for the sake of humans.

White argues that Christianity has inherited two ideas from Judaism that are of crucial importance in the ecological context. First, there is a linear and progressive view of history, which is seen as moving toward an ultimate goal. By contrast, other ancient societies, whether in European classical antiquity or in China or India, had

1. Lynn White Jr., "The Historical Roots of Our Ecologic Crisis," *Science* 155 (March 10, 1967): 1203–7. This article was reprinted in *The Care of Creation: Focusing Concern and Action*, ed. R. J. Berry (Downers Grove, IL: Inter-Varsity Press, 2000), 31–42. The page references that follow are to the latter source.
2. "Especially in its Western form, Christianity is the most anthropocentric religion the world has seen." Ibid., 38.
3. Ibid., 40, 42.

generally taken a cyclical, less teleological view of history. Second, there is the role assigned to humankind in the Genesis story (or stories) of creation.

According to Genesis, God created humans in God's own image and gave them "dominion" over the nonhuman world. Paganism attributed guardian spirits both to other animals and to groves of trees, sacred rivers, and mountains. These beliefs protected nature from overexploitation. But in Judaism, and subsequently in Christianity, respect for the sacredness of natural creation was seen as idolatrous. There was no longer any religious inhibition that might prevent the development of science and technology so as to use natural resources on a huge scale. And the further belief in linear progress encouraged such exploitation. From these arguments, White claims, it follows that "we shall continue to have a worsening ecologic crisis until we reject the Christian axiom that nature has no reason for existence save to serve man."[4]

In terms of our classificatory criteria, White focuses particularly on the interaction of ideology and technology. Thus, an ideology that denies the sacredness of nature allows us to apply science to determine the most efficient ways to derive output from natural inputs, with little concern for the ecological impact.

A common response to White's criticisms, particularly though not exclusively from evangelical commentators, has been to claim that the Genesis story allocates to humans the role of careful steward, rather than crass exploiter, of creation. This argument too has been questioned, as we shall see later. But many others have accepted the main thrust of White's argument while developing it in various ways.

White's theory appears to be based on a particular direction of causation from ideas to behavior: "What people do about their ecology depends on what they think about themselves in relation to

4. Ibid., 42.

things around them."[5] But this, while no doubt true as far as it goes, begs a fundamental question: how do people come to think what they think? An influential answer, emphasized by but not confined to Marxists, is that what people think about themselves depends on the material conditions of their lives and the social relationships that flow from these conditions. On this view, those who dominate the economic system also dominate the belief system: "The ideas of the ruling class are in every epoch the ruling ideas."[6]

This perspective on economic power and its implications for ideology is apparent in a number of the other approaches to religion and our relations with the environment, to which we now turn.

The Ecofeminist Critique

Ecofeminists are very much concerned with issues of power and ideology. Ecofeminism includes a wide range of theological opinion, from relatively orthodox Christianity to pantheism and neo-pagan spirituality. Here, as noted earlier, I shall focus only on ecofeminist views on the relationship of economy and environment. Even with this limitation, these views are diverse, touching on many of the economic issues listed at the beginning of this chapter. While many contributors have a common desire to see the remodeling of economic and social systems around matriarchal structures, others who share some ecofeminist sympathies may be prepared to pursue a more limited agenda.[7]

Since at least the 1980s, many feminist writers have been taking a strong interest in environmental issues. They would probably agree

---

5. Ibid., 37.
6. Karl Marx and Frederick Engels, *The German Ideology*, ed. and intro. C. J. Arthur (London: Lawrence and Wishart, 1974), 64.
7. Celia Deane-Drummond, *Eco-Theology* (London: Darton, Longman and Todd, 2008), 146.

with White that the mindset encouraged by the Judeo-Christian account of creation is indeed seriously implicated in crimes against the environment. But they ask where this attitude came from and whose interests it reflects. They find the answer in the general theory of patriarchy.

Patriarchal Religion and the Environment

In some feminist interpretations of theology, the Fall is seen as a "fall into patriarchy."[8] The roots of this idea lie in nineteenth-century anthropology, in particular the work of Johann Jakob Bachofen and Lewis Morgan; these ideas were subsequently taken up by Frederick Engels, Marx's collaborator, whose work served as an important source for the feminist movement of the 1970s.[9] Morgan developed a three-stage theory of social development: *savagery*, by which he meant the hunter-gatherer communities of the old stone age; *barbarism*, associated with the development of pastoralism, animal husbandry, and the cultivation of edible plants; and *civilization*, involving the creation of a permanent surplus over subsistence needs. These changes initially took place in areas especially suited to agricultural activity, such as the plains around the great rivers of China, India, and the Middle East, and occurred over a period of several thousand years between 15,000 and 10,000 B.C.E., though in

8. The phrase is used by Rosemary Radford Ruether in *Gaia and God: An Ecofeminist Theology of Earth Healing* (San Francisco: HarperCollins, 1992), ch. 6. However, she later suggests that it is "more misleading than helpful" to describe the change in social relationships associated with the spread of agriculture as a "fall" (257).

9. Johann Jakob Bachofen, *Das Mutterrecht* (Stuttgart: Verlag von Krais & Hoffman, 1861); Lewis H. Morgan, *Ancient Society, or Researches in the Lines of Human Progress from Savagery through Barbarism to Civilization* (Chicago: Charles H. Kerr, 1877); Frederick Engels, *The Origin of the Family, Private Property and the State*, 4th ed., trans. Ernest Untermann (1891; Chicago: Charles H. Kerr, 1908).

some parts of the world, of course, hunter-gatherer societies have continued to exist until modern times.

Building on Morgan's system, Engels characterized the social relations of the hunter-gatherer communities as "primitive communism," with rough equality among members of the group, whether male or female; sexual relations within the group were also thought to be nonexclusive. But during the stage of barbarism that followed, as pastoralism and cultivation developed, a change took place. Instead of gender relations based on group marriage, women became attached to a particular male. Engels suggested that this occurred when people became aware of the connection between individual acts of intercourse and subsequent pregnancy. Further, as productive assets multiplied (for example, as formerly wild herds of sheep and cattle became domesticated), questions about who was to take possession of them and how they were to be transferred from generation to generation emerged. The eventual solution was that the property would be passed down through the male line. Deprived of matrilineal right, women themselves became in effect the property of their husbands.

The institution of monogamy, with the close policing of women's sexuality, was designed to ensure that the children born in a man's family were genuinely his heirs. The consequent restrictions on women's freedom built conflict into the relationships between men and women: "The first class antagonism appearing in history coincides with the development of the antagonism of man and wife in monogamy, and the first class oppression with that of the female by the male sex."[10] To Engels and most other Marxists, patriarchal oppression, even if it is the first, is still just one aspect of the class conflict that has divided, and continues to divide, society—the

10. Engels, *Origin of the Family*, 79.

conflict, that is, between those who create the economic surplus and those who take control of it. But to many feminists, patriarchy seems not just the earliest but also the fundamental and ongoing source of social conflict and the destruction of the earth's resources, a point of particular relevance here.

The feminist critique of patriarchal theology claims that religion was at first "matriarchal," or at least "woman centered"—that is, it was devoted to the worship of a maternal Earth Goddess, to whom the Greeks subsequently gave the name "Gaia."[11] If patriarchal men have made God in their own image, it seems matriarchal women did something similar before them; the Goddess was seen as the giver and nurturer of life, just as women give birth to and care for children. This nurturing, so it is argued, did not simply apply to social relationships but extended to the relationship between human beings and the natural environment. As patriarchy took over, the dominant value system changed from one of nurturing to one of manipulation and exploitation.

Feminists point to creation myths in support of this argument. Ruether notes that the Babylonian creation myth, derived from earlier Sumerian sources, involves the overthrow of the dominant mother goddess, Tiamat, by the male Ea; Ea's son Marduk subsequently slays Tiamat and constructs the cosmos from her dead body while fashioning humans from the blood of her (subordinate male) consort. Ruether interprets this myth as reflecting a move not only from matriarchy to patriarchy but also from "reproductive" to "artisan" models of creation, which in turn she takes as implying "a deeper confidence in the appropriation of 'matter' by the new ruling class." Since in the myth humans are created to be slaves to the gods,

11. The name was applied by James Lovelock to his controversial views on the self-regulation of earth systems: see James Lovelock, *Gaia: A New Look at Life on Earth* (Oxford: Oxford University Press, 1979).

it also mirrors the hierarchical distribution of power in the growing city-states of the Middle East.[12]

Turning to the Hebrew creation myth, feminists would agree with White that it stresses, and appears to justify, man's domination over other creatures. But they are particularly interested in the version of the creation story in Genesis 2 and 3 in which Eve is created from Adam's spare rib; the implication of inferiority is reinforced when Adam is assigned to rule over Eve because of her role in tempting him to eat the forbidden fruit. The Old Testament creation story thus implies a hierarchy: God, the angels, man, woman, animals, vegetable life, and inanimate matter.

Christianity, of course, is not simply an offshoot of Judaism; its development included a (sometimes uneasy) attempt to link Athens with Jerusalem in a synthesis of Greek philosophy with Jewish ideas about God's action in history. Ruether argues that the Hellenistic strand has been influenced by the dualistic cosmology found in Plato, particularly in the *Timaeus* and the *Phaedrus*, which sees the time-bound and mutable material world as an imperfect manifestation of the eternal and changeless world of ideas.[13] True, by insisting on the doctrine of the incarnation orthodox Christianity could never go as far as Gnostic versions of the gospel in rejecting the material world. Nevertheless, the antimaterialist strand in Christianity has arguably encouraged a downplaying of the importance of the nonhuman created world and a suspicious and even confrontational attitude to its attractions; it is often seen as something to be subdued rather than accepted on its own terms. Feminists consider the fault line in Western culture, and in Christianity in particular, to lie not between the human and the nonhuman but rather within the human category: between men who are identified with "reason and spirit" and women

12. Ruether, *Gaia and God*, 16–19.
13. Ibid., 122–24.

who are identified "with the body and with nature" and hence liable to subjugation.[14]

"Patriarchal Science" and the Environment

For some ecofeminists, though not all, the dualism inherent in patriarchy and its downgrading of both women and nature casts doubt on the validity of the modern scientific approach.

The criticisms made of Western science by feminist authors such as Vandana Shiva, Evelyn Fox Keller, Carolyn Merchant, and Sandra Harding are wide-ranging.[15] As it developed from the seventeenth century onward, modern science, they allege, was produced "almost entirely by white middle-class males" bent on dominating "nature" as men dominated women.[16] Early scientists, in describing their relationship with nature, used the metaphors of torture (to compel nature to give up "her" secrets) and of rape (forcing her to yield to exploitation).[17] For all its claims to universality and objectivity, such science has from its foundation been "western, bourgeois and masculine."[18]

Shiva's analysis is particularly interesting in this context. Unlike some postmodern critics of Western science, Shiva cannot be faulted for attacking from a position of ignorance; she has an undergraduate

---

14. Sallie McFague, *The Body of God: An Ecological Theology* (Minneapolis: Fortress Press, 1993), 14–15.
15. Vandana Shiva, *Staying Alive: Women, Ecology and Development* (London: Zed, 1989); Evelyn Fox Keller, *Reflections on Gender and Science* (New Haven: Yale University Press, 1985); Carolyn Merchant, *The Death of Nature: Women, Ecology and the Scientific Revolution* (San Francisco: Harper and Row, 1980); Sandra Harding, *The Science Question in Feminism* (Ithaca, NY: Cornell University Press, 1986); Harding, "Why Physics Is a Bad Model for Physics," in *The End of Science? Attack and Defense*, ed. Richard Q. Elvee (Lanham, MD: University Press of America, 1992).
16. Keller, *Reflections*, 7.
17. Examples of this use of language are given in Shiva, *Staying Alive*, 16–18.
18. Harding, *The Science Question*, 8.

degree in physics, and her PhD was on the foundations of quantum mechanics. Her particular target is what she calls "maldevelopment": the application of modern science and technology to force the pace of change in traditional societies. In so doing, Shiva claims, scientists and technologists have neglected the expertise of women in these societies and "excluded ecological and holistic ways of knowing,"[19] instead destroying traditional cultures and perpetuating the subjugation of women, by violence when necessary. Thus, science stands condemned as "reductionist and mechanistic." It reduces knowledge to what can be discovered by its own narrow methods, and these methods themselves treat nature as a machine that can be taken apart and studied piece by piece in controlled laboratory experiments rather than as an organic and living system that must be studied as a whole.

It is easy, of course, to find examples of ecological disasters caused by attempts to exploit nature using modern science and driven by the profit motive: every major oil spill, exploding chemical plant, or devastated forest habitat could be listed on a lengthening charge sheet. But the feminist critics of science make a more fundamental allegation. Shiva explicitly dismisses the notion that the fault lies not with science per se but with the misuse of its findings.[20] In her view, it is the reductionist scientific method itself, deeply rooted in the violence of patriarchy and serving the interests of bourgeois commerce and industry, that by its neglect of feminine and holistic ways of knowing has led to ecological crisis.

19. Shiva, *Staying Alive*, 14–15.
20. Ibid., 26ff.

Alternatives to Patriarchy

So what sort of social and economic changes would ecofeminists like to bring about, and how would these affect the environmental problem? The answers depend on the particular version of ecofeminism.

The more radical authors have seen the environmental crisis as so deeply rooted in male psychology that only a very drastic reduction of the male role can put matters right. In 1982, Sally Miller Gearhart produced a manifesto titled "The Future—If There Is One—Is Female" in which she proposed, as an essential part of any solution to the environmental problem, not only that the dominant culture should become female but that "the proportion of men must be reduced to and maintained at approximately ten per cent of the human race." This suggestion won the support of Mary Daly, one of the best-known radical feminist theologians; Daly expected some such reduction to be brought about through the "decontamination" of the earth as the outcome of an evolutionary process.[21]

Other feminists have taken a more inclusive view of men's role, even if this role is not to be a dominant one. Heide Goettner-Abendroth, organizer of two world congresses on matriarchal studies, envisages rebuilding society on principles developed from the women-centered societies depicted in "mother goddess" literature.[22] Whereas prehistoric matriarchal clans were based on kinship

---

21. Daly supports the suggestion in Susan Bridle, "No Man's Land: An Interview with Mary Daly," *Enlightenment*, Fall–Winter 1999, http://www.scribd.com/doc/6146237/No-Mans-Land-Mary-Daly-Susan-Bridle. Daly's own critique of patriarchal culture is to be found in *Gyn/ecology* (Boston: Beacon, 1978).

22. Heide Goettner-Abendroth, "Modern Matriarchal Studies: Definitions, Scope and Topicality," trans. Jutta Ried and Karen P. Smith, Societies of Peace, 2nd World Congress on Matriarchal Studies, http://www.second-congress-matriarchal-studies.com/goettnerabendroth.html. The use of the term *matriarchy* to describe a system that is in fact intended to be strongly democratic has been queried by other feminists on the grounds that it suggests "rule by women" as a mirror image of patriarchy's "rule by men"; this, however, is far from the intention of those who use the term.

relations, those of the future will be based on "affinity groups" of people who are "siblings by choice," brought together by shared spiritual attitudes. Decisions will be made by consensus, which Goettner-Abendroth describes as "the genuine democratic principle." While men will be "fully integrated" in these societies, women will "guide the economy" (as they allegedly did in the matriarchal societies of ancient times).

So how would such a society resolve the basic economic problems listed at the beginning of this chapter? What sort of goods would be produced, by what methods, where, and for whose benefit? These societies would turn their backs on large-scale industry, with all its adverse environmental effects, in favor of self-sufficient, small-scale, local or at most regional economic communities. The emphasis on self-sufficiency necessarily implies that trade over a distance would be much more limited than in the present global world order. Although the communities would not necessarily be engaged solely in agriculture, this sector would make a relatively more significant contribution to output and employment than in industrial societies at present.

The preference for small-scale and egalitarian forms of economic organization, and for devolution of decision-making power to local levels, is common among ecofeminists and indeed many other ecotheologians, as we shall see. But this does not necessarily imply a neglect of global issues. Some feminists have seen the way forward as involving cooperation with antiglobalization and environmentalist groups; while giving due weight to feminist insights and concerns, these authors do not necessarily see the establishment of matriarchy as the ultimate goal.

Ruether argues vigorously for "integrating ecofeminism, globalization and world religions," in the words of the title of her 2005 book.[23] In her final chapter, she instances social movements such as the Zapatista revolt in Mexico, the anti–World Trade Organization (WTO) demonstrations that began in Seattle in 1999, and the World Social Forum (WSF) gatherings of nongovernmental organizations (NGOs); these movements, she believes, point the way forward toward an alternative world and away from "corporate globalization." They seek this through direct action against the major components of the present global system, which Ruether identifies as "transnational corporations, the Bretton Woods institutions (the IMF, World Bank, and the WTO), and the American military."[24] Among several examples of direct action, she cites the burning of genetically engineered crops in India and Brazil. The ultimate object of such social action, she believes, should be to replace the dominant power structures with "locally accountable, democratically governed, and environmentally sustainable forms of human society."[25]

Ruether recognizes that it is not enough to attack institutions without also attacking the ideologies that support them. In particular, she singles out neoliberal economics and "the ideology of messianic nationalism that dictates the vision of American world empire."[26] The second of these issues, though no doubt important, is beyond the scope of this book, but the role of neoliberal economics will be further considered in later chapters.

Meanwhile, we look at some alternative views that, while often drawing on or overlapping with feminist ideas, also bring in a broader range of cultural and economic issues.

23. Rosemary Radford Ruether, *Integrating Ecofeminism, Globalization and World Religions* (Lanham, MD: Rowman and Littlefield , 2005), ch. 4.
24. Ibid., 160.
25. Ibid., 164.
26. Ibid., 166–68.

The Deep Ecology Critique:
Anthroprocentrism versus Ecocentrism

Like the ecofeminists, deep ecologists would agree with Lynn White's criticisms of anthropocentrism, whether or not this is taken to have Judeo-Christian origins. Thus Arne Naess, who coined the term *deep ecology*, has criticized the biblical concept of stewardship as based on "the idea of superiority which underlies the thought that we exist to watch over nature like a highly respected middleman between the Creator and the Creation."[27] The deep ecology movement has perhaps carried this criticism as far as it can go.

Economists, as we saw at the beginning of the chapter, are concerned with the question of how resources are used in the interests of members of society. They take it for granted that *human* desires and preferences will determine these interests. Naess is arguing for a shift from the anthropocentric to the ecocentric. His use of the term *deep ecology* is intended to differentiate his concerns from those of "shallow" ecologists, who, while willing to "fight against pollution and resource depletion," do so in the interests of "the health and affluence of people in the developed countries" rather than in the interests of the ecosystem as a whole.[28]

Perhaps the most fundamental change in perspective for which Naess in particular has argued concerns the notion of self-realization. Naess's use of the term is to be distinguished from more popular notions of self-fulfillment, such as the idea of expressing identity through conspicuous display of the right sort of branded products. By contrast, in Naess's version, self-realization implies acceptance of the ineradicable links between the individual self, other human

27. Arne Naess, *Ecology, Community and Lifestyle: Outline of an Ecosophy*, trans. David Rothenberg (Cambridge: Cambridge University Press, 1989), 187.
28. Arne Naess, "The Shallow and the Deep, Long Range Ecology Movements," *Inquiry* 16 (1973): 95–100.

and animal selves, and inanimate nature, and it requires active engagement in the relationships implied by these links. From this perspective, "altruism becomes unnecessary. . . . [W]e must see the vital needs of ecosystems and other species as our own needs; there is thus no conflict of interest."[29]

The principles of the movement were helpfully summarized by Arne Naess and George Sessions in an eight-point platform; sympathizers were encouraged to work out their own formulations.[30] These principles included the notion that nonhuman life has *intrinsic* value, independent of its usefulness to humans; biodiversity should not be reduced "except to satisfy vital needs"; humans are interfering excessively, and increasingly, with the nonhuman world, and their own numbers need to undergo a "substantial" decrease; and, finally, major changes in economic, technological, and ideological structures are required, changes deep ecologists are obliged to attempt to bring about.

Interpreting this last requirement in terms of our classification criteria would imply very similar changes to those sought by the ecofeminists: changes in the types of goods produced, the methods used in producing them, the location of production, the distribution of the products, and the nature of economic power. Thus Naess envisages greater self-sufficiency in production and consumption (such as home-baked bread and recycling), reduction in energy use, reliance on local sourcing and local materials, and the use of "soft" technology—that is, a shift away from mass production toward craftsmanship.[31] Income differentials would be low in Naess's model, but he goes beyond many who support egalitarianism by asking for justice "not only with regard to human beings but also for animals,

---

29. The quotation here is from the introduction to Naess, *Ecology, Community and Lifestyle* by the translator David Rothenberg, 9–10.
30. The platform is reproduced and discussed in *Ecology, Community and Lifestyle*, 29–32.
31. Ibid., 92–100.

plants and landscapes."[32] Power would be devolved to local communities.[33] The main difference from the proposals of the ecofeminists is the lack of emphasis on the importance of gender relations.

Some of the arguments of the deep ecologists are of course shared with shallower ecologists. For instance, both groups insist that the ecosystem is a delicate web of complex interrelationships within and between both its animate and inanimate elements. Humans, themselves firmly embedded in the animate sector, are both arrogant and foolish if they imagine that they can either isolate themselves from the system or hope to control it. Both also contend that in attempting to manipulate nonhuman elements of the system for their own convenience, human beings have in many ways, some obvious and some more obscure, caused a great deal of damage.

Although there is a strong spiritual element in Naess's desire to achieve self-realization through identification with nature (he uses the phrase "nature mysticism" in this context), he does not explicitly adopt a theological perspective.[34] Some Christian writers who share his strong sense of the sacredness of the created world would no doubt prefer a theocentric (or, if influenced by feminists, theacentric) system of values to either an anthropocentric or an ecocentric one. Among such writers, those who are perhaps closest to the deep ecologists would include Sallie McFague, for whom the world (indeed, the entire universe) is "the body of God," and "creation spiritualists," such as Matthew Fox, who also emphasize the embodiment of the divine in the cosmos.[35] These views are seen by

---

32. Ibid., 173.
33. Ibid., 144–46.
34. Ibid., 176
35. McFague, *Body of God*; McFague, *A New Climate for Theology* (Minneapolis: Fortress Press, 2008), esp. 112–19. On "creation spiritualists," see, for example, Deane-Drummond, *Eco-Theology*, ch. 3.

more mainstream Christian theologians as uncomfortably close to pantheism, though the authors themselves deny this. Fox claims that his view is based not on pantheism (the belief that God *is* everything) but on "panentheism" (the belief that God is *in* everything and everything is in God); in similar vein, McFague argues that God is not identical with everything but rather is the *source* of everything (hence transcendent) while simultaneously being embodied in everything (hence immanent).[36]

While these writers reject a purely instrumentalist approach to creation, they do not all give the same attention to the implications of their views for social structures and economic justice; Celia Deane-Drummond criticizes the creation spiritualist school, in particular, for neglecting this.[37] Here she is not referring to McFague, who has written at some length on what she sees as the inadequacies of market capitalism and the overindividualistic approach to welfare in mainstream economics.[38] These criticisms follow from the metaphor of the body, and her argument here is reminiscent of the apostle Paul's use of the metaphor (1 Cor. 12); if each part of creation, even the humblest, contributes to the well-being of the whole, it makes no sense for that part's well-being to be neglected in the supposed interest of any other part. Whether and to what extent such criticisms of economics are justified, however, is a matter we will pursue later.

Some theologians have sought to provide a perspective that draws both on Scripture and on the created world as sources of divine guidance on environmental issues, and to such arguments we now turn.

---

36. McFague, *A New Climate*, 76–77.
37. Deane–Drummond, *Eco-Theology*, 43.
38. Deane–Drummond treats McFague as an eco-feminist writer (ibid., 150–53).

Theological Critiques of the Ills of Modernity

A prolific contributor to this line of argument is Michael Northcott, a professor of ethics at the University of Edinburgh and a priest in the Scottish Episcopal Church. Although in places he covers similar ground as both ecofeminists and deep ecologists, his arguments are more firmly rooted in the Judeo-Christian ethical tradition; Christian environmentalists made nervous by any suggestion of pantheism or by the paganism of the Mother Goddess may feel more comfortable with Northcott.

Northcott identifies those changes in social organization, technology, economy, and ideology that created "modernity" as the source of the environmental problem (among other evils). Thus his critique is eclectic and wide-ranging. It is developed in particular in three works: *The Environment and Christian Ethics* (1996), *A Moral Climate* (2007), and, most recently, *A Political Theology of Climate Change* (2014).

The earliest of these identifies four major determinants of the problem.[39] First, the development of agriculture, even in ancient times, often led to overuse of the soil and environmental degradation; the colonial expansion of Europe since early modern times, however, has intensified this and given it a global dimension. Second, and also arising in early modern Europe, is what Northcott terms the "commodification of nature"; this came about through the spread of market relationships. The activities of buying and selling, instead of being an occasional feature of life in societies where people mainly produced for their own needs, as in the past, now became the dominant purpose of production. In the process, traditional ways of relating to others, for example through the obligations of kinship

---

39. Michael S. Northcott, *The Environment and Christian Ethics* (Cambridge: Cambridge University Press, 1996), 40–85.

or neighborliness, were replaced by more exploitative ones; labor and natural resources came to be treated as commodities for sale and sources of profit. Greed, hitherto considered a vice, became the motive force driving the system and hence "one of the strongest roots" of the environmental crisis. Third, echoing the feminist critique of the alleged male urge to dominate nature, Northcott sees a further cause of crisis in the development of mechanistic models of the universe and their application to industrial technology in the name of "progress." Last, he attacks the utilitarian philosophy that dominates policymaking in industrial societies; in particular, he criticizes its alleged assertion of a strong link between happiness and consumption.

In view of Northcott's reservations about modern technology, it is not surprising that he is critical of some attempts to remedy environmental problems through further technology. In his latest work he particularly mentions the risks of proposals for "Solar Radiation Management" through the injection of sulfates into the atmosphere to reflect solar energy.[40]

Northcott's criticism of markets for encouraging the commodification of nature echoes the analysis of Marx.[41] But while Northcott agrees with Marx about the alienating effects of capitalist production, he takes issue with Marx's solution: "Marx's repair of the problem is inadequate, as its origin is in the instrumentalism of industrial making."[42]

Given his views on markets, it is not surprising that Northcott criticizes the creation of "carbon trading" markets as a means of

---

40. Michael S. Northcott, *A Political Theology of Climate Change* (London: SPCK, 2014), 92–100. However, he does not rule out all forms of geoengineering, such as the promotion of reforestation to absorb carbon dioxide from the atmosphere.

41. Michael S. Northcott, *A Moral Climate: The Ethics of Global Warming* (London: Darton, Longman and Todd, 2007), 134–50.

42. Ibid., 307n68. Marx's views will be further considered in chapter 3.

putting a price on the emission of greenhouse gases; as other writers have done, he criticizes such developments as equivalent to the medieval practice of issuing indulgences in return for money.[43] A further argument against this strategy, in his view, is that it tends to reflect and accept existing distributions of property rights without considering whether these entitlements were honestly come by.[44] Similarly, he is critical of cost-benefit analysis, a tool economists use to measure alternative social outcomes in monetary terms (see chapter 5, below).[45]

Although much of his attack on modernity echoes the arguments of the deep ecologists, Northcott is at pains to distinguish his position from theirs and from some of his fellow ecotheologians, such as Teilhard de Chardin, Matthew Fox, and Sallie McFague, whom he considers (despite their denials) as taking an overly pantheistic approach.[46] He sees natural theology as an important source of guidance.[47] The universe is not God, but it is God's created order and as such reflects the divine goodness. It follows that humans have to live in harmony with creation and treat it reverentially rather than exploitatively; Northcott links the ethical code of the Old Testament, with its strong demands for social justice and protection of the weak, with "the wisdom of natural systems."

Northcott shares the preference for natural systems over industrial systems, including the belief that the former are more in harmony with Christian principles, with other Christian writers critical of the

---

43. Northcott, *A Political Theology,* 138–39. The "indulgencies" argument will be considered in detail in chapter 6.

44. Michael S. Northcott, "Anthropogenic Climate Change, Political Liberalism and the Communion of Saints," *Studies in Christian Ethics* 24, no. 1 (2011): 42. Here he is referring to a particular approach to the issue of carbon credits known as "grandfathering." Carbon credits will be considered in chapter 6.

45. *A Moral Climate,* 143–150.

46. Northcott, *Environment and Christian Ethics,* 161.

47. Ibid., ch. 5, esp. 196–98.

modern social and economic order. Timothy Gorringe of Exeter University quotes with approval Wendell Berry's contention that the industrial economy is "firmly founded on the seven deadly sins and the breaking of all ten of the Ten Commandments."[48] Thus, in answer to the economist's question of what is to be produced, these writers would likely respond, "more agricultural and fewer industrial goods"; to the question of means, the response would be, "by traditional, labor-intensive technologies"; to the question of where, the writers would say, "in small and largely self-sufficient local communities"; and to the question of who says, the critics would explain that decisions should be taken cooperatively. Gorringe envisages a future in which, as oil runs out and global industrial systems, based on energy-intensive techniques, start to break down, a return to small-scale, low-technology production organized in local communities will become not merely ethically desirable but inevitable. He suggests that such communities could be seen as somewhat analogous to Noah's ark. As examples, he cites the Benedictine monasteries of the European Dark Ages following the collapse of Roman civilization and the modern example of the Transition Towns movement. The latter, which began in Britain in 2006, consists of local communities that seek a self-sufficient lifestyle to ensure local "resilience" in the event of problems arising from peak oil, climate change, or other threats to the functioning of modern complex economic systems. The idea has spread with surprising rapidity to other countries.[49]

48. Timothy J. Gorringe, "On Building an Ark: The Global Emergency and the Limits of Moral Exhortation," *Studies in Christian Ethics* 24, no. 1 (2011): 31. The quotation from Berry is to be found in Wendell Berry, *Sex, Economy, Freedom and Community* (New York: Pantheon, 1993), 100.
49. For background detail see Transition Network, "About Transition Network," http://www.transitionnetwork.org/about. The US network is Transition United States: see Transition United States, "The Transition Town Movement," http://transitionus.org/transition-town-movement.

Northcott, like others, identifies globalization as a major source of environmental and social ills, particularly insofar as it allows the free movement of goods and capital. He follows John Cobb and Herman Daly in arguing for "bioregionalism": the devolution of power to communities at lower levels than existing nation-states; those communities will then use that power to create more self-sufficient local economies.[50] This critique of modern industrial society has much in common with some of the feminist criticisms and also with those of the deep ecologists, although it approaches the issues from a rather different theological base. It is not surprising, then, that its remedies are so similar. However, in commenting on the Transition Towns movement in his latest work, Northcott also points out that it is not enough simply to opt out of the international order, where substantial power over resource use (or misuse) continues to rest with nation-states. He argues that groups like Transition should continue to "stimulate government and the state to recover their duties to foster national and sustainable economies rather than collude with the corporate agents of empire."[51]

Evangelical Theologies of the Environment

Both read the Bible day and night
But thou read'st black where I read white.

–William Blake, *The Everlasting Gospel*

Among evangelicals there has at least until recently been some reluctance to engage with environmental concerns; this has lately been changing, revealing a growing split within this theological

---

50. Northcott, *Environment and Christian Ethics*, 300; Herman E. Daly and John B. Cobb Jr., *For the Common Good: Redirecting the Economy towards Community, the Environment and a Sustainable Future* (London: Green Print, 1990), 269–70.
51. Northcott, *A Political Theology*, 312.

approach. For some, continuing rejection of environmentalism may simply reflect a focus on otherworldly, even apocalyptic, concerns. Motorists who carry stickers announcing that "in the event of the Rapture this car will be driverless" are unlikely to care whether the car in question is a gas-guzzler or not. More generally, however, the rejection may result from hostility to modern science, though for reasons very different from those given by some ecofeminists. Katherine Hayhoe, an evangelical who is herself a climate scientist and reviewer for the Intergovernmental Panel on Climate Change, attributes this hostility to long-standing quarrels between scientists and evangelicals over "evolution, age of the earth and stem cell research. . . . Along comes this new issue, climate change. What side are the scientists on? So it only makes sense that evangelicals have taken the other side."[52]

A second reason suggested by Hayhoe is the lack of a clear leadership structure among disparate groups of evangelicals, who in consequence have tended to accept leadership on political matters from the politicians whom they support. In recent years, evangelicals in the United States have tended to support Republicans, and most Republicans have been hostile to environmentalism, though this has not always been the case.[53]

Increasingly, however, evangelicals have begun to take an interest in environmental matters. A relatively early example in the United States was the founding of the Evangelical Environmental Network (EEN) in 1993; in 1994 the new organization published an influential document, *An Evangelical Declaration on the Care of the Environment.*[54]

---

52. Quoted in Lisa Palmer, "Preachable Moments: Evangelical Christians and Climate Change," Yale Climate Connections, June 28, 2012, http://www.yaleclimatemediaforum.org/2012/06/preachable-moments-evangelical-christians-and-climate-change/.
53. It is possible, of course, that there is two-way causation here; some Republican politicians may be responding to what they perceive as the current concerns of their constituency. It should be remembered that the Environmental Protection Agency was created in 1970 under President Nixon's Republican administration.

The EEN's website proclaims the group's biblical basis and its commitment to "creation care" to discharge the Genesis stewardship mandate. Its concerns cover a wide range of environmental issues.

The *Declaration* begins by acknowledging failure in the stewardship of creation, attributable to human sin, and specifically taking the form of seven "degradations": these are listed as "1) land degradation; 2) deforestation; 3) species extinction; 4) water degradation; 5) global toxification; 6) the alteration of atmosphere; 7) human and cultural degradation." Poverty is acknowledged as" both a cause and a consequence of environmental degradation."

While noting that some concerned environmentalists "are exploring the world's ideologies and religions in search of non-Christian spiritual resources for the healing of the earth," the authors of the *Declaration* opt for a Biblical response under four headings. The first requires confession and repentance for the abuse of creation and neglect of the stewardship mandate. Secondly, there is to be resistance to ideologies which either "presume the Gospel has nothing to do with the care of non-human creation" or, alternatively, "reduce the Gospel to nothing more than the care of that creation". Thirdly, there is commitment to seek to learn "all that the Bible tells us" about creation and human responsibilities. Finally, there is a commitment to learning from creation about God, and about its own "God-given order". While acknowledging that human beings are themselves part of creation, "embedded in the same systems...which sustain other creatures," the *Declaration* also considers that they have a "unique responsibility" for creation. Failure to discharge this stewardship role properly has led not only to environmental damage, but also to social injustice, seen as the "denial of God's created bounty" to both

---

54. The text of the declaration is reproduced in Berry, *Care of Creation*, 17–22. This source contains much useful commentary on the declaration, and on Christian environmentalism, from an evangelical perspective.

present and future generations. In the concluding section, the authors call upon their fellow Christians to reject consumerism and opt for a frugal lifestyle, while working for "godly, just and sustainable economies" which implement "responsible public policies".

The *Declaration* proved controversial in evangelical circles, and its detailed claims regarding the risks to the environment led to a debate in *World*, a Christian weekly. E. Calvin Beisner, at the time an economics lecturer at Covenant College in Tennessee, was a major critic.[55] But notwithstanding these criticisms, the environmentalist cause continued to gain ground. In the early years of this century, there was increasing debate on Christian responsibility toward the environment within the major evangelical lobby group, the National Association of Evangelicals (NAE). In 2008, Richard Cizik, the NAE vice president for governmental relations, had to leave his post, in part because of his support for the notion that humans have caused climate change. Yet the NAE itself has since published a paper on climate change and the need to take action to protect the vulnerable.[56]

Even those evangelical Christian commentators who are most critical of many of the claims of the environmental movement often now acknowledge some obligation to protect the natural world. A useful source for this perspective is the Cornwall Alliance for the Stewardship of Creation, whose national spokesperson is Calvin Beisner. As we have just seen, Dr. Beisner was critical of the EEN's position on the environment, and it is unlikely that his views had to change significantly, if at all, to allow him to accept his new post. The alliance was formed in order to implement the principles of the Cornwall Declaration on Environmental Stewardship, drawn

---

55. For details of the debate and further references, see Richard T. Wright, "The Declaration under Siege," in Berry, *Care of Creation*, 74–79.
56. Palmer, "Preachable Moments."

up in 2000 by "a coalition of scholars and religious leaders" and subsequently endorsed by "over 1500 clergy, theologians, policy experts and other people of faith."[57] Although the driving force behind this declaration appears to be conservative evangelicalism, signatories are drawn from the Jewish, Catholic, and Protestant communities ("joined by others of good will"), though it is made clear that they are signing in a personal capacity.

The Cornwall Declaration includes three sections listing the "concerns, beliefs, and aspirations" of the signatories. An overarching concern is to define the alliance's position in contradistinction to that of others who have contributed to the discussion of the environment. True, the first section includes an admission common to all environmentalists that human activity can harm both people and the nonhuman environment. This, in the view of the signatories, gives rise to the need for "stewardship." But much of the remainder of this section of the declaration consists of a list of what are described as "misconceptions about nature and science, coupled with erroneous theological and anthropological positions." In particular, these are said to include opposition to economic progress, together with a view of humans "as principally consumers and polluters rather than producers and stewards"; "romanticism" that leads some to "deify nature or oppose human dominion over creation"; and exaggerated fears about "manmade global warming, overpopulation and rampant species loss." The environmental problems the Cornwall Declaration acknowledges are principally those arising from too little rather than too much economic growth, including "inadequate sanitation, widespread use of primitive biomass fuels like wood and dung, and primitive agricultural, industrial, and commercial practices."

---

57. Cornwall Alliance: For the Stewardship of Creation, "About," http://www.cornwallalliance.org/about. The alliance was originally formed as Interfaith Stewardship Alliance.

It is clear, then, that the Cornwall Alliance takes a very different view from most of the other theologians discussed in this chapter. It is skeptical not only about global warming but also about threats to biodiversity while being strongly in favor of economic growth, modern science, and technology. Far from praising the ecological wisdom of traditional communities, it considers their environmental practices to be "primitive" and a major source of their health problems. Christian belief and practice are seen not as the cause of any ecological crisis, but as the remedy.

How would the different evangelical approaches answer the economic questions raised at the start of this chapter? As compared with other theological commentators, both tendencies within evangelicalism seem less concerned with achieving structural changes to the economic order, though this is particularly true of the supporters of the Cornwall Alliance. Since the latter group does not appear to envision major reforms in the modern industrial system, they would presumably expect much the same goods to be produced as at present, and by much the same methods. On the question of for whom the economy is designed, their linking of poverty to environmental degradation implies that the more rapid spread of capitalist institutions and enterprise, and the adoption of modern technologies, might be expected to improve the environment by lifting people out of poverty.

By contrast, as we have seen, the EEN is convinced of the reality of global threats such as climate change and species destruction, which is a major point of difference between the groups. Thus on the question of what is to be produced, the emphasis on avoiding wastefulness and greed would imply some shift away from production of consumer goods in advanced industrial economies. The *Declaration*'s call for sustainability would also suggest a switch to less energy-intensive technologies. On the question of who benefits from the economy, there is explicit mention of the need to "empower the poor," though it is not clear from the *Declaration* just what this would involve. But for some evangelicals, working with poorer communities, it has included collective action to develop local resources in a sustainable way and in accordance with a Christian stewardship ethic.[58]

On the exercise of economic power, indeed, the EEN is clearly at odds with the Cornwall Alliance. The EEN is more than willing to lobby for tighter restrictions on US business in the interests of removing pollution and limiting greenhouse emissions; it sees support for the Environmental Protection Agency and the standards it seeks to apply, as being a Christian duty. By contrast, the Cornwall Declaration aspires "to a world in which liberty as a condition of moral action is preferred over government initiated management of the environment as a means to common goals." However, the EEN, like the Cornwall Alliance, is a biblically based Christian group; it can have no truck with quasi-pantheistic or neo-pagan arguments or mother goddesses, nor can it accept White's view of the Genesis creation story. As we have seen, it too agrees with the concept of environmental stewardship, even if its interpretation of how to implement it differs from that of the Alliance.

The idea of stewardship is by no means an uncontroversial interpretation of Genesis, even among those who base their approach to ecology on the Bible. For instance, Richard Bauckham's book *Bible and Ecology* takes issue with the stewardship concept as it is often applied.[59] Bauckham makes the interesting comment that before the seventeenth century the term *stewardship* would not have been regarded as synonymous with the biblical idea of "dominion."

---

58. See Stephen Rand, "Love Your Neighbor as Yourself," in Berry, *Care of Creation*, 140–46; Susan Drake Emmerich, "The *Declaration* in Practice: Missionary Earth-Keeping," in Berry, *Care of Creation*, 147–54.

59. Richard Bauckham, *Bible and Ecology: Rediscovering the Community of Creation* (London: Darton, Longman and Todd, 2010), esp. ch. 1.

According to Bauckham, the stewardship concept was introduced by Matthew Hale and others associated with the Royal Society, established in 1660. The concept served as a corrective to the more anthropocentric view of science expressed by Bacon and his followers and was intended to imply that dominion over the rest of nature should be exercised not only for human benefit but also in the interests of nonhuman creation, which had an intrinsic value beyond its contribution to human welfare. While this might be regarded as an improvement on the Baconian concept, Bauckham nevertheless believes it is still open to criticism on the grounds that human beings are very far from achieving the understanding of complex natural processes required to exercise effective control over them. He rejects any notion of a hierarchical, "vertical," or "middleman" relationship that fails to recognize our community with other living creatures, which he sees as an important message of the Bible taken as a whole. In a commentary on the EEN's *Declaration*, he takes issue with its concluding call that we should be "faithful stewards of God's good garden"; this, he suggests, comes "still too freighted with the baggage of the modern project of technological domination of nature."[60] Instead of treating the world as a garden to be brought under control, he recommends that we respect it as a wilderness.

Economy and Environment: Is There a Consensus?

Clearly, there are important differences in the theological and ethical starting points of the groups we have been considering. Yet apart from those evangelicals who would agree with the Cornwall Declaration, most writers whose views have been outlined come to very similar conclusions about the baleful influence of economic

60. Richard Bauckham, "Stewardship and Relationship," in Berry, *Care of Creation*, 103.

activity on the environment, as we have already seen. We might say that they have weighed in the balance the answers that modern industrial societies give to the basic economic questions and have found them wanting because of their effects on the ecosphere. It may be helpful to summarize their criticisms of these answers.

What sort of goods? The critics consider the range and types of outputs produced in modern economies to be the wrong sort. Our societies create material abundance in terms of manufactured goods but at the expense of destroying "natural" goods: the beauty of the world and the diversity of plant and animal life.

By what methods? Production uses energy-intensive technologies that use up irreplaceable resources, degrade the land, pollute air and water, and threaten to destroy climate stability.

Where? Goods are produced on a global scale, which means that traditional ways of life even in formerly remote areas are disrupted. Goods, resources, and people are transported around the world, and the transportation networks thus created cause further pressures on energy resources and climate stability.

For whose benefit? The critics see the main beneficiaries as being rich rather than poor people, and rich rather than poor countries. Some foresee, however, that even the well-off will not be protected forever from looming environmental catastrophes.[61]

Who says? Most of the critics believe that large business corporations have too much power to determine what to produce, where, and by what technologies.

The widely shared (even if not universal) agreement on problems also extends to many aspects of policy. Most consider that businesses need to be subjected to tighter regulations to protect the environment. Some, however, see a difficulty here: what if the power

---

61. See, for example, Northcott, *A Political Theology*, 16.

of businesses extends to controlling the governments that are supposed to regulate them?

At this point in the argument, as perhaps in any discussion of power, ideology becomes central. For ecofeminists, the key issue is that both governments and businesses are dominated by men, who share a common belief system that encourages a hubristic and uncaring exploitation of nature. Ultimately, at least for those who hold a strong version of this view, only the rejection of patriarchal attitudes and the dismantling of the power structures that embody them can resolve the environmental problem (and, indeed, a host of other problems). Other critics share the feminist concern with exploitative attitudes to the natural world without necessarily seeing patriarchy as the sole or primary cause. They agree, though, in criticizing the human-centered, instrumentalist attitude to the use of the natural world, which, like the feminists, they relate to the development of "mechanistic and reductive" scientific approaches.

Another important ideological stance many of the critics share is a dislike of the market system that characterizes modern industrial economies. Often, behind this criticism is the suspicion that the control of markets is what gives big business much of its power and, further, that neoliberalism hinders governments from protecting the environment by intervening to regulate markets. But these are not the only reasons for criticism of the market. Even if economic power were more evenly spread, some would still consider it inappropriate to value nature in monetary terms, treating it as a commodity to be bought and sold, and basing decisions on a balancing of actual or imputed costs and benefits arising from protection or destruction of environmental "goods."

The critical attitudes to both national governments and globalized market systems, which many environmentalists share, may help to explain the preference for local, community-based decision making and for replacing reliance on globalized markets with self-sufficiency. However, it is also true that most critics do not despair of exerting a beneficial influence on environmental policy through pressure on existing national government structures.

A further policy issue on which most would agree is the need for the protection of indigenous communities and traditional ways of life. In particular, indigenous communities should have their rights both to territory and to traditional ways of life respected against the attempts of multinational companies (or, presumably, local ones) to exploit their resources for profit.

Hostility to Western science and technology makes some ecotheologians reluctant to accept that there could be technological fixes for environmental problems. To those who feel this way, using technology to solve the ecological crisis would be like trying to cast out devils through Beelzebub, the prince of devils. Similarly, while some authors acknowledge that technology has contributed to economic growth and its attendant advantages, the general tenor of the argument seems to be that growth is now causing more harm than good. Population growth, in particular, is seen by many as a major threat.

In the literature surveyed, there is also some hostility toward mainstream economics. This arises partly from suspicion of the economists' perceived enthusiasm for markets, technological innovation, and economic growth and partly because of the utilitarian and individualistic philosophical underpinnings of much economic analysis.

Finally, while acknowledging that structural social and economic change is required, many theological critics claim that only a change in both individual attitudes and individual behavior will ultimately solve the ecological problems they identify. For some, this is linked to broadening the definition of sin to incorporate offenses against nonhuman creation. In some versions, this seems to cover a high proportion of economic activity.

Appraisal

How do the views outlined in this chapter strike economists, and this economist in particular? Much of what follows in the rest of this book will be concerned with answering this question. But it will perhaps be helpful at this point to outline some significant points of agreement and disagreement on the key issues, which I take to be the following:

- How serious is the environmental problem?
- How well do the critics explain its causes?
- How adequate are the recommended policy responses?

The Extent of the Problem

On the first issue, there is no doubt in my mind that many of the environmental concerns raised in the literature reviewed in this chapter are serious and require an urgent and energetic response. In particular, it is very likely that the current rate of increase in greenhouse gas emissions, if left unchecked, will cause unacceptably rapid rises in global temperatures in the course of the present century, with adverse consequences for food security, health, and flooding of coastal regions. These emissions also contribute, through acidification, to the pollution of the oceans, for which there are of course many other sources. Atmospheric pollution, too, is a major problem for the health of both animal and plant life. Nonrenewable resources are being depleted; renewable ones are being used at unsustainable rates. There are alarming threats to biodiversity. The critics are right to be worried.

I am not completely convinced, however, that the breakdown of the modern industrial system is inevitable or that it will happen any time soon. As will be explained in chapter 4, I find some of the gloomier and more apocalyptic forecasts of disaster overstated, particularly those that rest on arguments about "peak oil" or population pressure.

The Explanation of Causes

From the point of view of the health of the natural environment, how have modern societies managed to produce the wrong sort of outcomes, using harmful technologies and distributing costs and benefits so unequally? As we have seen, the critics have offered a range of explanations in which issues of power and ideology feature prominently.

Some of the explanations could perhaps be criticized as influenced by the golden age fallacy: the nostalgic belief that "things used to be better than this." Thus, the characterization of early societies by some feminists as predominantly peace loving, egalitarian, woman centered, and environment friendly is by no means universally accepted, even among feminist academics.[62] Some argue that evidence of widespread goddess worship (such as is suggested by the ubiquity of female figurines in early Neolithic sites) does not *necessarily* imply an egalitarian or even a nonpatriarchal political system. Similarly, the preference of some feminists for traditional knowledge rather than modern science seems in danger of being carried to unreasonable lengths. It is unwise to attack scientific

62. Cynthia Eller, *The Myth of the Matriarchal Prehistory: Why an Invented Past Won't Give Women a Future* (Boston: Beacon, 2001); Ruether, *Gaia and God*, 149–55.

methods when, in practice, one must rely on them. The connection between carbon dioxide emissions and climate change is by no means obvious to common-sense observation or to women in rain forests living by the traditional wisdom of their ancestors. The significance of this connection can only be established by complex modeling using the most advanced techniques of modern scientific investigation. It is inconsistent to accept the findings of such investigation when they support the antigrowth case while rejecting *on principle* the techniques by which they are obtained. None of this implies that the *rights* of traditional communities should be ignored, and, as we will see in chapter 6, there are also many circumstances in which local communities have developed efficient mechanisms for promoting collective action that outsiders should leave well alone.

I am also not persuaded that the agricultural societies of medieval Europe were better or more wholesome places to live than modern industrial societies. Michael Northcott comments on the happiness of the medieval peasant under feudalism, drawing explicitly on G. K. Chesterton's romantic enthusiasm for the Middle Ages, but his attempt to support this perspective by citing economic historians is not entirely convincing.[63] Similarly, the Berry-Gorringe comments on the moral failings of industrial civilization, quoted earlier, are no doubt accurate, but the practice of the seven deadly sins and neglect of the Ten Commandments seem to have been no less a feature of Chaucer's time than of ours, if the *Canterbury Tales* are any guide.

One very fundamental ideological conviction common to most of the critics, following White, is that modern ways of looking at the

---

63. Northcott, Environment and Christian Ethics, 49, 336 n. 35. In support of Chesterton's "Merry Peasant" thesis, Northcott quotes a 1937 work by H. S. Bennett, Life on the English Manor (Cambridge: Cambridge University Press). This source does not seem entirely supportive of the thesis. The pages referred to by Northcott give an account of an imaginary peasant's life at what Bennett admits to be "a particularly favourable moment of the year," and are followed by the comment that "the remainder of this book will show clearly enough the difficult existence which was all that most peasants could hope for" (Bennett, Life, 25).

world take an anthropocentric and instrumentalist view of nature. Economists appear fully complicit in this approach, as we saw in the discussion of deep ecology.

However, it seems to me there is an incoherence in the deep ecology approach and in that of others who echo this kind of criticism. A key dispute is whether it makes sense to consider nonhuman entities as having intrinsic value independent of their contribution to human goals. To suggest they do not seems, indeed, to be very anthropocentric. But if we say they do, then how do we find out what that value is? Have all living things equal value? Do the Streptococcus, the rabies virus, and the mosquito have a claim to our affections equal to that of our fellow humans?

Deep ecologists urge us to replace an anthropocentric system of values with an ecocentric one. But who is to determine what these latter values are? As Naess himself has remarked, "Value statements . . . are formulated by humans in human language, not by mosquitoes in mosquito language."[64] Deep ecologists are therefore obliged to "channel" for the ecosystem, and what emerges can look uncommonly like just another anthropocentric list of preferences. Thus, the deep ecology platform emphasizes the desirability of maintaining species diversity. Many of us who are not deep ecologists would also agree that this is desirable. But can we say that this reflects anything more than a very human delight in the variety and color of the universe of which we are part, together perhaps with the no less anthropocentric view that biodiversity may be desirable to protect our food supplies against plant disease? The universe itself appears indifferent to species diversity. As William Grey has pointed out in a critique of deep ecology, nonhuman processes caused quite

64. Naess, *Ecology, Community and Lifestyle*, 176.

remarkable mass extinctions long before humanity made its appearance.[65]

So ecological values cannot avoid being human ones; even if we claim they are God's values, they still reflect what human beings take to be God's will. But any system of values intended to serve as a guide to action has to resolve a crucial problem: what do we do when desirable outcomes are in conflict? Ideally, in such cases, we need to weight different values in order to trade off outcomes against each other. Thus, in the situation mentioned in the Naess-Sessions statement of principles, we want to be able to say *how much* of a reduction in species diversity would be acceptable in return for a given increment of satisfaction of human "vital needs." Deep ecologists do not give a clear answer to this problem. Economists, as it happens, have devised mechanisms to help tackle it. But these mechanisms have not always proved acceptable to environmentalists. This is because they make use of "market" concepts; that is, they seek to impute *prices* to environmental goods or bads.

When they identify the market as a crucial part of the environmental problem, the critics are not wrong, for reasons that will be explained in detail in chapter 3. But I will argue in chapters 5 and 6 that they are too ready to dismiss the market as part of the solution, though it cannot simply be left to itself.

Policy Responses

This brings us to the third question: what actions need to be taken, and by whom, to solve the problems of the environment before it is too late? Some of the those surveyed above are clearly very critical about the role of national governments and what they see

---

65. William Grey, "Anthropocentrism and Deep Ecology," *Australasian Journal of Philosophy* 71, no. 4 (1993): 468.

as governments' bias toward economic growth and toward private business corporations as agents of growth. Nonetheless, when they turn to questions of policy, the critics often take the pragmatic view that, despite their inadequacies, governments have a role to play and should be put under pressure to perform more adequately.

Michael Northcott is one theologian who has commented perceptively on both the failures of governments to protect the environment and on how policy might be improved. In the present context, his views on the role of governments in relation to markets are particularly interesting. As we have already seen, he rejects the creation of markets for carbon emissions. In particular, he criticizes their operation in practice both under the Clean Development Mechanism set up under the Kyoto Protocol to limit emissions and also under the European Emissions Trading Scheme. In the course of his criticisms, he comments that "carbon taxes are much more efficient than markets in carbon emission offsets."[66] I believe he is correct to criticize these particular schemes because of their vulnerability to political manipulation, but not for the theological reasons concerning indulgences that he also gives. And while he may well be right to argue that carbon taxes would be more efficient, these are equally to be regarded as market incentives to reduce carbon emissions because they operate by increasing their price. These issues will be further discussed in chapter 6.

Conclusion

In the rest of the book I shall argue that economists may have a more constructive role to play in environmental policy than some theological critics have so far acknowledged. I begin in the next

66. Northcott, *A Political Theology*, 124–25.

chapter with an introductory account of what mainstream economic theory has to say about environmental issues. A fair criticism of economic theory, at least as most commonly presented in many textbooks, is that it tends to take a number of important ethical issues for granted without giving them sufficient consideration. I shall therefore endeavor to bring these out clearly both in the general survey in chapter 3 and in the more detailed applications that follow in subsequent chapters. Throughout, I shall try to relate the discussion to the concerns reviewed in the present chapter.

3

———

Economics, Ethics, and the Environment

A Beginner's Guide

In this chapter the economist's explanation of the environmental problem is set out. As with all explanatory models, certain issues are played down while others are highlighted. In the later part of this chapter, therefore, the implications of reintroducing some of these issues, in particular those relating to ethical questions, to assumptions about technology and also about human behavior, will be explored.

How the Market Works: Successes and Failures

I begin with a model to which novice economists are generally introduced at a very early stage in their studies: the circular flow. This gives a simplified picture of how resources are coordinated to create income in a system of markets. The simple picture may be complicated in a variety of ways. Since we are concerned with environmental issues, I will first complicate the model by placing the economy within the natural environment. We can then explore a question not always included in the first-year textbooks: does this picture leave out, or divert our attention from, any important issues—in particular, ethical ones?

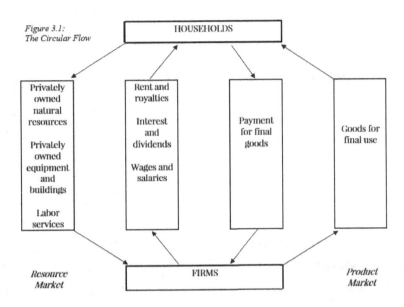

Figure 3.1:
The Circular Flow

HOUSEHOLDS

Privately owned natural resources

Privately owned equipment and buildings

Labor services

Rent and royalties

Interest and dividends

Wages and salaries

Payment for final goods

Goods for final use

Resource Market

FIRMS

Product Market

The simplest possible version of the model is presented in figure 3.1. It takes no account of the role of government or of international trade. All resources are privately owned. Only two types of economic agent are considered: households and firms. Households have two roles to play in this picture: as purchasers of goods in the product market and as suppliers of productive inputs in the resource market. The role of firms is to use the resources supplied by households to produce the goods households want to buy.

We could imagine various ways in which households could be made to supply the resources to the firms. For example, in a completely centrally planned economy the government could "conscript" the resources and direct households to deliver them to particular firms, then could requisition the goods produced by the firms and supply them to the households through a system of rationing. Something like this, in varying degrees, happened in many countries during the Second World War. But the model here, as we have noted, allows no such role to government planners. Instead, everything is done through markets, where goods and services (the outer ring of the circular flow) are exchanged for money payments (the inner ring).

In the resources market, firms offer financial incentives, such as wages for labor services or rent for the use of property, to encourage households to supply these services. In the goods market, households offer payments for the goods they want to the firms who have produced them. The households get the money for these payments from the firms to whom they have hired out their resources, and the firms in turn get the money to recompense the households from the payments received for the goods. So everything hangs together.

Note two points about the goods produced for final use. First, some firms will not produce goods sold directly to households; instead, they will produce goods to be sold to other firms further down the chain of production. Thus a farmer's grain may be sold to a miller who will sell flour to a baker who will produce bread for the households (the final consumers) who buy it. The grain and the flour are intermediate goods in this example; only the bread is a final good. Second, not all final goods are for consumption. Some take the form of factory buildings or machinery: investment goods that will add to the stock of productive resources and help increase the output of goods in the future.

Clearly, such a system can work, but does it work well? In theory (and, most orthodox economists would argue, in practice too) it has a number of advantages, two in particular. First, the market provides *information*. By bidding up prices for the goods that are most highly valued, consumers indicate the strength of demand for them; in effect, by being willing to pay more for some goods than others, consumers are "voting" for the production of these goods. But the market also provides *incentives*: as the prices of goods in high demand go up, any firm that increases production of these goods will gain higher profits; conversely, firms in industries where demand and hence price are falling will start to have losses, and some firms will move out. Thus, as the patterns of consumer demand change, prices will also change, and the flow of resources among different lines of production will adjust automatically in response.

The model thus implies the decentralization of economic *power*, which is often claimed as a key political advantage of the market system. No single politician or bureaucratic agency is responsible for deciding which goods society should produce or for whose benefit. Instead, sovereignty over the economy is vested in a multitude of individual consumers, whose willingness to pay for different products and services will influence the decisions of suppliers.

The incentive effects of the profit motive are also said to encourage economic growth. The first firm to work out how to produce a better product will be able to attract customers from rivals; the first to innovate in ways that achieve higher output levels with fewer resource inputs will be rewarded by higher profits. Competition among firms will ensure that innovations in both products and production methods will quickly be copied or improved on.

But if the market works so well, why does economic activity cause environmental problems? To see this, we need to extend the model a little. This has been done in figure 3.2, which situates the market economy within the ecosystem: the complex system of interactions among living organisms and between those organisms and the nonliving environment that supports them.[1]

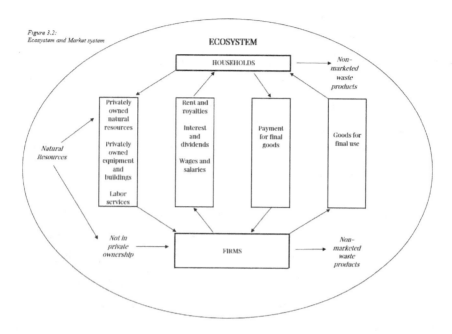

Figure 3.2:
Ecosystem and Market system

ECOSYSTEM

HOUSEHOLDS

Non-marketed waste products

Privately owned natural resources

Privately owned equipment and buildings

Labor services

Rent and royalties

Interest and dividends

Wages and salaries

Payment for final goods

Goods for final use

Natural Resources

Not in private ownership

FIRMS

Non-marketed waste products

The core of this diagram, as before, is the circular flow. But we now introduce two more things into the picture: first, the presence of natural resources (whether animate or inanimate) *not* owned by any private individual or firm and, second, the existence of waste outputs that are produced by economic activity but have negative values and are therefore dumped on the environment. Obvious examples of unowned natural resources would be fish swimming around in the open sea and the ozone layer that protects us from ultraviolet radiation. Waste released to the environment would include all sorts of environmental pollution, some from firms and some from private households: harmful gases such as those that cause acid rain and global

1. This is not the only way to show the interaction between economy and environment. Other treatments emphasize the exchange of matter and energy between the two. See, for example, Michael Common and Sigrid Stagl, *Ecological Economics: An Introduction* (Cambridge: Cambridge University Press, 2005), 2, Fig. 1.2. My own approach is intended to bring out the role of property rights in creating an environmental problem.

warming, mounds of plastic-based packaging materials, empty beer bottles, untreated sewage discharged in rivers, and so on.

Pollution appears to be a major problem for the free market economy; does it, then, constitute an argument for some form of government intervention in the market system? This was certainly the conclusion drawn by one of the first economists to study the problem systematically. In *The Economics of Welfare*, A. C. Pigou distinguished between the "private" and "social" costs and benefits arising from economic activity.[2] Consider a firm in the chemicals industry that manufactures soap. The firm has to pay for the raw materials and energy used to produce the soap, for the labor time of its workers, and for the rent of the factory premises: all these are private costs, and it will be in the interests of the firm's owners that such resources should be used carefully so as to maximize profits.

But suppose that the manufacturing process yields as a by-product a poisonous effluent; further, suppose that the cheapest way to get rid of this effluent is to dump it in a nearby river. In consequence, the stock of fish in the river may be greatly reduced, perhaps to zero, to the detriment of local fishers. This cost, known as an "externality," is external to the firm; it does not affect profits, and the firm has no incentive to take steps to minimize or avoid it.

Internalizing Externalities

If there were no external costs, such that private and social costs were identical, a policy of *private* profit maximization would also be *socially* profitable. Prices would be providing information to direct resources to their socially most desired uses and supplying incentives to persuade their owners to send them there.[3] But the presence of external costs implies that prices are giving *misleading information*

2. A. C. Pigou, *The Economics of Welfare*, 4th ed., (London: Macmillan, 1946), 134–35, 192–94.

and also creating *perverse incentives*. The price the consumer pays no longer takes full account of the true cost of producing the good because some of this cost has been unloaded on members of society who are not party to the contract between buyer and seller. In industries with substantial external costs, there is an incentive to produce more than would be socially ideal.

Pigou's solution was for government to intervene in such cases and to impose taxes on such goods at a level fixed to reflect the external cost. Thus, in our example the price paid by the consumer for a bar of soap would have to cover the additional (or, in the jargon, *marginal*) private cost incurred in order to produce that extra bar, as before, plus a tax equal to the value of the fish sacrificed to pollution.

Another economist, Ronald Coase, subsequently pointed out that such "Pigovian" taxes would not be necessary as long as property rights were created and enforced for all scarce resources.[4] In our example, if property rights in fish were assigned in law to owners of the riverbanks downstream of the factory, and if the damage to the fish stocks could be clearly demonstrated to be caused by the effluent, the riverbank owners could charge the firm for the stock's loss in value, backing this up if need be by court action.[5] This would ensure that the value of the fish would be taken into account in the decision about how much soap to produce; prices would again be performing their socially useful function.

---

3. Strictly speaking, we need to allow for external benefits as well as external costs. In the example given, this could arise if one person's consumption of soap benefited his or her neighbors, as would perhaps not be implausible.

4. Ronald H. Coase, "The Problem of Social Cost," *Journal of Law and Economics* 3 (October 1960): 1–44.

5. Coase argued that it did not matter from the viewpoint of social *efficiency* if the right to pollute the river were assigned to the soap manufacturer; in this case the riverbank owners could get together to "bribe" the soap manufacturer to cut back production. The final output of soap should be just the same, but the assignment of property rights will clearly determine the *distribution* of gains and losses—that is, who will pay for the cost of pollution.

The relative merits of these two methods of pollution control, and of others, will be examined much more fully in chapter 6. But note that neither of these methods, strictly speaking, is an *alternative* to the market system for allocating resources; each involves an attempt to repair a malfunction in the mechanism rather than to replace the system. This is most obvious in the case of the Coase solution, which in effect allows prices for pollutants to be found by negotiation with holders of property rights, backed by civil sanctions to protect these rights. But it is also true of the Pigovian solution, whereby governments tweak prices through taxation. Either way, the external costs are being made internal to the firm; once this has been done, the market can be left to allocate resources efficiently.

Public Goods and the "Prisoner's Dilemma"

In the particular case of fishing rights, the Coase solution can work quite effectively in practice.[6] In England and Wales, the Anglers' Conservation Association raises funds to enable anglers' clubs and owners of riparian rights to bring civil cases against those who are polluting rivers. Often these cases are settled out of court, and the streams are effectively protected. But such cases have some crucial features not present in many important instances of environmental pollution. There are generally a small number of clearly identifiable sources of pollution, and the complainants are easy to organize—members of a local angling club, often in conjunction with a local landowner who leases fishing rights to club members. There are clearly defined obligations under common law and legal remedies if the rights of the clubs and owners are infringed.

---

6. Roger Bate, *Saving Our Streams* (London: Institute of Economic Affairs, 2001).

Contrast this situation with another case: air pollution in major cities. A striking example of this was the Great Smog of London in 1952. From December 5 to 9, a combination of adverse weather conditions interacting with the emissions from factories and domestic chimneys meant that the city was blanketed in a very thick fog, so much that visibility was reduced to a few feet. Apart from the inconvenience, there were serious medical consequences for many Londoners, particularly those with weak chests; as many as twelve thousand people died prematurely as a result of the smog.[7]

How could we apply the Coase solution in these circumstances? The conditions that make this feasible in the fishing rights case (a single source or a small number of sources of pollution and a well-organized group of plaintiffs) are not present here. In particular, we do not have a clear division between victims and polluters; even those who suffered from the pollution were guilty of helping to cause it, through the smoke from their own chimneys. Yet it would have made no sense for them to cut their individual consumption of coal during the cold December weather since this would have had a negligible effect on the total volume of emissions and hence on their health (indeed, the loss of a heat source might well have rendered them more liable to illness).

We have here a classic case of the *public goods problem*. As we have seen, markets are well able to supply us with goods that satisfy purely private wants. A commodity like a cake has two important characteristics. First, the more I consume, the less there will be for you; we are rivals in consumption. Second, it is a simple matter to exclude either of us from having any cake at all if we are not willing to pay for it. Public goods, by contrast, are *nonrival* and *nonexcludable*.

7. M.L. Bell and D.L. Davis, "Reassessment of the Lethal London Fog of 1952: Novel Indicators of Acute and Chronic Consequences of Acute Exposure to Air Pollution," *Environmental Health Perspectives,* 109 Suppl. 3, June 2001, 389-94.

For such goods, the more there is for me, the more there will be for you, but at the same time it will be impossible to prevent either of us from benefiting from the good once it has been provided. This latter characteristic gives rise to what is called the *free rider problem*: if people can enjoy the benefits of provision without paying, why should anyone bother to pay? But if everyone is looking for a free ride, no one will in fact bear the costs of provision.

Consider the case of clean air. In big cities like London this is costly to provide. For example, the obvious way to improve air quality in the 1950s was to replace smoky coal with more expensive smokeless fuel for every fireplace or industrial location in the city. This would benefit everyone living in or visiting the city, each of whom would now have the same access to clean air. There would be no rivalry in the consumption of clean air, and no one could be excluded from breathing it, even if they had done nothing to pay the cost of the more expensive fuel. So there would be a free rider problem, as we may see with the aid of a prisoner's dilemma matrix, as in figure 3.3.

		Everyone else's strategies	
		Buy smokeless fuel	Don't buy
My strategies	Buy smokeless fuel	Second best	Worst
	Don't buy	Best	Third best

Figure 3.3 Clean Air Dilemma

This grid lays out the alternative strategies I may adopt, with the boxes showing my payoffs from each strategy; these payoffs depend on what everyone else decides to do.

I will get the best payoff if I decide *not* to buy the more expensive smokeless fuel while everyone else decides to buy it, as the bottom left box shows. This is because everyone else's decision will be enough to bring about clean air; my own continuing pollution will be too little to make a difference to the citywide outcome. This is better for me than the payoff if I join the others and change to more expensive fuel (top left), though that would still offer quite a good outcome because of the benefits in health and convenience. If none of us decide to pay for smokeless fuel, I will be left with the status quo, which is third best (bottom right). But the worst payoff of all for me will occur if I buy the smokeless fuel and no one else does (top right). I then get no benefits and incur an additional cost. For obvious reasons, this is often referred to as the "sucker's payoff."

The advantage of laying out the decision problem in matrix form is that we may at once see that the strategy "don't buy" is better for me *whatever* the others decide: If they buy smokeless, I get best rather than second best. If they don't, I get third best rather than worst. In the jargon of game theory (of which this is a famous example), "don't buy" is the *dominant strategy*.[8] The final stage of the argument is to note that everyone else will be making the same calculation as I am making; if they are behaving as rational and self-interested people, they too will decide on a strategy of "don't buy." So we remain with the status quo and have to continue suffering the air pollution, even though we would all end up with a superior outcome if each of us were to choose the apparently "inferior" strategy!

---

8. Game theory concerns the study of strategic behavior in a huge variety of situations, including war, marriage, politics, and economics. The prisoner's dilemma game is generally thought to have been developed in 1950 by Merrill Flood and Melvin Dresher, who were working on Cold War strategy for the RAND Corporation; it was popularized in the version that gave it its title by Albert Tucker. See Steven Kuhn, "Prisoner's Dilemma," *The Stanford Encyclopedia of Philosophy*, Fall 2014 edition, ed. Edward N. Zalta, http://plato.stanford.edu/archives/fall2014/entries/prisoner-dilemma/.

So are Londoners still enduring the sort of pea-soup fogs that killed so many in 1952? No, because in 1956 the UK government brought in the Clean Air Act, which obliged people in built-up areas, over a brief transitional period, to switch to smokeless fuel. In terms of the matrix, individuals were forced by law out of the lower right-hand box into the upper left-hand one. This rather successful example of state intervention in the free market quickly led to greatly improved air quality in Britain's cities.

Although measures like the Clean Air Act have been effective in many countries, administrative regulation by a central authority is not the only way to solve the free rider problem analyzed in the prisoner's dilemma matrix, nor is it always the best. Rather than mandate socially responsible behavior, the authorities may create market incentives to encourage it. In certain circumstances, too, local communities may find ways round the apparently rigid logic of the prisoner's dilemma and develop mechanisms for cooperation independent of government control; these initiatives appeal to those who are suspicious of both the market and the state. All such options will be considered in detail in chapter 6.

The Market, Economic Growth, and the Environment

We saw earlier that a competitive market is alleged to foster economic growth through innovation and technological change. But what exactly do we mean by economic growth?

The growth rate of the economy measures the rate of increase in the value of the output of goods and services produced by an economy from year to year. A commonly cited measure of this value is the gross domestic product, or GDP. To see how this might be estimated, refer again to the circular flow in figure 3.1. Recall that the inner ring shows the money flows. Thus the inner left-hand box shows that the value of incomes created in the economy over a year is the sum of the different types of income paid out by firms in the course of a year. Since the firms get the money for such payments from the receipts from the sales of the goods they produce, this money is necessarily the same as the sum of all expenditure on these goods, in the inner right-hand box. While there are always "errors and omissions" in practice, in countries with efficient central statistical offices the measure of total expenditure on different types of goods and services generally does match pretty closely the measure of total income paid out by firms and received by households.

"Gross" implies that the measure used makes no allowance for wear and tear in the buildings and equipment used in the process of production. Would it not be more meaningful to deduct such an allowance and obtain a figure for "net" domestic product? It would, and sometimes this is the figure cited in comparisons—a point to which we return shortly. However, such estimates are in practice rather difficult to make. "Domestic" means that the output is produced by facilities and people located within the geographical boundaries of the country. But some factories located in one country are owned, in whole or in part, by investors in another. So if we want a more accurate view of the income entitlements of people in different countries, we should deduct "property income paid abroad" and add "property income received from abroad" to get a measure of gross *national* product, or GNP. A final point to note is that when measuring growth over time we have to allow for changes in the value of money. For various reasons, modern industrial economies have been characterized for most postwar years by a fall in this value, which implies that some of the apparent increases in GDP result from price inflation, not from actual increases in output volumes. We may estimate the effects of inflation by comparing price changes of representative samples of goods over time and then deduct these effects when measuring growth in "real" or "constant-price" GDP rather than "nominal," "money," "current price" GDP.

GDP, Economic Success, and Sustainability

Reports on the state of the economy make much use of the concept of GDP. Growth in GDP is considered to be a measure of a country's economic success. Comparisons of growth rates across economies show whether the country is doing better than its rivals. When we divide a country's GDP by its population to get "income per head," we often take this as a measure of economic welfare and of whether the country is better off or worse off than others (though this requires converting GDP for different countries to a common currency, usually dollars, which raises some technical problems). But serious issues of principle arise from such comparisons.

We saw that the circular flow diagram points to ways of estimating the value of economic activity over the course of a year. Some, particularly feminist writers, reasonably query whether these approaches give adequate credit to the contribution of work done within the households themselves. Because such work by members of the household is not paid for, it appears not to be valued. Yet somebody has to do it, and in most societies, however unfairly, women have found themselves undertaking a much greater share of unpaid household duties.

It follows that changes in women's involvement in the paid workforce may distort GDP comparisons, whether over time or between countries. Suppose a woman who had previously specialized in unpaid household services decided to hire someone else to do them while she pursued a paid career. This would apparently increase the country's domestic product in two ways. The entry of the woman to the labor market would create a paid income for her; the payment to the hired housekeeper would create another paid income. But only the first of these represents an actual increase in output. The second income would represent simply a market valuation of work that had previously been unpaid. This is just an example of a more general point: as the boundary of the market's "domain" shifts, so too will the estimate of GDP, even if no actual change in output has occurred. In developing countries with a large subsistence-farming sector, a shift of labor into the market economy can exaggerate the apparent increase in GDP if the fall in subsistence output has not been fully taken into account. Similarly, many countries have a large "informal" (perhaps in part illegal) sector that operates below the government statistician's radar. Estimates of per capita income that do not include the market value of such activities will give a misleadingly low figure for GDP.

When we consider the effects of economic activity on the environment, the limitations of GDP as a measure of economic success or human welfare become even more apparent. An oft-quoted example will bring this out. In 1989, the tanker *Exxon Valdez* ran aground off the coast of Alaska, resulting in the spillage of millions of tons of crude oil. This disaster led to a temporary *increase* in Alaska's GDP, reflecting the incomes earned by all the workers drafted to clean up the mess. Yet diverting labor to clean up pollution is surely a cost to society rather than a benefit (as its inclusion in the category of income would seem to imply).

When we estimate the net benefits of economic activity, as we saw before, we would ideally like to deduct the effect of wear and tear, or depreciation, of buildings and equipment—that is, of those productive resources created by human beings themselves. But why stop there? What about the natural resources, whether or not privately owned, that have been used up or in some way degraded in the process of production? These resources, like factory buildings and machinery, are in scarce supply; using them up will make us poorer in years to come—or, if not us, then future generations. Incomes earned cleaning up the environment are like incomes earned repairing or replacing machines and buildings. At best, they merely restore the status quo and should logically be deducted from gross domestic product to obtain a net figure.

Considerations such as these have led some economists and environmentalists to suggest other ways of measuring the true "value added" by the economy that take proper account of the consumption of both artificial and natural resources. One such measure is the Index of Sustainable Economic Welfare, or ISEW. This was initially proposed by Herman Daly and John Cobb in 1989; they have since developed a related index, the Genuine Progress Indicator, or GPI.[9] These approaches deduct expenditures from GDP that represent the destruction of either natural or artificial resources and add sources of income ignored by GDP estimates. Thus the ISEW measure includes estimates of nonmonetary economic activity from economic activity within the home and deducts estimates of the costs of environmental degradation and the consumption of both artificial and natural capital. Such measures are controversial and difficult to make with accuracy, but they do suggest that GDP growth measures significantly exaggerate improvements in welfare over time.[10]

From Mainstream to Ecological Economics

The above picture is drawn from the perspective of a mainstream, or neoclassical, economist with an interest in environmental issues. For

9. Herman E. Daly and John B. Cobb, *For the Common Good* (Boston: Beacon, 1989).
10. For an examination of the underlying theory for such estimates, see Philip A. Lawn, "A Theoretical Foundation to Support the Index of Sustainable Economic Welfare (ISEW), Genuine Progress Indicator (GPI), and Other Related Indexes," *Ecological Economics* 44, no. 1 (2003): 105–18.

the most part, such economists would accept many of the criticisms of the adverse effects sometimes associated with economic growth in our real-world, imperfectly functioning market economies. But they would not argue for the complete replacement of the market system, only its reform. Similarly, the alternative measures of economic progress use modifications of market values rather than dispensing with them altogether. More fundamentally, this approach retains the assumptions on which mainstream analysis is based, concerning such issues as technology, human behavior, the institutional framework for decision making, and the appropriate criteria for decisions.

This kind of approach still serves as the basis for many of the policy recommendations developed in later chapters. But it is far from uncontroversial, and we have to consider the criticisms that may be made of it to see what modifications may be desirable. We saw in chapter 2 that many criticisms have been made from outside the economics profession, by ecotheologians and others writing from a range of ethical perspectives. But some criticisms have come from economists themselves, a number of whom seek to differentiate themselves from the mainstream by practicing what they term *ecological economics*. This covers a wide range of different approaches, and it is not easy to give a brief account of the concept. For some, the ecological approach reflects a difference of emphasis rather than a fundamental rejection of all mainstream economic theory. Thus, they complain that mainstream economics treats environmental issues as an "add-on" for those who are interested in these matters (a final-year option rather than a compulsory core unit, perhaps) rather than seeing the interaction between economy and environment as fundamental to the prospects for both.[11] Others, while not quarrelling with this criticism, would push it much further, seeking a radical

---

11. See Common and Stagl, *Ecological Economics*, 4.

replacement of the methodology and assumptions of the mainstream. As will become apparent as we go along, my own view on these matters is closer to the mainstream than to the radical end of the spectrum.

Some beliefs, however, would probably be held in common by all economists who adopt the ecological label. An important one concerns the need for a cross-disciplinary approach. Readers will have noticed a family resemblance between the words *economy* and *ecology*: the common prefix comes from the Greek *oikos*, or household. Thus introductions to the subject will often point out that it seeks to integrate the study of "human housekeeping" with that of "natural housekeeping."[12] This requires students to develop some awareness of physics, particularly the laws of thermodynamics, and also of biology, to an extent that goes beyond the treatment of such matters in standard introductory economics texts.

Ecological economists are also much more explicitly engaged with ethical concerns. They often criticize mainstream economists for seeking to develop an objective, value-free "scientific" approach to the subject; the critics believe, by contrast, that economics is inevitably value laden and that the pretense of scientific objectivity is merely an ideological smokescreen intended to obscure the fact that many apparently economic arguments justify some exercise of power.[13] Here I think we have to be careful. It is true that some concepts used in economics are indeed based on value judgments. As we have seen, for example, GNP measures cannot be constructed without making a whole range of assumptions about what to include or exclude; many of these assumptions will express political beliefs

---

12. Ralf Eriksson and Jan Otto Anderson, *Elements of Ecological Economics* (London: Routledge, 2010), 54; Common and Stagl, *Ecological Economics*, 1.
13. See, e.g., Clive L. Spash, "The New Environmental Pragmatists, Pluralism and Sustainability," *Environmental Values* 18 (2009): 255.

about what is important. But there are other issues in economics that do not seem to me to involve values directly. Consider the statement that a rise in the price of pears, other things remaining equal, will lead to a fall in the number purchased. This statement may be true or false, but it is a statement about cause and effect, not about values; it may be tested by scientific methods, though with difficulty, by looking at information about prices of pears, the quantities purchased, and often a great many other things as well (the ones that in real life refuse to remain equal). Quite a lot of economics is concerned with questions of cause and effect, though in setting policy objectives it is of course true that political or moral values will have to be taken into account.

Values, along with science, shape the effects of policy on income distribution. The question of who bears the costs and who receives the benefits of any policy can be determined through scientific questions: that is, the answer may be predicted using theoretical models of the economy, the validity of which may be tested against statistical data. Whether the policy is a good one or not, given the distributional outcomes, is certainly a matter of values, and economists who wish to argue for particular outcomes should make clear the value judgments that underpin their advocacy. Issues of income distribution will in fact be a central concern of the chapters that follow.

Another criticism made by most ecological economists concerns the mainstream's belief in *substitutability*—in particular, the belief that inputs may generally replace each other in the production process in response to changes in price signals. This becomes particularly relevant in the environmental context through the (perhaps tacit) assumption that manufactured inputs will be able to replace natural ones, should the latter become increasingly scarce. This question will be considered at more length when we come to consider *sustainability* in chapter 4.

There is perhaps less agreement among ecological economists on certain other aspects of mainstream theory. Those closer to the mainstream appear willing to accept much economic analysis based on the traditional model of *rational economic behavior*. In essence, this assumes that economic agents are able to rank all achievable outcomes in order of preference and will choose the most preferred. An alternative way of expressing the rationality axiom is to say that agents choose the course of action that will *maximize their utility.* Other ecological economists cite recent work that integrates economics with psychology and that reveals a number of situations the rationality assumption cannot plausibly explain.[14] Such anomalies often arise in the context of decision making under conditions of uncertainty and also in situations in which people are influenced by the behavior of others. They will be discussed in more detail as we come to them at various points in the course of this text.

The more radical ecological economists often display a hostility to market institutions reminiscent of some of the theological criticisms of the market we encountered in chapter 2. Like the theologians, though basing their arguments on a humanist rather than a religious philosophy, they reject, together with the market, the closely associated anthropocentric and instrumentalist approach to the natural world, which is rather taken for granted in traditional economic analysis. In the remainder of this chapter we will explore those criticisms of the market in particular, drawing in part on the arguments reviewed in chapter 2.

---

14. The alleged inadequacies of the rationality assumption are among the many criticisms of mainstream economics made in John Gowdy and Jon D. Erickson, "The Approach of Ecological Economics," *Cambridge Journal of Economics* 30, no. 2 (2005): 207–22.

Criticisms of the Market as a Social Mechanism

A common criticism of the mainstream model is that the role it assigns to the individual household conceals the true nature of the system. This approach has a long history, going back to Thorstein Veblen at the start of the twentieth century.[15] Veblen argued that as people become wealthy, they spend not for their "autonomous" individual wants but to impress others and to emulate the even wealthier: he is perhaps best known for coining the phrase "conspicuous consumption." But probably the most cogently and entertainingly expressed critique of the model is to be found in the works of the late John Kenneth Galbraith, particularly in this context *The Affluent Society* and *The New Industrial Estate*.[16]

Manipulation of Consumer Preferences

Galbraith argues that the ideological persuasiveness of the traditional market model depends to an important extent on the notion of consumer sovereignty: the belief that the force to which the system responds is the spending power of households. He uses the term "the accepted sequence" to describe the one-way "flow of instruction from consumer to market to producer" that the model implies.[17] But in fact, Galbraith claims, if we really want to understand what is going on in modern industrial societies, our focus should be not the household but the *technostructure*. This term he uses to refer to the key planners and decision makers within the large corporations that were coming to dominate industry in the postwar era. Members of the technostructure include all those with the specialized knowledge of

15. Thorstein Veblen, *The Theory of the Leisure Class* (London: Macmillan, 1899).
16. John K. Galbraith, *The Affluent Society*, 2nd ed. (Boston: Houghton Mifflin, 1969), and *The New Industrial Estate*, 2nd ed. (Boston: Houghton Mifflin, 1972).
17. Galbraith, *New Industrial Estate*, ch. 19.

technology and markets such enterprises require. The motivation of the technostructure, Galbraith argues, rather than being profit per se, is to secure the survival and if possible expansion of the organization of which they are a part. In pursuit of this aim, they seek to control the corporation's environment as far as possible—not least, to control and manage consumer demand for the firm's products. Thus, while in the accepted sequence producers do what consumers want, in the "revised sequence" postulated by Galbraith consumers are made to want what producers want them to want.

While Galbraith accepts that a significant part of the modern economy remains outside the domain of the large corporations, and that even within this domain consumers may and sometimes do resist the persuasions of corporate marketing agencies, he considers the revised sequence sufficiently important to cast serious doubt on the notion of consumer sovereignty in the modern industrial system. His arguments, which are controversial, lend support to those who see this system not so much as meeting human needs but as generating artificial demands for more and more elaborate and diverse forms of output, regardless of the environmental consequences.

A Marxist Critique: Commodity Fetishism

A second line of criticism, this time from a Marxist perspective, focuses not on relations between consumer and producer so much as on relations within production. A Marxist might very well characterize the circular flow model in its standard form as ideologically motivated: an exercise in mystification, taking the form of *commodity fetishism*. This criticism, as we saw in chapter 2, has also found favor with some authors writing from a Christian perspective, such as Michael Northcott.

The concept of commodity fetishism is not to be confused with the obvious notion, the topic of many a sermon, that people tend to idolize material possessions, according them a reverence they owe to God alone. Few Christians would disagree with this, or with the claim that it helps to explain the environmental problems facing us today. But this was not what Marx had in mind. As a materialist himself, he was not concerned with the relations between human beings and God, but he was very interested in the relationships among human beings. His argument was that under the capitalist mode of production "the relations connecting the labor of one individual with that of the rest appear, not as direct social relations between individuals at work, but as what they really are, material relations between persons and social relations between things."[18]

Under previous economic systems, goods had mostly been produced by households for their own consumption or that of their social superiors; market exchange of any surplus goods had been limited. Under market capitalism, goods had become commodities produced for exchange, made by workers who no longer owned any means of production and had only their labor power to offer, as yet another "commodity," in the marketplace. Thus, Marx argued, the complex social relationships involved in the production process were disguised as exchange values reflecting the relative market prices of the commodities produced as outputs or used as inputs to the process. Just as social relationships appeared as relations between things—through *reification*—so, conversely, did inanimate things appear as persons: "It is an enchanted, perverted, topsy-turvy world, in which Monsieur le Capital and Madame la Terre do their ghost-walking as social characters and at the same time directly as mere things."[19]

18. Karl Marx, *Capital*, vol. 1: *A Critical Analysis of Capitalist Production*, ed. Frederick Engels (London: Lawrence and Wishart, 1974), 78.

Thus, in the circular flow diagram given earlier, manufactured resources and privately owned natural resources are treated as fellow contributors with workers to the process of production; as such, those resources are entitled to their own (or at least their owners') remuneration through interest and profits in the first case and rents in the second, just as workers are entitled to their wages.

Commodity fetishism thus obscures the process of exploitation, as the term is understood by Marxist writers. Marx took over from earlier economists the *labor theory of value*, according to which commodities would exchange at prices reflecting the labor time required for their production, but he gave this a particular twist. Labor power, as a commodity, would also exchange at such a price, determined by the labor time needed to provide a subsistence income sufficient to maintain a worker and allow the reproduction of a new generation. But labor power was capable of producing "surplus value" over and above this. By virtue of their monopoly of the means of production, as a class, capitalists would be entitled to retain this surplus after paying the workers their wages.

In earlier times exploitation had taken a more obvious form. Under slavery or feudalism, the exploitative nature of social relationships was clear. It involved the straightforward exercise of power by one social class over another (slave owner over slave, lord of the manor over serf) backed by law. By contrast, in industrial capitalism, workers were free of legal restrictions on their labor and movements. When it came to enforcing the contracts into which they voluntarily entered with employers, both sides were equal in the eyes of the law. Nonetheless, the dominant social class continued to appropriate the workers' surplus output, through the apparently impersonal process of the exchange of commodities on the free market. To both workers and

---

19. Karl Marx, *Capital*, vol. 3: *A Critique of Political Economy* (London: Lawrence and Wishart, 1972), 830.

capitalists, this might seem to be a "natural" process, outside any individual's control, but in fact it was a feature of the social institutions of capitalism, in particular the concentration of private property rights in the hands of a small group.

For technical reasons at least as much as for ideological ones, mainstream economists have not found the labor theory of value a helpful analytical tool for explaining the allocation of resources in a modern economy. Yet there are aspects of Marx's argument that cannot be gainsaid. Clearly, the production of output does require inputs of human labor time: natural resources and machinery will not put food on the table or clothes on our backs without human effort. Yet not everyone is obliged to make this effort: ownership of property may bring in a substantial income without the owners having had to work for it. Private property ownership is in fact a major source of inequality in industrial societies. The idea of a "free market" may seem to legitimate such inequalities, but it is questionable whether the propertyless laborer is really free rather than subject to an implicit duress: in a truly free market in the absence of state welfare provision, and in conditions where there was a surplus of workers looking for jobs, the only alternative to accepting poor pay and wretched conditions would be starvation, unreliably mitigated by voluntary charity.

But the fetishism of commodities does not merely conceal the true nature of social relationships in production. In the words of the Hungarian Marxist Georg Lukács, "it stamps its imprint upon the whole consciousness of man."[20] Lukács gives as an example the commodification of the marital relationship. Arguably, this very much predates capitalist society, but in any case there seems no reason to confine the argument to relations between people; it presumably

20. Georg Lukács, *History and Class Consciousness*, trans. Rodney Livingstone (London: Merlin, 1971), 100.

applies to relationships between humanity and the natural environment as well. As we have seen, one theologian who has developed this argument is Michael Northcott, who does so as part of his general critique of industrial society. But the commodification critique, which concerns the important question of where the boundaries of the market's domain should ideally be drawn, has also been put forward by other writers from both theological and philosophical perspectives.

Should We Restrict the Market's Domain?

Most societies do place limits on market exchange: most obviously, people are no longer allowed to sell themselves or their families into slavery, and many societies limit or prohibit the sale of body parts. Yet as we have seen, there are also arguments for extending the scope of the market, particularly to include the sale of property rights in environmental "assets." Not everyone agrees this is a good idea.

Michael Sandel of Harvard University is an eloquent critic of current attempts to extend the scope of the market—a process he describes as "market triumphalism." In 2009, Sandel gave the Reith Lectures hosted by the British Broadcasting Corporation; the first of these was titled "Markets and Morals."[21] In an argument reminiscent of Lukács's, Sandel claimed that "the market leaves its mark"—that is, the market is not an ethically neutral mechanism but affects human consciousness and how we perceive social relationships. Some of Sandel's criticisms concerned efficiency. For example, he repeated the argument first put forward by Richard Titmuss that the US system of paying for blood discouraged a high-quality supply from volunteer donors and replaced it with sometimes-contaminated blood from

21. Michael Sandel, *Reith Lectures 2009: A New Citizenship*. Transcript produced by the British Broadcasting Corporation, London, 2009.

paid ones.[22] But both in his presentation and in the discussion that followed, Sandel made it clear that his opposition to the market did not depend on such efficiency considerations. Even if the use of market incentives did increase some socially desired outcomes, there could be an argument against them if they also encouraged a decline in altruistic impulses.

In his lectures and also in a subsequent book, Sandel has applied his criticism of the market to its use in the protection of the environment, explicitly mentioning schemes for creating markets in carbon emissions.[23] There are certainly problems with making such schemes effective, but it is not clear—to me at any rate—that Sandel has made a convincing case *in principle* for excluding market forces from environmental protection. But further development of the arguments for and against this approach will be postponed until the detailed examination of policy techniques in chapters 5 and 6.

Inequality within and between Generations

As we saw earlier when discussing Marx, market capitalism is a source of inequality. Marx's focus was on the inequality caused by class differences, arising from the power of the owner of property ("capitalist") vis-à-vis the propertyless worker ("proletarian"). But even within the class of those who have to work for a living, the market creates many inequalities. While these may arise because some workers work harder than others, they often reflect differences in acquired or innate skills. In a market economy, wage differentials

---

22. Richard Titmuss, *The Gift Relationship: From Human Blood to Social Policy* (London: George Allen and Unwin, 1970). The argument was that the practice encouraged the concealment of diseases such as hepatitis by donors who relied on the payments to finance a drug or alcohol habit (in an expressive phrase, they were prepared to "ooze for booze").

23. Michael J. Sandel, *What Money Can't Buy: The Moral Limits of Markets* (London: Allen Lane, 2012), 72–78.

act like any other price differential; they "signal" those skills the market requires and give an incentive for workers to acquire them. But changes in technology or shifts in market demand may render painfully acquired skills obsolete, through no fault of the worker. Opportunities to retrain may be limited, particularly for older workers. The instability to which market economies are subject may also lead to long periods of unemployment, however willing the worker; this is another important reason for inequality.

But the market system does not merely create inequality *within* generations, it may also be a source of inequality *between* generations. Look again at the circular flow diagram. Whether consumer preferences are autonomous or are partly determined by the marketing efforts of large companies, as Galbraith argues, the price of goods will depend on the willingness of consumers to pay for them. Fish, for example, are scarce, and thus their price reflects the demands for fish by the households who wish to purchase them and are in a position to pay for them. But what about households as yet unborn, who may not be born for decades to come? How will the market take account of their future demand for fish? Presumably, if the prospective demand of generations of consumers stretching into the distant future were reflected in today's marketplace, the price of fish would be a great deal higher than it is, implying that households today would be encouraged to be much less profligate in their consumption of this scarce resource and would leave more for their successors. As it is, however, the market price will be determined only by the preferences of the present generation, not of future ones.

So we have two distributional problems arising from the use of the market, both of which result from the same fact: the market can only respond to preferences backed up by the willingness of the current generation to spend on different options. Members of today's generation who are deficient in money income are unable to exert much influence on what is produced, however great their needs may be. This means that resources may be used to satisfy the whims of rich people rather than the urgent needs of poorer ones. Members of future generations, who currently have zero spending power, obviously can neither exert any influence at all nor prevent vital resources from being frittered away by the present generation.

These distributional issues cast further doubt on the use of any aggregate single figure index of economic progress, whether GDP, ISEW, or GPI. It has long been argued that not only the total output produced, as measured by the GDP, but also how that outcome is distributed among different people is important for human welfare. More recently, broader indexes try to take the distribution of benefits into account. But the further we go in giving weight to questions of income distribution, the more our index may be criticized on the grounds that it represents the particular political or philosophical values of the estimator rather than a universally agreed consensus.

More General Criticisms of the Economic Approach

As we will see in chapter 5, the appraisal of the effects of different environmental policies on less well-off groups is something many economists have tried to integrate into decision-making procedures. Economists have also made proposals for incorporating the interests of future generations into decisions made today, for example through the rate at which future income is discounted in investment calculations. This, too, will be considered in chapter 5. But there are criticisms even more fundamentally hostile to the underlying economic philosophies, whether mainstream or Marxist. Such criticisms go back to the earliest days of the subject's emergence as a social science, as a famous quotation from Edmund Burke demonstrates: "—But the age of chivalry is gone.—That of sophisters, economists, and calculators, has succeeded; and the glory of Europe is extinguished forever."[24]

Economists, now as then, attempt to analyze social affairs using the methods of the natural sciences but with access to less satisfactory sources of data than are available to most of their natural science colleagues. In particular, in many (though not all) areas they would like to investigate, they are unable to conduct controlled laboratory experiments. Nonetheless, they attempt to observe social phenomena, formulate theories based on rigorous assumptions about underlying behavior, and collect data to test such theories. As in many natural sciences, such as medicine, they try not merely to understand what is going on but to make recommendations about how to respond. In economics, such recommendations are often about important issues for national policy; the old name for the subject, "political economy," brings this out.

Once we start making recommendations, however, we have to define what would constitute an improvement in social affairs and to measure how far such an improvement has occurred. Burke was correct to lump economists together with "calculators," if by this he meant statisticians. This focus on the measurable often gets economists into trouble. Sometimes the hard figures may disprove, or cast serious doubt on, popular and strongly held theories; most people, whether politicians, newspaper editors, or members of the general public (or, of course, economists themselves), dislike having their pet beliefs challenged. But there is also a sense that important human values may fall through holes in the statisticians' net. Burke seems to imply that the excesses of the French Revolution arose at

24. Edmund Burke, "Reflections on the Revolution in France," in *Edmund Burke: Revolutionary Writings,* ed. Iain Hampsher-Monk (Cambridge, UK: Cambridge University Press, 2014), 78.

least in part from an overemphasis on a rational approach to human affairs and the neglect of traditional insights.

Modern economics is certainly a product of the seventeenth- and eighteenth-century intellectual movement known as the Enlightenment, which was very much an attempt to examine with a critical eye beliefs and institutions that had evolved over time and to suggest how they might be improved or replaced. In establishing criteria for social improvements, mainstream economists were attracted by *utilitarianism*. The essence of this philosophy is encapsulated in a famous remark by Francis Hutcheson: "That action is best, which procures the greatest happiness for the greatest numbers."[25] This principle was reiterated in a 1768 pamphlet by Joseph Priestley, and there, apparently, it was found by Jeremy Bentham, who proceeded to build a whole system of "morals and legislation" upon it.[26]

Bentham refers to the greatest happiness concept, interpreted as the pursuit of the greatest aggregate happiness of the whole community, as "the principle of utility." He defines utility as "that property in any object, whereby it tends to produce benefit, advantage, pleasure, good or happiness (all this in the present case comes to the same thing)."[27] He seems prepared to include in the community its nonhuman but sentient members, which should make the philosophy attractive to those environmentalists concerned with the interests of

---

25. Frances Hutcheson, *Inquiry into the Original of our Ideas of Beauty and Virtue Treatise II*, 2nd ed. (London: Printed for J & J Knapton, 1729), sec. 3.8.

26. Although Bentham attributes the "greatest happiness" phrase itself to Priestley's pamphlet, it does not in fact appear in it, though similar sentiments are certainly expressed. See Joseph Priestley, *The First Principles of Government and the Nature of Political, Civil and Religious Liberty*, 2nd ed. (London: Printed for J. Johnston, No. 72, St Paul's Church-Yard, 1771). Bentham nowhere mentions Hutcheson as a source for the principle, though he does acknowledge Beccaria as a possible alternative source to Priestley. See *The Works of Jeremy Bentham, published under the superintendence of his executor, John Bowring* (Edinburgh: William Tate, 1843), vol. 10, 142.

27. Jeremy Bentham, *Works*, vol. 1, ch. 1.III.

nonhuman animals. Bentham believed that traditional arguments for ignoring these interests were irrelevant: "The question is not, *Can they talk?* nor, *Can they reason?* but, *Can they suffer?*"[28] However, Bentham also believed it legitimate to use animals both for food and, even more controversially (especially in an age before anesthetics), for medical experimentation; this is consistent with the utilitarian view that what matters is the net balance of pleasures and pains in the aggregate. So perhaps those who have suggested that Bentham should become the patron saint of animal rights should stick with St. Francis.[29]

Whatever our views on the treatment of animals, the notion that government policy should seek to maximize welfare seems an obvious one, but there are problems that concern both the underlying morality of the principle and the task of rendering it operational.

While some Christians, notably Joseph Fletcher in his book on situation ethics, have come close to embracing a utilitarian approach, many others are put off by its *consequentialism*, the view that the morality of actions is to be judged solely by their outcomes—in effect, that the end justifies the means.[30] Also, many are concerned not simply with numbers but with the treatment of individuals. In this regard, they may cite scriptural justification. In his vision of the day of judgment Christ expresses concern for "one of the least of these brothers of mine" (Matt. 25:40); in the parables of the lost sheep and the lost coin, there is similarly a focus on the individual, not just the majority (Luke 15:3–10).

28. Ibid., ch. 17, n. 122.
29. For more detail on Bentham's views on this topic, see Jeremy Bentham, "To the Editor of the Morning Chronicle," Morning Chronicle,(London, 9 March 1826).
30. Joseph Fletcher, *Situation Ethics: The New Morality* (London: ,SCM, 1966). Fletcher argues that "as the love ethic searches seriously for a social policy it must form a coalition with utilitarianism" (95).

Aside from its consequentialism, utilitarianism has also been criticized for choosing individual happiness as its maximand. The Nobel prizewinning economist Amartya K. Sen labels as *welfarism* this use of happiness as a means of assigning value to different situations.[31] He criticizes welfarism on the grounds that a person's well-being is not the only issue that is important for that person and that utility, in the sense of people getting what the prefer is in any case an inadequate measure of well-being. An example of the first criticism would be a situation in which people live in comfort and prosperity but lack agency, which Sen sees as the ability to pursue a whole range of goals, including but possibly also transcending personal well-being. An example of the second is a situation in which desires are so constrained by poverty or persecution that the victims "tend to adjust their desires and expectations to what little they see as feasible."[32] This poverty of expectations, Sen argues, makes the disadvantages they suffer appear less important for their well-being than an impartial outsider might consider them to be. Sen also argues that freedom to choose is of value in itself and not merely because it may further economic prosperity.[33] Rather than seeing utility maximization as a single overarching goal, Sen prefers policymakers to focus on providing or protecting a range of "instrumental freedoms" or *capabilities*: political rights, economic and social opportunities, transparency guarantees against corruption, and material security.[34]

A further difficulty with the utilitarian approach concerns the nature of the pleasures that make up utility. This issue was addressed

---

31. Amartya K. Sen, "Utilitarianism and Welfarism," *Journal of Philosophy* 76, no. 9 (1979): 463–89; Amartya Sen and Bernard Williams, eds., *Utilitarianism and Beyond* (London: Cambridge University Press, 1982), 2–5.
32. Amartya Sen, *The Idea of Justice* (London: Allen Lane, 2009), 283.
33. Amartya Sen, *Development as Freedom* (New York: Knopf, 1999), 36–37.
34. Ibid., 38–40.

by one of Bentham's most distinguished followers, the philosopher and economist John Stuart Mill. Mill's view was that "the pleasures of the intellect, of the feelings and imagination, and of the moral sentiments" should be considered much more valuable as pleasures than "those of mere sensation." He supports this view with the (perhaps doubtful) claim that those who have experienced both sorts of pleasures will always rank the former above the latter. Thus "it is better to be a human being dissatisfied than a pig satisfied; better to be Socrates dissatisfied than a fool satisfied. And if the fool, or the pig, are of a different opinion, it is because they only know their own side of the question."[35] To some, however, this insight seems to allow for a degree of paternalism (which in another essay Mill strongly condemns).[36] This will be considered again toward the end of the present chapter.

Meanwhile, even if we were to accept the principle of utility as a guide (perhaps with some limitations on its domain of applicability or as only one of a variety of decision criteria), how are we to implement it? In particular, how shall we measure the quantity we are inviting policymakers to maximize? Here we encounter a question economists have in the past considered to be a particularly troublesome one. In order to obtain a measure of aggregate happiness, we obviously have to add together the utilities of individual members of the relevant community. This implies two things. First, we have to compare the happiness of different individuals in a whole variety of situations. Second, those happinesses have to be capable of being expressed in figures that it makes sense to add together. The first of these, interpersonal utility comparison, is questionable, if only because of Sen's point about "poverty of expectations" in some groups. The second, the additivity of utility

35. John S. Mill, *Utilitarianism*, 7th ed.(London: Longman, Green, 1879), ch. 2.
36. John S. Mill, *On Liberty*, 4th ed. (London: Longman, Roberts and Green, 1869).

measures, is also doubtful, even if we confine the additions to a single individual, much less to members of a group.

Consider the following mental experiment. Choose a piece of music you enjoy and another you also like, but not as much. Presumably, it would make sense to say that the experience of listening to the first gives you greater utility than you would derive from listening to the second. You might even be prepared to say it would give you a lot more utility. But could you be more precise than that? Would you be prepared to say that you liked it twice as much? Or 1.753 times as much?

If you were comparing your weight with that of your best friend, it would obviously be perfectly possible to make such statements. It would also be possible to add the weights together—for example, to discover whether you both could occupy a small elevator without infringing safety restrictions. But if the only information you had was that you weighed more than your friend did, no such numerical total could be given.

Faced with such difficulties, many economists chose to abandon the notion that utility was a quantity that could be compared across individuals or even added up for a single individual. Instead, it was allowed to be no more than "ordinally" measurable.[37] That is to say, individuals were assumed to be able to say of any situation whether it gave them more utility than another situation, but not by how much it did so. It turns out that ordinal utility allows economic analysis to proceed a long way in making predictions about how economic agents will behave in different situations. Clearly, the predictions of such models, if well supported empirically, can help policymakers who are trying to devise incentives to encourage citizens to conform to their policies. But what if the policymakers want to measure the

---

37. Weights satisfy the criteria for cardinal measurement; they can be meaningfully added together. Where quantities can only be ranked in order of size, they are described as ordinal.

impact of these policies on welfare? Here the limited information base of ordinal utilitarianism is less helpful.

If we are unable to compare utilities between different people or to add them up, then what can we say about whether a policy is a good one or not? Everyone affected by the policy may agree that it is better than the status quo. If so, it seems reasonable to adopt the policy. Even if some people do not benefit from the policy but agree that they are no worse off, while others do benefit, the change should be implemented. This is the basis of a *Pareto improvement*, named after the Italian social scientist who first proposed it.[38] But what if a policy benefits some but disadvantages others? If we cannot add or subtract utilities, and if they are in any case incomparable, it would seem that the situations before and after are also incapable of being compared.

It did not take economists long to come up with a possible way around this difficulty. In 1938, Roy Harrod initiated a discussion on *compensation criteria*, using a historical example: the repeal of the Corn Laws in Britain in 1846.[39] This was not a Pareto improvement, as it harmed landlords by removing agricultural protection but benefited other social groups by reducing the price of food. So how could it be said to be either a good idea or a bad idea? From the resulting debate there arose a criterion that, for better or worse, is the basis of much economic policy appraisal.[40]

The *Kaldor-Hicks criterion*, as it is known, suggests that a change in economic policy will be worthwhile if those who gain can afford to overcompensate the losers—that is, if they would be willing to pay more for the change than the losers would be willing to pay to prevent it. Note that the criterion does not require that compensation

38. Vilfredo Pareto, *Manual of Political Economy*, trans. Ann M. Schweier, ed. Ann S. Schweier and Alfred N. Page (New York: A. M. Kelley, 1971).
39. Roy Harrod, "The Scope and Method of Economics," *Economic Journal* 48 (1938): 383–412.
40. Nicholas Kaldor, "Welfare Comparisons of Economics and Interpersonal Comparisons of Utility," *Economic Journal* 49 (1939): 549–52.

actually has to be paid; it is designed to handle cases where this would be impracticable, as is true of most real-world policy changes. In effect, the Kaldor-Hicks criterion does not require a Pareto improvement but merely a *potential* Pareto improvement. We may perhaps see it as an attempt to make utilitarianism operational by using "willingness to pay" as a proxy for utility and thus reintroducing cardinal utility by the back door. This criterion is the basis of the economic technique of cost-benefit analysis. But it has always been ethically controversial for an obvious reason, which was noted earlier in the discussion of GDP as a measure of welfare: the unequal distribution of income. Suppose the losers from a policy decision were low-income families while the gainers were the well-off. The criterion would then have led to a policy which made the rich richer and the poor poorer. If each dollar gives much more utility to a poor person than to a rich one, as seems plausible, then the link between willingness to pay and utility is broken.

Some economists are quite happy to accept this conclusion, arguing that the implications for fairness are no concern of theirs. To employ the usual metaphor, they see it as the economist's job to determine which policies will maximize the size of the cake; it is for politicians to determine how the cake is to be sliced up. But others—including many ecological economists—have argued that equity criteria should be built into the procedure of analyzing the costs and benefits of distributional consequences. This is seen as more reliable than simply hoping that the politicians will follow along behind (perhaps, indeed, a considerable distance behind) and tidy up the distributional consequences of decisions taken on efficiency criteria alone. Amendments to the cost-benefit algorithm have been proposed to take distributional issues into account; we consider them briefly in chapter 6.

In Defense of Utilitarianism

Recently, there has been a vigorous attempt to restore the concept of happiness as a guide to policy decisions: a kind of "neo-Benthamism." Perhaps the most distinguished protagonist of this approach is Richard Layard, emeritus professor of economics at the London School of Economics and member of the House of Lords. Layard believes that developments in psychology have brought us much closer to an understanding of what constitutes happiness and how it can be achieved.[41]

Layard acknowledges the importance of a range of capabilities like those identified by Sen; however, he considers these simply to be instrumental to the pursuit of the overarching goal of happiness. Since he thinks it should be possible to measure how much each capability contributes to happiness, he assumes that one capability outcome can be traded against another as long as overall happiness will be increased by doing so.[42] He is therefore an enthusiast for the economist's technique of cost-benefit analysis but is well aware of the limitations of "willingness to pay" measures, given the inequality in the distribution of the means of payment. Thus, he supports the approach that weights money payments so as to show how they affect the ultimate happiness of those who pay the costs or receive the benefits.[43] Such weighting allows policymakers to show what some theologians like to call "a bias to the poor."

On the question of the quality of different types of happiness, Layard explicitly rejects Mill's distinction between higher and lower pleasures. He appears to argue that it would have been better for Socrates to have been a satisfied fool than a dissatisfied philosopher; if he had been, the sum of happiness in Athens of the fifth century B.C.E.

41. Richard Layard, *Happiness: Lessons from a New Science*, 2nd ed. (New York: Penguin, 2011)
42. Ibid., 113 and note 4.
43. Ibid., 131–32.

would have been greater. However, this would not have been better for subsequent generations, who have benefited from the insights Socrates suffered in order to produce.[44] In rejecting Mill, Layard is perhaps motivated by a desire that policymakers avoid paternalistically substituting their own views about what people *ought* to want for what people actually *do* want.

Layard appears to be a "rule utilitarian": that is, he believes societies have to use the greatest happiness principle to establish basic rights conducive to happiness in the long run. These may be enshrined in law and should not be violated even where in a particular instance it might seem that to do so would increase utility.[45] Arguably, this goes some way to overcome the objection that utilitarianism allows the persecution of a small minority if doing so would increase the happiness of a large majority.

Does Layard succeed in mounting an effective defense of utilitarianism? His version of the doctrine certainly includes features that go some way to meeting ethical concerns by emphasizing its egalitarian aspects and the need to respect the rule of law. Yet his arguments are still open to question.[46] Why choose happiness as the overarching principle rather than other desirable objectives, such as freedom or human solidarity? Is there a danger that by considering such goals only as instrumental to the pursuit of happiness we will lose aspects of them that are nonetheless of value in their own right? True, it is very convenient for policymakers to have a single goal in terms of which all alternatives may be judged instead of having to balance a plurality of noncomparable goals, but perhaps the cost of this restriction is too high. Is Layard right to see the ban on paternalism as absolute, even in the circumstances described by Sen,

44. Ibid., 118.
45. Ibid., 123.
46. See, for example, Sen, *Idea of Justice*, 273–75.

where deprivation or oppression has limited the capacity for preference formation? If so, has he not introduced nonpaternalism as a value additional to happiness and worth pursuing for its own sake?

It is not clear, in fact, that Layard accepts the full rigor of his argument for the solitary preeminence of the happiness principle. In the second edition of his book, he goes into more detail on the question of the distribution of utility, using the following example. Suppose in one state of affairs Person A has a utility of 8 and Person B of 2, while in the second state of affairs A has 5 and B has 4. The first state has the greater total and average utility, but in the second the lower total is more equally distributed. Which state should be chosen? Bentham would have chosen the first, but Layard chooses the second. Christian ethics, based on the notion that we should love our neighbor as ourselves, seems easier to square with Layard's more egalitarian choice. But for our present purposes it is sufficient to note that fairness has been smuggled in as a governing principle additional to utility. Layard argues, not entirely convincingly, that "there is no conflict between happiness and fairness, since fairness is ultimately about how happiness is distributed."[47] But, as was noted earlier in the context of nonpaternalism, it does seem that the notion of giving policymakers a single overriding objective has been breached.

The view I take in later chapters is that policymakers should not seek to replace the multiplicity of social objectives with a single goal, even as important a goal as happiness. But they should nevertheless include an appraisal of their proposals in utilitarian terms, if only to see what the cost of preferring nonutilitarian options is likely to be.

---

47. Layard, *Happiness*, 246. An obvious question, which Layard accepts as a controversial one, is how much average utility should be traded off in the interests of fairness. On this, Layard seems to be placing himself somewhere between Harsanyi, who follows Bentham in arguing for maximum average utility, and Rawls, who focuses on the welfare of the worst-off member of the society. See John Harsanyi, "Morality and the Theory of Rational Behavior," in Sen and Williams, *Utilitarianism and Beyond*, 39–62; John Rawls, *A Theory of Justice* (Cambridge, MA: Harvard University Press, 1970).

Ecological Economics and Christian Environmental Perspectives

It is clear from the foregoing that there is at least some common ground between ecological economists and those Christian writers who have a strong environmental concern. Both groups take a strong view on the need for ethical issues to be included explicitly in the appraisal of policy; both condemn the assumption, implicit in much economic policy, that economic growth is unambiguously desirable.

Many who sympathize with ecological economists, however, would perhaps not wish to accept the whole package of criticisms outlined toward the end of chapter 2. Particular areas of disagreement for some would include the abhorrence of markets and the refusal, or at least reluctance, to acknowledge the gains from trade and globalization or to accept the continuing need for economic growth and modernization in the poorer countries of the world. These areas of disagreement will be explored further in the chapters that follow.

4

Sustainability

We came across the notion of sustainability in the previous chapter when considering the limitations of the gross domestic product as a measure of economic progress. There, we saw that any such measure ought to take into account the need to replace both artificially produced resources, such as equipment and buildings, and natural resources used up in the process of output creation. Presumably, then, economic activities are only sustainable if they do not allow the world's stocks of natural and produced capital to diminish over time. This, however, is not as simple a statement as it looks, and not everyone agrees on how the sustainability requirement should be interpreted.

Alternative Concepts of Sustainability

Look again at the phrase "do not allow the world's stocks of natural and produced capital to diminish over time." Should we interpret this as requiring us to preserve stocks of natural capital *independently* from those of produced capital, or is it acceptable to run down natural capital if we make up for it by increasing the stock of produced capital we bequeath to future generations? As soon as we start talking about substitution of produced for natural resources, we find ourselves having to consider the question: how effective is the substitution?

The Weak Sustainability Concept

Mainstream economists have a ready solution in principle to such problems (though, as usual, it is not so easy to implement in practice). Even if in some cases substitution of synthetic for natural goods is imperfect, in other cases it may be an improvement. Overall, we have to ensure that we substitute manufactured resources of equal *value* for natural resources we use up. That is, we have to estimate what a future generation would require in compensation for the natural capital used up by the present one, which will depend on willingness to pay for the prospective stream of goods or services that would have arisen from this capital and compare it with what they would be willing to pay for the benefits stream from the produced capital offered in replacement. By imputing money valuations to both natural and produced capital in this way, we may add together and compare all sorts of different types of resources, from rain forests to cruise ships to fast food outlets, since all are expressed in a common standard of value. As long the total value of what has been used up is no greater than the total value of what is being offered in replacement to the next generation, we will have achieved sustainability. In the jargon, this is known as the *weak sustainability* principle.[1]

---

1. For more details on sustainability concepts and debates, see Tom Tietenberg, *Environmental and Natural Resource Economics*, 6th ed. (Boston: Pearson Addison Wesley, 2003), 94–99; Simon Dresner, *The Principles of Sustainability*, 2nd ed. (London: Earthscan, 2008), 81–95.

Donald Hay, a distinguished Oxford economist, notes that the mainstream view within the profession is generally optimistic about sustainability.[2] If we take the concept in its weak form, as just defined, there are many reasons for this optimism, which certainly reflects much past experience. Synthetic resources have often been substituted for natural ones in the productive process: an early example, from among a great many in the textile industry, would be the substitution of nylon for silk in the production of stockings. Improvements in technology have also allowed reductions in the ratio of material inputs (whether natural or artificial) to outputs; as Charles Leadbeater has pointed out, such improvements may be interpreted as the substitution of "knowhow" for materials.[3] To the extent that natural resources become scarcer, these developments will be stimulated by price signals, which will also encourage prospecting for and exploiting additional sources of natural materials, as well as the more efficient recycling of materials in scrapped equipment.

But we need to look more closely at the mainstream economist's optimism. In the second part of this chapter, we consider specific environmental situations that may pose a threat to sustainability, but for the moment the discussion can remain at a more general level. Take, for example, the question of substituting synthetic for natural resources. The first law of thermodynamics states that matter and energy can neither be created nor destroyed.[4] Hence, synthetic goods cannot be created ex nihilo; they need an initial input of natural raw materials. Nylon and other synthetic fibers may substitute for

---

2. Donald Hay, "Sustainable Economics," in *When Enough Is Enough: A Christian Framework for Environmental Sustainability,* ed. R. J. Berry (Nottingham: APOLLOS, 2007), 113–14.

3. Charles Leadbeater, "Welcome to the Knowledge Economy," in *Tomorrow's Politics: The Third Way and Beyond,* ed. Ian Hargreaves and Ian Christie (London: Demos, 1998), 11–12. Economists would describe this as substituting human capital for physical capital.

4. See, for example, David W. Pearce and R. Kerry Turner, *Economics of Natural Resources and the Environment* (Hemel Hempstead: Harvester Wheatsheaf, 1990), 37, 49; Hay, "Sustainable Economics," 114.

silk, wool, or cotton, but they are themselves derived ultimately from carbon products such as crude oil. But perhaps the inputs can come, if not from raw materials, then from recycled ones? The second law of thermodynamics, or entropy law, has implications for recycling; it reminds us that there are limits to this process. The entropy law lends itself to anthropocentric interpretation because it implies that, although energy cannot be destroyed, as it is used to do work energy becomes less "ordered" in ways that make it less useful for human purposes.[5] Thus, when we recycle materials, we need to replace "degraded" energy with new usable sources of energy. In addition, the conversion of energy from one form to another will be less than 100 percent efficient.

What about Leadbeater's point, that over time we are able to reduce material requirements in production through improved knowledge? This is part of a more general argument about the use of human ingenuity to find technical solutions to problems arising from earlier applications of technology; another instance would be the invention of new methods for extracting raw materials from less accessible sources as those materials become scarcer. Pessimistic commentators, however, point out that it is an act of faith to assume that the necessary inventions will always be available in time to avert catastrophe.

Other Concepts of Sustainability

Those who believe it not always possible to substitute artificial for natural capital may look for a tougher criterion than is implied by weak sustainability. One stronger possibility would be to treat the two forms of capital, natural and produced, as separately maintained,

---

5. For further discussion of this law, see Michael Common and Sigrid Stagl, *Ecological Economics: An Introduction* (Cambridge: Cambridge University Press, 2005), 30–32.

so that the value of useful services *from each type* would not diminish from one generation to the next. This would still not be strong enough for some environmentalists; for example, it would allow the overfishing of cod to the point of extinction as long as the total value of the edible fish stock as a whole did not fall. Those concerned about species diversity might prefer a yet stronger criterion that would impose defined limits on the consumption of at least some natural resources.

Part of the problem in defining sustainability is that we often do not know exactly what the impact of economic activity on the environment will be. This reflects the complexity of both economic and ecological systems. We cannot always tell in advance whether particular types of economic development will be sustainable or disastrous in the long run. This is the sort of issue to which we will frequently return, both in the present chapter when looking at specific threats to sustainability and in chapter 5 when we consider decision making in uncertain situations.

Fairness and Sustainability

The weak sustainability concept, as we saw earlier, makes use of "willingness to pay" when aggregating different types of resources, and indeed any concept of sustainability that compares values of diverse goods and services cannot avoid this. As we saw in chapter 3, a willingness-to-pay criterion is suspect as a measure of social welfare because the connection between money expenditure and welfare depends on the distribution of income. So should we build in a further sustainability requirement that world income distribution not become less equal over time? For many, this would not go nearly far enough, inasmuch as the present distribution of world income is already very unequal; they would be opposed to any concept of sustainability that simply preserved this inequality.

Whole books have been written to quantify and illustrate global inequality, but a few figures will give some idea. In the United States, gross national income per capita was $50,610 in 2012; that same year in the African country of Zambia it was $1,620, measured not at the dollar exchange rate but in "purchasing power parity" terms that allow a more accurate comparison of relative command over resources. True, national income statistics may be criticized, as we saw in chapter 3, but they do give a rough indicator of differences in prosperity. In very many respects, Zambians are clearly worse off than US citizens. If we doubt the monetary estimates, it will perhaps be enough to note that their children are much more likely to die in infancy: in Zambia, fifty-six per thousand live births in 2012 did not survive infancy, while in the United States only six per thousand did not survive (other rich countries do even better). Not surprisingly, Zambians make less of an impact on the environment than do their American counterparts. In 2010, carbon dioxide emissions per Zambian amounted to only 0.2 metric tons, while for US citizens the figure in that year was 17.6 metric tons.[6]

Sub-Saharan Africa, where Zambia is located, is the poorest region in the world. In 2010, 48.5 percent of the people in the region had to live on $1.25 or less per day (this figure is currently taken as representing the direst level of poverty). Around 875 million people live in sub-Saharan Africa, so about 424 million of them were at or below this poverty level. But extreme poverty is widespread in other, more heavily populated regions: in South Asia, the corresponding figure for the *poverty headcount ratio*, as it is known, was 31 percent, and in East Asia and the Pacific region it was 12.5 percent.[7] Overall,

6. The figures in this paragraph were sourced from the World Bank, accessed November 30, 2013, http://data.worldbank.org/indicator/EN.ATM.CO2E.PC

a little more than 1.2 billion people, 20.6 percent of the world's population, satisfied this stringent poverty criterion in 2010.[8]

Now, it is important and encouraging to note that this very gloomy picture is actually improving rapidly. The sources just cited also tell us that by 2010 the poverty headcount ratio had fallen by more than half from its level of 43.1 percent in 1990.[9] True, world population had increased over the period, but even in absolute numbers the fall had been substantial, from 1.9 to 1.2 billion. Much of this has to be attributed to globalization and opening opportunities for world trade, which may help to explain why economists are for the most part much more enthusiastic about globalization than are some social activists, who tend to focus on its (admittedly still serious) flaws. But the faster world poverty is reduced, the greater the potential threat to environmental sustainability. As the very poorest become a little less poor, those at higher income levels also tend to become better off and increasingly seek to emulate the lifestyles of the rich industrialized countries; this may be seen very clearly in China, India, and the growing number of other "emergent" nations. Does the world have sufficient resources to allow "the rest" to catch up with "the West"?

The equity issue we have just been considering is essentially about moving toward *intragenerational* fairness, implying a more egalitarian distribution of income on a worldwide scale among members of the same generation. I will explore both the rationale for this and the question of *intergenerational* fairness, which is also very relevant to the concept of sustainability, in chapter 5.

---

7. For regional comparisons, see "Data: Poverty," World Bank, http://data.worldbank.org/topic/poverty.
8. See "Poverty and Equity Data," World Bank, http://povertydata.worldbank.org/poverty/home.
9. For the earlier year the poverty line used was one dollar a day. See Martin Ravallion, Shaohua Chen, and Prem Sangraula, "Dollar a Day Revisited," *World Bank Economic Review* 23, no. 2 (2009): 163–85.

Criticisms of the Economic Approach to Sustainability

So far, the discussion has followed a broadly economic approach to sustainability. But as we saw in earlier chapters, some environmentalists offer fundamental criticisms of the economist's approach.

There is the *commodification* issue: is it appropriate to put a price on natural resources or ecological systems, as we implicitly do when suggesting that a sufficient increase in produced capital may compensate for a loss of natural capital (in other words, that they may be assigned an equal monetary value)? Treating natural systems as commodities, of course, only makes sense in the context of *anthropocentrism*: only humans can express a willingness to pay. But anthropocentrism raises another issue. Does sustainability only require that each generation of human beings leave a resource inheritance to future *human* generations that is, in some sense at least, no worse than the inheritance they themselves received? Or does it require each generation to *protect* the nonhuman world for reasons that transcend the interests of humans?

But what might this wider interest be? In chapter 2 we saw that some writers claim to adopt an *ecocentric* approach, one that protects the environment for its own sake rather than simply for ours; others demand a *theocentric* approach that would see the protection of the environment as part of our duty toward God as creator. Both these perspectives would require a stronger version of sustainability. The strongest would perhaps come from the ecocentrists. As we saw when considering the deep ecologists, these writers are reluctant to accept any suggestion that human beings might play a stewardship role toward the natural world. The theocentrists might be more willing to accept trade-offs between natural and produced capital, as some of them, particularly the evangelical ones, are comfortable with and indeed strongly committed to the concept of stewardship. As stewards, they consider themselves permitted to intervene in the environment in ways that inevitably interfere with, perhaps even destroy, some ecosystems. Thus, Bookless, in a discussion of the Christian concept of sustainability, allows for "farming, animal husbandry, forestry, mining and resource extraction, hunting, fishing and industry," subject to "never taking from natural systems beyond their capacity to renew and replace" (a requirement especially hard to meet in the case of mining or fossil fuel extraction).[10]

In subsequent chapters, we will return to the question of how much difference in practice these alternative perspectives might make to our decisions about the environment. For the present, as we look at some of the pressing environmental problems facing our own generation, we consider what sorts of decisions are becoming urgently necessary.

Population: Is It a Problem?

How pressing is population growth as an environmental issue? Trends in population growth were certainly one of the earliest environmental topics to attract the attention of economists. In 1798, Thomas Robert Malthus, an Anglican clergyman and amateur economist, wrote a famous essay that predicted that any increase in prosperity could only be temporary.[11] Taking food supply as his measure of prosperity, he argued that any increase in this would simply encourage people to have more children, given "the passion between the sexes." But with a limited supply of land for cultivation,

10. Dave Bookless, "Towards a Theology of Sustainability," in Berry, *When Enough Is Enough*, 44.
11. Thomas Robert Malthus, *An Essay on the Principle of Population As It Affects the Future Improvement of Society with Remarks On the Speculations of Mr Godwin, M. Condorcet and Other Writers* (London: Printed for J. Johnston in St Paul's Churchyard, 1798).

the ability to reproduce would outrun the ability to increase agricultural output: "Population, when unchecked, increases in a geometrical ratio. Subsistence increases only in an arithmetical ratio. A slight acquaintance with numbers will shew the immensity of the first power in comparison with the second." Thus, population growth would eventually be checked by the arrival of too many mouths to feed, with resulting famine reducing the surplus population and restoring the balance.

This prediction, that most people could never expect to rise for long above a bare subsistence standard of living, was an influential one among many early classical economists; not surprisingly, it colored the reputation of economists, famously described by Thomas Carlyle as "respectable professors of the dismal science."[12] In more recent years, as we saw earlier, many mainstream economists have become much more cheerful about the prospects for continuing growth in prosperity. The mantle of Malthus has instead fallen upon environmentalists, in some cases with a double portion of his spirit.

In industrializing societies, Malthus's predictions were already being refuted even as he made them; between his time and ours, there have been sustained increases both in population *and* in absolute living standards even for the poorest groups. The population of England and Wales, the first industrial society, has been estimated at 5.5 million at the beginning of the eighteenth century; by the first census in 1801, three years after Malthus's first edition, it had risen to 9 million, doubling to 18 million by the 1851 census.[13] A century later it stood at 44 million, and by the 2011 census it had reached 56.1 million.[14]

---

12. Thomas Carlyle, *Latterday Pamphlets No. 1: The Present Time*, Project Gutenberg, Ebook 1140, last updated November 30, 2012, http://www.gutenberg.org/ebooks/1140.

13. Data for the beginning of the eighteenth century is drawn from D. C. Coleman and S. Pollard, "Introduction: The Industrial Revolution," in *A Survey of English Economic History*, ed. M. W. Thomas (London: Blackie, 1957), 234.

Why was the population increase not checked by famine, as had often been the case in earlier periods? Malthus had failed to take account of the improvements in agricultural productivity spreading throughout England and Wales during the eighteenth century. These increases had a variety of causes, among them the introduction of new techniques of production; the enclosure movement, which amalgamated smaller strips of land into larger units under a single owner; and the stimulus to agricultural enterprise from growing demand in industrial cities.[15]

Similar changes in agricultural organization, techniques, and productivity occurred in other industrializing countries, permitting a huge expansion in population worldwide. This population increase became particularly clear (and, to some, alarming) in the course of the twentieth century. UN estimates show that the world population in 1950 was 2.5 billion; by 2010 it had risen to 6.9 billion.[16] It is particularly interesting to note where this increase has occurred. In "More Developed Countries" the increase was from 0.8 billion in 1950 to 1.2 billion in 2010, but in "Less Developed Countries" population rose from 1.7 billion to 5.7 billion in the same period. Thus, while in 1950 the richer countries accounted for 32 percent of the world's population, by 2010 this share had fallen to only 17 percent.

These figures are consistent with the *theory of demographic transition*.[17] According to this theory, much of human history since the Neolithic revolution in agriculture around 10,000 B.C.E. was

---

14. Census figures from ibid.; for 2011, see UK Office for National Statistics, *2011 Census*, Table 2: Usual Resident Population.
15. Phyllis Deane, *The First Industrial Revolution* (Cambridge: Cambridge University Press, 1965), 37–50.
16. United Nations, Department of Economic and Social Affairs, Population Division, *World Population Prospects, the 2012 Revision*, http://esa.un.org/unpd/wpp/index.htm.
17. Tom Tietenberg, *Environmental Economics and Policy, 2e* (Reading, Mass.: Addison Wesley, 1998), 93–4.

characterized by very slow population growth—birth rates and death rates were almost in balance, with a slight tendency in the long run for birth rates to exceed death rates (and subject, of course, to violent short-run fluctuations in population caused by war, famine, and disease). In the early stages of industrialization, death rates typically fell rapidly at first while birth rates remained high. During this stage, the population growth rate increased sharply, as we saw in the case of England and Wales. Subsequently, however, as societies became richer, the birth rate fell as well. Thus, population in those early-developing societies that had become rich by the mid-twentieth century has grown slowly relative to the population of those still in the intermediate stage of transition, as the UN figures show.

How can these trends be explained? The rapid fall in the death rate as development begins seems attributable to improved food supplies, sanitation, and the spread of medical knowledge; these can all take effect quite quickly. But birth rates take longer to change. In times past, parents knew that many children would fail to survive to adulthood; when families are needed for support in old age, it makes sense to have large ones as a form of insurance. Even when falling child mortality rates meant that people were no longer under the same economic pressures to have large families, the motivation may for a time have outlived its rationale. But other factors were also at work to change attitudes. The growth of urbanization, coupled with child protection legislation, meant that children remained a financial burden on families for longer periods than before. Whereas in traditional rural societies children could do useful work on the farm from an early age, in towns they faced increasingly severe restrictions on factory employment. Over time, both in rural and urban areas, children were obliged to attend ever-lengthening periods of compulsory education. Eventually these influences increased the motive to limit family size.

The means of limiting population were also being transformed. Malthus was correct to argue that the passion between the sexes appears to be a basic human constant. But copulation does not have to generate population. The spread of knowledge about contraceptive methods, and their increasing variety, convenience, and affordability, has helped people in the richer countries reduce their family sizes. This has come to apply even in Roman Catholic countries where religious taboos on efficient methods of contraception tended for a time to reinforce traditional attitudes.

By contrast, many poorer countries are still at the stage where death rates have fallen but birth rates remain high; while there may be some access to modern health services, especially in towns, and (with some exceptions) there is greater food security than before, substantial sections of the population often remain in subsistence agriculture and social attitudes continue to set a high value on family size. In consequence, rapid population growth continues.

Clearly, the theory draws with a very broad brush, and individual countries may be affected by disruptions such as war or a run of crop failures, causing temporary fluctuations in their population statistics. One such disruption has been the modern plague of HIV/AIDS, particularly in Africa south of the Sahara. Government intervention to control population growth may also have an independent impact on its rate. The most striking example of this is China, which since the late 1970s has pursued a strong family planning policy that attempts to restrict couples in urban areas to a single child. This has been achieved principally through fines for those exceeding their quota, but implementation has sometimes included forced abortions. The policy does seem to have reduced the birth rate, and it is possible the one-child rule will soon be relaxed. Under Indira Gandhi, India also tried, less successfully, to use coercive state power to limit families; the unpopularity of this policy, which included compulsory sterilizations, helped cause the fall of her government in 1977.[18]

While demographic transition theory cannot be regarded as rigidly deterministic, there is some empirical support for it; enough, in the view of some writers, to suggest that the upward trend in human numbers will not continue indefinitely but will level out in due course as the final stage of transition becomes the global norm.[19] Even if this is true, there remains the question of the level at which population may be expected to plateau and how long the process will take. The most recent forecasts from the United Nations predict that population will rise from 7.2 billion in 2013 to 9.6 billion in 2050 and may still be rising to nearly 11 billion by the end of the present century.[20]

Pressure on Resources

Although the figures just quoted do suggest a slowing rate of population growth in the course of the present century, they still suggest to some that population growth will eventually be a major factor in environmental catastrophe.[21] In effect, Malthus was not wrong, merely premature. A neo-Malthusian viewpoint, verging on the apocalyptic, was controversially expressed in the book *The Population Bomb*, written in 1970 by two biologists specializing in animal populations, Paul Ehrlich and Anne Ehrlich.[22] This book predicted that the pressure of population on resources, exacerbated by

---

18. For a comparison of population policies in India and China, see Jean Drèze and Amartya Sen, *India: Development and Participation*, 2nd ed. (Oxford: Oxford University Press, 2002), 134–40.
19. Danny Dorling, *Population 10 Billion: The Coming Demographic Crisis and How to Survive It* (London: Constable, 2013), 113–14.
20. United Nations, *World Population Prospects.*
21. The slowing in the rate of population growth may easily be seen from the fact that between 2013 and 2050 population is expected to grow in total by 33 percent over thirty-seven years, whereas from 2050 to 2100 it will grow by only 15 percent over fifty years.

pestilence and war, would lead to mass starvation by the mid-1970s or at any rate the 1980s; of three scenarios the book presented, the most favorable (not considered to be the likeliest) would still have involved half a billion people starving to death.[23] In fact, none of the predictions turned out to be true, and there has so far been no population crash of the kind envisaged. Ehrlich has nonetheless continued to insist on the problems posed by growth in population linked with the demand for an ever-increasing standard of living.

Paul Ehrlich's pessimism led to a famous wager with Julian Simon, from the more optimistic wing of the economics profession. In 1980, Simon invited Ehrlich to select any five commodities he wished and invest a hypothetical $200 in the purchase of each. In 1990, the total value of the quantities purchased would be recalculated at 1990 prices and an allowance deducted for general inflation over the period. If the total exceeded the initial notional investment of $1,000, Simon would write a check for the difference and send it to Ehrlich; if it were less, Ehrlich would do the same for Simon. The check, for $576.07, went to Simon. In other words, the value of the five commodities (chrome, copper, nickel, tin, and tungsten) had actually fallen in real (noninflationary) terms by about 58 percent over the decade. So does this story mean that Ehrlich's doom-laden forecasts may be ignored? Not necessarily. It has since been pointed out that if the end date of the forecasts had been moved to 2011, Simon would have lost the bet.[24]

---

22. The book was published in Paul Ehrlich's name only: see Paul Ehrlich, *The Population Bomb* (New York: Ballantine, 1968). A sequel on the same topic was credited to both authors: Paul R. Ehrlich and Anne H. Ehrlich, *The Population Explosion* (New York: Simon & Schuster, 1991).
23. Ehrlich, *Population Bomb*, 39–44.
24. For the period to 2011, see Jeremy Grantham, "Resource Limitations 2: Separating the Dangerous from the Merely Serious, Appendix 1," GMO Quarterly Bulletin, July 2011. For an interesting account of the wager and subsequent developments, see a recent study by Paul Sabin, *The Bet: Paul Ehrlich, Julian Simon and Our Gamble over Earth's Future,* (New Haven: Yale University Press, 2013).

What, then, does all this signify? It is tempting to conclude that there are two lessons to be learned:

- Don't believe everything environmentalists tell you about imminent disaster.
- Don't believe everything economists tell you, either.

These are both quite useful lessons for any who need them, but there are others as well.

One important point is that trends in both environmental and economic phenomena (as, indeed, in other matters) are crucially dependent on the start and end dates of the relevant statistical series. We shall see this again as we consider other predictions. It is surprising that Simon was so ready to bet that prices of the commodities chosen by Ehrlich would not rise over a period as short as a decade; his own argument allows for price increases in the short term, but he claims that they will only be temporary, as the initial increases encourage substitution and technological innovation to limit use of the scarce commodity. To test Simon's claim properly, a longer period is required. In addition, we should ideally be testing it over a wider range of commodities, as Ehrlich's pessimism is very wide-ranging. Just such a test has been undertaken recently by Mark Perry, using the Dow Jones-AIG Commodity Index adjusted for inflation and covering prices of nineteen commodities across a range of categories: not just metals (two of Ehrlich's five, copper and nickel, are included) but also agricultural products and fuels.[25] Over the period from January 1934 to January 2013, when world population increased from two to seven billion, there was a clear long-term *downward* trend in the index, though there have certainly been sharp

---

25. Mark Perry, "Julian Simon: Still More Right than Lucky in 2013," *Carpe Diem*, American Enterprise Institute, http://www.aei-ideas.org/2013/01/julian-simon-still-more-right-than-lucky-in-2013/.

peaks within that trend: in the long upswing following World War II, from the late seventies to the mid-eighties, and most recently for much of the first decade of the millennium, doubtless reflecting pressures from emerging countries, though this increase too has fallen away in the current recession.

These figures certainly seem to support Simon, but do they conclusively refute Ehrlich? They are inconsistent with the more extreme claims Ehrlich has made from time to time; he is in some danger of acquiring the same reputation as the boy who cried wolf. But the fact that the wolf has not yet turned up does not mean there is no wolf. Also, we have been focusing in this section on the availability of *specific* natural resources, but there is an even more important general question about the impact of economic activity on the global ecosystem within which all such activity has to take place. In an interview given after he lost the bet with Simon, Ehrlich raised this question, mentioning such issues as the depletion of soil and groundwater systems and the potentially catastrophic effects of global warming.[26]

At this point, it may be helpful to introduce a distinction made by Dresner between *nonecospheric* and *ecospheric* natural capital.[27] The former includes specific resources, such as the minerals and other commodities about which Simon and Ehrlich had their wager. Such resources, Dresner argues, can often be replaced by synthetic substitutes. They are therefore less a source of concern than ecospheric resources, which are (or may be) links in complex networks of interrelationships.

As an example, we might compare copper mining with timber harvesting. While the process of extracting copper will no doubt

26. John Tierney, "Betting on the Planet," *New York Times Magazine*, December 2, 1990, http://www.nytimes.com/1990/12/02/magazine/betting-on-the-planet.html.
27. Dresner, *Principles of Sustainability*, 89–90.

have some adverse effects on the local ecosystem, it is likely less potentially damaging than cutting down a rain forest, which will damage biodiversity and remove a sink for greenhouse gases; using the timber as fuel will also release more carbon dioxide into the atmosphere.

The strength of the environmentalist position is that the earth has ultimately limited resources for human beings to take advantage of. The strength of the more optimistic position is that human beings have so far shown great ingenuity in responding to shortages by discovering new resources or economizing on existing ones. The weakness of both positions is that nobody really knows how long this process can continue. Where ecospheric resources are concerned, the element of uncertainty is particularly acute and the risks of causing irreparable environmental damage correspondingly greater.

Given this uncertainty, what are the implications for sustainability? All versions of the concept imply that we should not be taking actions today that may reasonably be expected to impoverish the options facing those who come after us. Retaining for the moment our focus on specific resources, we will examine the implications of this principle for different kinds of resources.

Nonrenewable Recyclable Resources

The metals involved in the wager, and indeed many other products of the mining and quarrying industries, are nonrenewable. However, they have not necessarily been destroyed; there is often a possibility of retrieving them from the use to which they have been put. Copper used in coaxial cables will still be available for future generations; if coaxial cables are no longer needed for telecommunications, the copper may be salvaged and applied to a more urgent use. Future generations will not have the expense of digging it up from deep below the earth's surface, though there will be energy and other costs involved in the recycling process. For this class of resources, our actions seem unlikely to impose a serious burden on our successors even if we cannot be sure how much of them remain to be exploited or how heavy a demand there may be for them in the future.

Nonrenewable Nonrecyclable Resources

Fossil fuels—coal, oil, and natural gas—are the most obvious examples of resources that are both nonrenewable and nonrecyclable, at any rate on a human rather than geological timescale. Once burned as fuel, they will cease to be available as anything other than waste products (which, furthermore, are responsible for a whole range of environmental problems).[28] So in what sense, if any, can they be used in a "sustainable" way?

For the moment, we are concerned only with the availability of fossil fuels to meet our energy needs (the broader environmental implications of using them will be considered later). There are few other areas in which predictions of imminent resource exhaustion have been more frequently made, only to be refuted. In 1865, the distinguished economist W. S. Jevons published a book in which he concluded that British coal reserves would soon be exhausted and that alternative sources of energy could never replace them.[29] While it is true that the UK coal industry went into a slow decline during the twentieth century, it proved possible to meet the continuing needs of the United Kingdom and many other countries through

---

28. Where carbon-based products are used as feedstock for the chemicals industry, however, they may be recyclable; for example, used plastic bottles may be converted into synthetic fabrics, such as fleeces. See "EcoSpun (Eco-fi) Clothing," Eartheasy Solutions for Sustainable Living, http://eartheasy.com/wear_ecospun.htm.

29. W. S. Jevons, *The Coal Question: An Inquiry Concerning the Progress of the Nation, and the Probable Exhaustion of Our Coal Mines* (London: Macmillan, 1865).

importation of coal from vast foreign coal deposits; furthermore, during that time oil was proving to be a major substitute energy source. But pessimistic predictions about oil were also being made, in this case within a few decades of its initial commercial exploitation. Daniel Yergin's recent study of the industry identifies five occasions on which it has been predicted that oil production would peak and then decline as oil wells dried up: in the mid-1880s, at the end of the First World War, at the end of the Second World War, in the 1970s, and in the early years of the new millennium.[30] As with earlier predictions, this latest prediction seemed plausible enough when made; for example, US oil production had fallen from around eleven million barrels per day in 1985 to just over eight million in 2005. Yet by 2012 production had increased to around the 1985 level, and it is becoming clear that the peak has again been indefinitely postponed.[31]

The reasons for this turnaround, which is not confined to the United States, serve as a classic illustration of Julian Simon's argument: shortages from increasing world demand have led to price increases, which in turn have generated a search for new sources and better ways of exploiting existing sources. In the case of oil, a useful distinction may be drawn between *resources* and *reserves*: the former include oil known to exist but for which economically efficient techniques of extraction are not yet available, the latter include only oil that can be economically extracted with existing technology. Some of the new reserves come from unconventional sources, such as Canadian oil sands, which have only been capable of significant commercial development since the early years of this century. Some are from oil fields that have been known about and exploited for some

30. Daniel Yergin, *The Quest: Energy, Security, and the Making of the Modern World* (London: Allen Lane, 2011), 227–41.
31. David Shukman, "The Receding Threat from 'Peak Oil,'" *BBC News: Science and Environment*, July 15, 2013, http://www.bbc.co.uk/news/science-environment-23280894.

time but can only now yield oil from less accessible locations as a result of new technology, perhaps involving horizontal drilling. The technique of *hydraulic fracturing*, more popularly known as "fracking," which fractures rock with high-pressure fluid and is often used in combination with horizontal drilling, promises to release large reserves both of shale oil and shale gas.[32]

But again we have to temper these optimistic predictions. First, and most obvious to environmentalists, the effects of both extracting the fuel and consuming it may be causing serious and perhaps irreversible harm to the ecosystem, particularly through climate change. This issue will be considered at length in a later section. For the sake of argument, let us assume this turns out to be less of a problem than most climate scientists currently anticipate (if, for example, anthropogenic warming were to be offset by planetary cooling from natural forces, such as the start of another "little ice age"). There would still be another problem: even if there are more fossil fuels accessible than was previously thought, they are still a nonrenewable asset. If we take the view that our sustainability obligations extend to distant generations as well as to those in the more immediate future, have we any right to continue using up this commodity at anything like the current rate? This seems to me a further argument for reducing the rate of exploitation of fossil fuels.

However, it is not an argument for reducing this rate to zero. If the principle of sustainability were taken to be "never run down the reserves of any resource that cannot be fully replaced because doing so will deny its use to some future generation," then acceptance of this very principle would also deny its use to any future generation, which seems a reductio ad absurdum. A more pragmatic solution that avoids this internal contradiction would be to continue to use fossil

32. Vikram Rao, *Shale Gas: The Promise and the Peril* (Research Triangle Park, NC: RTI International, 2012).

fuels, as they are at present the cheapest source of usable energy, while at the same time investing in innovations seeking to make renewable sources of energy cheaper. Whether or not we accept the anthropogenic global warming hypothesis, there is still a strong case for switching to sources of energy not based on fossil fuels.

Renewable Resources

In principle, renewable resources do not seem to impose the same ethical dilemma as nonrenewable and nonrecyclable ones. The object of sustainability here is for each generation to use a resource only up to its natural rate of increase. But problems arise both in cases in which the resources are not owned by anyone and thus are openly available and in cases of private ownership.

The case of open resources would apply in circumstances where there is open access to grazing, hunting over an area of forest, or sea fisheries beyond territorial limits. The problem may be analyzed in terms of a prisoner's dilemma model like the one in figure 3.3. In this case, the two strategies would be "use with restraint" and "maximize your own take." The first strategy, if generally applied, would ensure that the resources were exploited sustainably, and the second that they would become exhausted over time. By the same logic as before, the dominant strategy would be "maximize take," yet everyone would be better off in the long run if each pursued a strategy of restraint.

Surprisingly, this logic is not always followed in circumstances where it seems to apply. Many ethical systems, of course, include an injunction that, if followed, would override the prisoner's dilemma outcome: Christianity's Golden Rule (Matt. 7:12) or Kant's categorical imperative would both have this effect.[33] In some communities, where access to grazing or forest resources is held in common by members of a clearly defined group, techniques have been devised to reinforce such moral principles by effective policing of the behavior of group members, as we shall see in chapter 6. But there are obviously important instances where neither morality nor community policing have been sufficient to prevent stocks of natural resources from being seriously threatened by overexploitation.

A striking example is the depletion of world fisheries, of which the overfishing of cod stock in the North Sea or off the Newfoundland banks is just one of the better-known examples. A joint report published in 2009 by the World Bank and the UN Food and Agricultural Organization attributes this in part to an excessive number of fishing boats and more intensive fishing technologies, as the prisoner's dilemma model would predict; at the same time, though, rising sea temperatures and sea acidity, and other forms of maritime pollution, have been exacerbating the problem by damaging habitats, and in some parts of the world misguided subsidy policies pursued by governments have helped ensure that more and more fishers would continue to pursue fewer and fewer fish.[34]

As we also saw in chapter 3, enthusiasts for the property rights approach consider that private ownership, where feasible, may resolve problems of overuse by giving owners an incentive to preserve their assets. But when considering issues of long-run sustainability, this may not always be the case. If I own a forest that is achieving net growth of 2 percent per year and this offers a return broadly comparable to similarly risky investments elsewhere, I may be inclined to manage the forest sustainably and sell only enough timber each year to allow for replacement, passing the estate on to my heirs. But I may prefer to sell off much of the timber

33. Immanuel Kant, *Groundwork of the Metaphysic of Morals*, trans. H. J. Paton (New York: Harper and Row, 1964), 70.
34. World Bank and Food and Agriculture Organization of the United Nations, *The Sunken Billions: The Economic Justification for Fisheries Reform* (Washington, DC: World Bank, 2009).

to provide funds that allow me to pursue my interests in gambling and fast cars while there is still time. In other words, we are back at the issue of intergenerational distribution of welfare; private market systems cannot guarantee the interests of future generations who have no voice in the market. Forests also raise a second problem, as they generate external effects through their role in the ecosystem; these in general will not be fully reflected in the private return to individual owners. To address this issue, we now turn to the question of ecosystems.

Sustainability and Ecosystems

In the final sections of this chapter we shift our focus from the impact of economic activity on specific natural resources to its effect on ecospheric resources, to use Dresner's terminology—that is, on ecosystems or their subsystems. We will look in particular at the impact of "waste": unwanted outputs from industrial activity that must be disposed of. We begin with one of the most controversial environmental issues: global warming. Before we do, note that even if there were no global warming problem, industrial waste disposal would still cause serious threats to ecosystems.

Global Warming: The Ongoing Debate

The emission of *greenhouse gases* to the atmosphere is alleged to cause potentially catastrophic climate change. The theory behind this was developed by a number of scientists from a diversity of disciplines, beginning with de Saussure and his "hot box" theory in the 1770s.[35] It became a matter for active (and frequently acrimonious) public

35. Yergin, *Quest*, 419–31.

debate in mid–1988, following the testimony of a NASA climatologist, James Hansen, to the US Senate Energy Committee in June, which was followed in November by the creation of the Intergovernmental Panel on Climate Change (IPCC) in Geneva; this body was jointly established by two United Nations agencies, the World Meteorological Organization (WMO) and the United Nations Environment Programme (UNEP).[36]

Climate scientists have written many explanations of the greenhouse effect, so only the briefest summary will be attempted here.[37] When the sun's energy reaches the earth, some is absorbed to warm the surface of the earth but some is reflected back into space. If the earth had no atmosphere, a lot more would be reflected, but, as it is, gases in the atmosphere trap part of the sun's energy. These gases include water vapor, methane, ozone, and some others, but carbon dioxide is the greenhouse gas on which much attention has been focused, as it is emitted in large quantities by the burning of fossil fuels and remains in the atmosphere for long periods. These gases prevent the temperature of the earth's surface from falling too low, but the theory asserts that as their presence in the atmosphere increases with global economic activity, more energy is being trapped and surface temperatures are warming.

When Hansen made his presentation to the Senate committee, he claimed that the rise in temperature had now been empirically verified. This view was highly controversial, as have been subsequent attempts to support it, including the work of three atmospheric scientists, Michael Mann, Ray Bradley, and Malcolm Hughes, who developed a controversial diagram known as the "hockey stick graph." It was based on a construction of Northern Hemisphere

36. Ibid., 453–70.
37. A simple explanation is given in Robert Henson, *The Rough Guide to Climate Change*, 3rd ed. (London: Rough Guides, 2011). A more technical but accessible explanation will be found in David Archer, *Global Warming: Understanding the Forecast* (Hoboken, NJ: Wiley, 2012).

climate records from 1000 C.E. to the late 1990s.[38] For most of this period, there were no instrumental measurements, so information came from proxies, observations of a range of natural phenomena, including two in particular: the rings of very long-lived trees, which vary in thickness according to the relative warmth of the climate, and borehole samples from the earth or thick ice sheets. Tree rings allow estimates for about twelve hundred years, while borehole records are considered sufficiently reliable for about five hundred.[39] Only from the late nineteenth century could these data be compared with, or modified by, thermometer records. The data were subject to large year-by-year variations but still appeared to show that the overall, long-run trend in temperatures had been slightly downward over the millennium until the later nineteenth century (the "shaft" of the hockey stick) but had since taken an increasingly rapid upturn (the "blade"); the 1990s were apparently the hottest decade of the second millennium. A version of the graph was prominently featured in the "Summary for Policymakers" from the IPCC Third Assessment Report in 2001.[40]

The validity of the data on which the hockey stick graph is based has been questioned, but that is only one of many controversies associated with the theory of global warming.[41] Is the recent upward trend caused by natural, nonhuman causes, often responsible for temperature variations in the earth's past before we came on the

38. Michael E. Mann, Raymond S. Bradley, and Malcolm K. Hughes, "Northern Hemisphere Temperatures during the Past Millennium: Inferences, Uncertainties and Limitations," *Geophysical Research Letters* 26, no. 6 (1999): 759–62, doi: 10.1029/1999GL900070.

39. Archer, *Global Warming*, 145–47.

40. Intergovernmental Panel on Climate Change, *Third Assessment Report: Climate Change 2001, Summary for Policymakers* (Cambridge: Cambridge University Press for the IPCC, 2011), Fig. 1(b), http://www.grida.no/climate/ipcc_tar/wg1/pdf/WG1_TAR-FRONT.pdf.

41. See Stephen McIntyre and Ross McKitrick, "Hockey Sticks, Principal Components, and Spurious Significance," *Geophysical Research Letters* 32, no. 3 (2005), doi: 10.1029/2004GL021750.

scene? And even if we are now entering a new period of global warming, how high and how quickly will temperatures rise? There are also a host of questions about the likely *consequences* of a sustained increase in temperatures. How will an increase affect food and water supplies and public health? Will some areas actually benefit at the expense of others? Will warming destroy or enhance biodiversity?

Since these are questions requiring both breadth and depth of relevant scientific knowledge to answer, those who lack the necessary scientific background naturally ask whether scientists have reached consensus on the issues. On the fundamental question of whether human activity really is causing global warming, environmentalists claim that a strong consensus does in fact exist. A recent survey by John Cook and his colleagues of abstracts of peer-reviewed scientific papers on climate change found that over 97 percent of abstracts that took a position on anthropogenic global warming (AGW) endorsed the view that it was indeed taking place. However, almost two-thirds of abstracts expressed no position on AGW, so Cook and his colleagues approached authors directly to ask their position on this issue. They obtained responses from 14 percent of those e-mailed; the usable sample amounted to 1,189 authors. Among these self-raters, 34.9 percent held "no position"; of those who did take a position, 96.4 percent were AGW endorsers. While not all of the endorsers stated that humans were the primary or only cause of global warming, Cook and his colleagues found only 3.6 percent of self-raters who totally rejected the AGW hypothesis.[42] The study was broadly consistent with earlier findings on scientific opinion, showing over time a slight increase in support for the theory.

42. John Cook et al., "Quantifying the Consensus on Anthropogenic Global Warming in the Scientific Literature," *Environmental Research Letters* 8 (2013): esp. tables 3 and 4, doi:10.1088/1748–9326/8/2/024024.

Notwithstanding the substantial proportion of abstracts that take no position on AGW, its endorsers are clearly much more numerous than its deniers. But climate skeptics argue that this appearance of consensus reflects groupthink among scientists that affects the peer-review process and ensures that any who challenge the consensus find it difficult to publish their research. Some consider this view vindicated by the release in November 2009 of some "hacked" e-mails from and to members of the staff of the University of East Anglia's Climatic Research Unit (CRU)—an episode known as "Climategate."[43] The CRU has been a major source of research supporting the global warning case. A number of the e-mails seemed to suggest that some of its members were reluctant to provide details of the evidence on which their work was based, and certain e-mails showed a willingness to discredit a journal that published research by scientists skeptical of climate change. Although some of the e-mail material was undoubtedly distorted in the media by being quoted out of context and subsequent official investigations cleared the CRU staff and their correspondents of serious misconduct, the episode lent support to the perception that the scientific "consensus" was seeking to make life difficult for its critics.[44] It also weakened the argument for action on global warming shortly before the United Nations Climate Change Conference opened in Copenhagen in early December (many suspected that the leaks had been timed with this end in view).

---

43. See James Delingpole, "Climategate: the Final Nail in the Coffin of 'Anthropogenic Global Warming,'" *Telegraph*, November 20, 2009, http://blogs.telegraph.co.uk/news/jamesdelingpole/100017393/climategate-the-final-nail-in-the-coffin-of-anthropogenic-global-warming/.

44. Thus the Science and Technology Committee of the House of Commons criticized the Climatic Research Unit's reluctance to share data and recommended greater openness, but cleared the unit of scientific malpractice. See House of Commons, Select Committee on Science and Technology, *The Disclosure of Climate Data from the Climatic Research Unit at the University of East Anglia*, Eighth Report of Session 2009-10, March 31, 2010 (London: Stationery Office, 2010), 47.

Of course, academics who have developed their reputations in establishing a particular theoretical approach will be reluctant to agree that they have spent their lives in a worthless pursuit; some may even engage in academic politics to strengthen their own position. Such behavior may be criticized, but it does not of itself invalidate their scientific work. While the Climategate affair may have damaged the global warming case in the eyes of politicians or the general public, it in no way demonstrated that the science was "wrong" or that it lacked empirical support. Of course, the opponents of the AGW hypothesis sometimes have unscientific reasons for their own stance; there are powerful financial interests in the energy industry who seek to discredit the view that further economic development based on fossil fuels threatens ecological catastrophe. The role of industrial lobbyists and other advocacy groups in the political process will be further considered in chapter 7. Here, it is enough to note that we cannot judge the validity of the science by the supposed interests of those who either support or attack it.

In a 2010 report on climate change, the Royal Society sets a good example of how to explain contested scientific issues to a wider public. It divides the science on this topic into three categories: "well established," "wide consensus but continuing debate," and "where there remains substantial uncertainty."[45] The report is concerned only with the causes and extent of climate change, not with its impact on ecosystems or human welfare.

As the report makes clear, a major problem for the study of climatic systems is that they are subject to strong but complex *feedback effects*; such systems are known as *chaotic* (financial systems provide another example). In chaotic systems, very small changes in initial conditions can lead to very large differences in final outcomes (the popular

45. The Royal Society, *Climate Change: A Summary of the Science* (London: Royal Society, 2010).

if perhaps mythical example is of the butterfly in the forest that causes hurricanes at sea by fluttering its wings).[46] Thus an initial warming effect caused by, say, a rise in atmospheric carbon dioxide may reduce the areas covered by snow and ice; this lowers the planet's *albedo*, or reflectivity, so that less solar energy is radiated back into space, which in turn causes further warming—a "positive" feedback effect reinforcing the initial impact. Feedback effects may be modeled in computer simulations of climate change, but because of their complexity they may sometimes be overlooked, with adverse effects on the predictions of the model.

The Royal Society report includes in its "well established" category the finding that the earth's surface had indeed warmed in the course of the twentieth century, by a little less than one degree Celsius on average, though not at a steady rate and with variations across the globe. In particular, the Arctic regions have experienced relatively more warming, and the area of sea ice has declined here (though it has increased slightly round Antarctica). This has been associated with increasing average concentrations of carbon dioxide and other greenhouse gases. The report, however, acknowledges that there is less certainty about the impact of nonhuman influences, such as volcanic eruptions and variations in solar energy emissions, on climate change. While increases in water vapor are thought to increase global temperatures, "substantial uncertainty" remains concerning this factor's precise role. In particular, there is uncertainty about how much water vapor will increase in consequence of the initial warming and thus how far this positive feedback will amplify the initial change (clouds may also have a negative feedback, reflecting solar energy before it reaches the earth's surface). Such

46. The term *butterfly effect* was coined by Edward Norton Lorenz: see Kenneth Chang, "Edward N. Lorenz, A Meteorologist and a Father of Chaos Theory, Dies at 90," *New York Times,* April 17, 2008, http://www.nytimes .com/2008/04/17/us/17lorenz.html?_r=0 (accessed September 29, 2014).

uncertainties make it more difficult to predict the degree of *climate sensitivity*—that is, the temperature change that would result from a doubling of atmospheric carbon dioxide. The report cites the mainstream estimate that such a doubling would produce warming in the range of 2 degrees to 4.5 degrees Celsius. Prior to industrialization, the gas was present in the atmosphere in a concentration of a little over 280 parts per million; in 2013, as the UK Meteorological Office notes, it passed 400 parts per million, about 40 percent higher.[47]

Recently, a gap appears to have opened between the temperatures predicted by the standard models of global warming and the temperatures observed. In the fifteen years between the 1998 "high" observed in the hockey stick study and 2013, there has been no sustained rise in surface temperatures, despite the continuing increase in emission of greenhouse gases into the atmosphere. A diagram circulated by Ed Hawkins of the Department of Meteorology at the University of Reading shows that the actual path followed by temperatures over that period has been heading for the lower boundary of the range of predictions provided in models of the warming process.[48] Possible explanations include the increase of heat uptake in the ocean depths rather than on the surface during the period, with perhaps more minor effects coming from changes in solar energy reaching the planet. Hawkins points out that "decadal variability" is not unexpected and indeed is sometimes built into climate models.

47. Meteorological Office, *The Recent Pause in Warming, Paper 1: Observing Changes in the Climate System,* accessed July 27 2013, http://www.metoffice.gov.uk/research /news/recent-pause-in-warming

48. In statistical terms, the temperature fell to the lower 95 percent confidence limit of these predictions. See Ed Hawkins, "Recent Slowdown in Global Surface Temperature Rise," *Climate Lab Book*, National Centre for Atmospheric Science, July 25, 2013, http://www.climate-lab-book.ac.uk/2013/recent-slowdown/

It should be noted, as the UK's Meteorological Office has explained, that other indicators of global warming, such as the decline in Arctic sea ice, have continued during these fifteen years.[49] But there has also been speculation that the long-run climate sensitivity to carbon dioxide emissions may have been overestimated in earlier work. If so, there will be more time to develop and implement an effective strategy for dealing with the problem, assuming that the time is not simply wasted in procrastination.

In September 2013, some of the findings of the Fifth Assessment Report of the IPCC were published; further material was released during 2014. The first release addresses the physical evidence for climate change; its main thrust is to confirm and update previous analysis.[50] Thus, it concludes that "warming of the climate system is unequivocal"; from 1880 to 2012, the combined land and ocean data suggest a surface warming of 0.85 degrees Celsius on average over the globe, though there are a few cold spots.[51] The report is dismissive of the recent slowdown in the rate of warming since 1998, pointing out (correctly) that short-run trends are highly sensitive to start and end points.[52] With "medium confidence," it repeats the suggestion noted earlier that part of the explanation for the slower rise of surface temperatures is a redistribution of heat within the oceans.[53] The fourth report considered human activity "very likely" to have caused global warming; the fifth, however, increased this probability to "extremely likely," implying that whereas there was

---

49. Meteorological Office, *Recent Pause in Warming*.
50. "IPCC, 2013: Summary for Policy Makers," in *Climate Change 2013: the Physical Science Basis. Contribution of Working Group I to the Fifth Assessment Report of the Intergovernmental Panel on Climate Change*, ed. T. F. Stocker et al. (Cambridge: Cambridge University Press, 2013).
51. Ibid., 2, 3 and 4 (figure SPM1).
52. Ibid., 3. It is also clear from figure SPM.1 in the summary that the generally strong upward trend during the past century was consistent with pauses from time to time, particularly in the 1950s to 1970s.
53. Ibid., 13.

previously one chance in ten that the hypothesis might be mistaken, there is now only one chance in twenty.[54] However, the temperature increase estimated to result from a doubling of atmospheric carbon dioxide concentrations was changed from a range of 2 to 4.5 degrees Celsius to a range of 1.5 to 4.5 degrees Celsius.

The warming of the oceans will cause sea levels to rise because of thermal expansion, and the rise in surface temperatures and the consequent melting of land-based ice sheets and glaciers will cause further sea-level increases. Estimates vary depending on the particular climate model used, but the increase from the end of the twentieth century to the end of the twenty-first century ranges from a low of 0.26 meters in the most optimistic projection to a high of 0.98 meters in the most pessimistic.[55]

The uncertainties associated with predicting the *rate* of global warming are compounded when predicting the *impact* of global warming. We now examine some areas where already existing threats to ecosystems would be intensified by significant global warming.

Biodiversity on Land and Sea

Extinction of species, of course, has often occurred as a result of natural processes, but our concern here is with the human impact on biodiversity. The media regularly report on the more spectacular examples, such as the threat to large animals from illegal hunting (elephants for their ivory tusks, rhinoceroses for the supposed aphrodisiac properties of their horns, gorillas for "bushmeat," and so on). The destruction of natural habitats for agricultural and commercial reasons has also had a serious effect on wildlife. The

54. Ibid., 15.
55. Ibid., 23–24 and figure SPM.9.

replacement of virgin forest on Borneo, first by rubber plantations and subsequently by the cultivation of palm oil, has much reduced an area rich in plant and animal life. In Madagascar, too, clearing of forests as part of the traditional slash-and-burn system of subsistence agriculture has seriously damaged a unique refuge for many species found nowhere else on the planet.

Waste generated by humans is an obvious threat to animal life. A traditional method for disposing unwanted by-products has been to use the oceans as a "sink," whether by dumping them from ships or by discharging effluents into rivers, as with chemical products (including fertilizer washed down from agricultural land) or sewage, and letting these products find their own way to the sea. This has been happening for centuries, but a more recent threat has come from the rapid growth of the plastics industry.

Remarkable amounts of plastic products have found their way into the sea. These tend to concentrate in particular areas, and in recent years there has been some media interest in the accumulation of plastic in the North Pacific subtropical gyre, an area of ocean to the north of Hawaii characterized by slow spirals of currents that tend to collect floating rubbish. The size of the garbage patch has been a matter of some controversy: "about the size of Texas," according to Greenpeace, but "less than 1 percent of the geographic size of Texas," according to an oceanographer at Oregon State University.[56] The important issue is not so much the relation between the size of the patch and the area of Texas as the implications of the plastic for the health of ocean inhabitants, and on this there is more agreement. Plastics do not readily biodegrade. Larger items such as plastic bags

56. Greenpeace International, "The Trash Vortex," http://www.greenpeace.org/international/en/campaigns/oceans/pollution/trash-vortex/; "Garbage Patch' not Nearly as Big as Portrayed in the Media," *Oregon State University News and Research Communications*, January 4, 2011, http://oregonstate.edu/ua/ncs/archives/2011/jan/oceanic-"garbage-patch"-not-nearly-big-portrayed-media.

may cause asphyxiation or entanglement; over time, plastics may break up into smaller particles that are harmful when ingested by seabirds and marine mammals, particularly since these particles may also absorb toxins found in the sea. Further, they may disrupt ecosystems by providing oceanic "transport" for species to areas in which they are nonnative.

Although areas of concentration such as the North Pacific subtropical gyre are particularly striking, plastic refuse is found widely dispersed throughout the oceans and has recently been discovered in the Southern Ocean round Antarctica, previously thought to be relatively unaffected.[57]

There are many reasons for being concerned about species diversity that are independent of global warming. What contribution might climate change make to the problem?

The shrinkage of the Arctic sea ice, particularly over the summer, is confirmed in the latest IPCC evidence; the size of the sea ice fell by around a quarter, from over eight million square kilometers in the early 1980s to a little over six million by 2010.[58] This shrinkage, it is feared, may well reduce the habitat for creatures that live on the ice: a media-friendly example is the polar bear. This argument has been queried by Bjorn Lomborg on the grounds that so far the main reason for any decline in polar bear numbers seems to have been bear hunting by local Inuit communities.[59]

Emissions of carbon dioxide have caused damage to coral reefs, an important marine habitat, for two reasons: first, they increase ocean acidification, which may prevent coral from forming, and, second, insofar as the emissions raise sea temperatures, they may kill off

57. Zoe Holman, "Plastic Debris Reaches Southern Ocean," *Guardian*, September 27, 2012, http://www.guardian.co.uk/environment/2012/sep/27/plastic-debris-southern-ocean-pristine.
58. "IPCC, 2013: Summary," 10, figure SPM.3(b).
59. Bjorn Lomborg, *Cool It: The Skeptical Environmentalist's Guide to Global Warming*, 2nd ed. (New York: Vintage, 2010), 4–8.

coral, which are very sensitive to heat, creating the phenomenon of coral bleaching. But there are other human sources of damage to coral reefs, such as a covering of rubbish, which reduces exposure to sunlight, or direct damage caused by clumsy scuba divers.

There remains the question of why preservation of species diversity should matter. As we saw in chapter 2, some argue for this from a religious standpoint or from an ethical perspective based on deep ecology. But for those who do not share these values, there is a more direct argument based on enlightened self-interest. Because of the complexity of the biosphere, we do not always know what contribution an individual species may be making to our present or future welfare as fellow members of that biosphere. As a general rule, it might be wise to give it the benefit of the doubt.[60]

Water Scarcity

Population growth implies a need for more fresh water, both for sanitation and for use in agriculture or industry. The growth of incomes has further increased demand, which has been rising at twice the rate of world population, according to the UN Food and Agricultural Organization's Water Unit.[61] The unit claims that at present there is no *global* water scarcity; this, however, is quite compatible with local shortages in the arid and semiarid regions. In 2012, it was estimated that 1.2 billion people were suffering from physical water scarcity while a further 1.6 billion were experiencing "economic" water scarcity, which occurs when there is sufficient water for an area's needs but an inadequate infrastructure to deliver it.[62]

60. For more detail on this, see Common and Stagl, *Ecological Economics*, 526–27.
61. "Hot Issues: Water Scarcity," FAO Water Development and Management Unit, 2013, http://www.fao.org/nr/water/issues/scarcity.html.

Although the most vulnerable areas are mainly to be found in the developing countries of Africa and Asia, shortages are by no means unknown in richer countries. In recent years they have become acute in some southern areas of the United States. In Texas on November 1, 2013, Governor Perry renewed the emergency disaster proclamation first issued in 2011 as a consequence of "exceptional drought conditions." Periods of low rainfall, of course, are not new in Texas, but the problem of drought has been exacerbated over the years by the demands of cattle ranching, cotton farming, thirsty cities, and, most recently, fracking, which makes very heavy demands on water.

To what extent will global warming exacerbate the problem? On one hand, warming is expected to cause greater humidity from oceanic evaporation and hence to increase precipitation; however, this is not expected to be uniform across the globe. The latest IPCC findings confirm the increases "with high confidence" in the midlatitude land areas of the Northern Hemisphere, but the findings are less confident for other areas. A recent report for the US government notes that annual average precipitation has increased by about 5 percent in the past half century but predicts that in future northern areas will become wetter while southern areas, especially the Southwest, will become drier.[63] Much of the additional precipitation has taken the form of "heavy downpours," and it is likely that such events will become more frequent, especially in the northeastern states.

62. UN Department of Economic and Social Affairs, *International Decade for Action: 'Water for Life' 2005–2015*, http://www.un.org/waterforlifedecade/scarcity/shtml.
63. US Global Climate Change Research Program, *Global Climate Change Impacts in the United States, 2009 Report* (New York: Cambridge University Press, 2009), 30, http://www.globalchange.gov/usimpacts.

Food Security

Water scarcity is obviously a factor in determining food security. One of the reasons the world has so far not suffered neo-Malthusian outcomes from rapid population growth has been the success of the Green Revolution. This term was coined by William Gaud of the US Agency for International Development (USAID) in a speech to the Society for International Development in 1968.[64] He was referring to the changes transforming agriculture in developing countries, based on the development of new high-yield seeds—"Mexican wheat, miracle rice"—supported by investments in fertilizer, pesticides, and infrastructure such as rural roads and irrigation. But the high water-intensity of modern agriculture, in particular, is a major cause of concern for the future of food supply, given the diversion of water to the needs of industry and growing urban centers.

As FitzRoy and Papyrakis point out, limited water availability is not the only environmental problem for food supply.[65] Others include loss of agricultural land to expanding urban areas, communications, soil erosion, and the spread of desertification. Modern farming techniques may also be implicated in the recent collapse of many pollinating insect populations, perhaps through destruction of habitat or reaction to chemicals, though there has been debate over the causes. In addition, the shift in food demand from direct consumption of cereals to consumption of animal-based food products (meat and dairy) exacerbates the problem of feeding the world, since eating animals fed grain uses much more grain per calorie than the direct consumption of grain itself would.

64. William S. Gaud, "The Green Revolution: Accomplishments and Apprehensions," address before the Society for International Development, Washington, DC, March 8, 1968, http://www.agbioworld.org/biotech-info/topics/borlaug/borlaug-green.html.
65. Felix R. FitzRoy and Elissaios Papyrakis, *An Introduction to Climate Change Economics and Policy* (London: Earthscan, 2010), 23–42.

The diversion of land to grow "biomass" as a renewable source of bioenergy has is another problem for food supply. The theory underlying this shift has been that biomass is "carbon neutral" because it provides a closed carbon loop; although the use of plant sources as fuel does release carbon to the atmosphere, the growth of new plants as replacement will absorb the carbon again. But as Dieter Helm argues, the loop is not really closed at all because the harvesting and transport of biomass itself requires energy use, which currently is often carbon based.[66] And there is also the loss of food supply—for example, from the diversion of maize output to bioenergy use. Not all biomass developments are harmful, however; FitzRoy and Papyrakis recommend the production of biogas from sources, such as waste, that do not compete with food production.[67]

The threats to food security noted so far would be present even if there were no further prospect of global warming. If temperatures continue to rise within the range anticipated by the latest findings of the IPCC, how will this affect the situation? Some have suggested that at least at the lower end of the range there are possible advantages for agricultural production. As we have seen, there are likely to be higher levels of rainfall overall, perhaps mainly concentrated in the higher northern latitudes. Thus, output may increase in those areas by more than it falls in the arid areas, increasing global supply. Greater amounts of carbon dioxide in the atmosphere may have a beneficial effect on plant growth (as, of course, the analogy of the greenhouse would suggest).

---

66. Dieter Helm, *The Carbon Crunch: How We're Getting Climate Change Wrong—and How to Fix It* (New Haven: Yale University Press, 2012), 91–94. Note that in 2011 the Scientific Committee of the European Environment Agency also criticized the case for biomass on grounds of misleading greenhouse gas accounting. See "Opinion of the Scientific Committee of the European Environment Agency on Greenhouse Gas Accounting in Relation to Bioenergy," European Environment Agency, http://www.eea.europa.eu/about-us/governance/scientific-committee/sc-opinions/opinions-on-scientific-issues/sc-opinion-on-greenhouse-gas/view.
The EU has, however, provided generous subsidies to farmers to encourage shifting to biomass.
67. FitzRoy and Papyrakis, *An Introduction to Climate Change Economics*, 40.

These issues are considered in a report from the current IPCC round, released on 31 March 2014.[68] This suggests that for a 2°C or more increase in temperatures, losses in production of major crops (defined as wheat, rice and maize) would, on a global scale, more than offset gains, particularly from 2030 onwards.

Conclusion

The IPCC's 2007 report claimed that the Himalayan glaciers could melt by 2035 if global warming continued at its current rate, with disastrous implications for regional agriculture. This timescale is well outside the realm of possibility, and the assertion attracted severe criticism; it turned out to have been made in an interview in a popular science journal in 1999, not in a peer-reviewed article. The IPCC was obliged to issue an apology that proper procedures for vetting its reports had not been followed in this case.[69] This serves as another reminder that the environmentalist cause may be harmed by overstating threats. In the foregoing brief review of the evidence, I have tried to take a cautious rather than a sensationalist approach. Yet, overall, there is much cause for concern.

This chapter has focused on sustainability, and we have seen that there are only limited opportunities to substitute produced for natural capital. While advantage should certainly be taken of such opportunities for substitution as do exist, these limitations mean that the weak sustainability principle is ethically suspect and must be replaced by a stronger version that would safeguard irreplaceable

68. IPCC, 2014, Summary for Policymakers". In *Climate Change 2014: Impacts, Adaptation and Vulnerability. Part A: Global and Sectoral Aspects. Contribution of Working Group II to the Fifth A ssessment Report of the Intergovernmental Panel on Climate Change* Field, C.B., *et al* (Cambridge University Press, Cambridge UK and New York, USA), 17-28 and Figure SPM.7.

69. Damian Carrington, "IPCC Officials Admit Mistake over Melting Himalayan Glaciers," *Guardian*, January 20, 2010, http://www.guardian.co.uk/environment/2010/jan/20/ipcc-himalayan-glaciers-mistake.

natural resources as well as crucial ecosystems. This is no easy task, given the effects of population growth, the demand by rich societies to increase their consumption, and the determination of poorer societies to catch up with the rich. It is difficult to see how all these aspirations can be fulfilled using known resources with existing technologies. Whether from overexploitation or pollution, there are too many threats to water supplies and food security as well as to biodiversity. And we have seen that a reliance on fossil fuel resources to meet our future requirements for usable energy raises two distinct issues. First, these resources are irreplaceable once used. The amounts that remain available for use are uncertain, though it is likely they will be more than sufficient for energy needs at least in the medium term, though at an environmental cost. Second, there is a plausible model, accepted by very many climate scientists, that their very use is causing global warming. There is still much debate over both its extent and likely effects. Unfortunately, there is a nonnegligible downside risk that these effects could be seriously damaging to the environment and hence to humans and other species who inhabit it. This risk makes it very unwise to continue with business as usual.

In chapters 5 and 6 I will consider how government policy should deal with the urgent environmental issues this chapter has explored.

5

Ethical Decision Making

How should policymakers approach the kinds of problems outlined in chapter 4? I will begin this chapter by proposing some guiding general principles that develop in part from earlier discussions in chapters 2 and 3. The second part of the chapter will consider how these principles should be made operational for planners deciding on particular environmental projects. Here, I shall consider the use and limitations of the economist's technique of cost-benefit analysis and will describe how it has been developed by some economists to take account of the ethical issues raised so far.

Principles for Policymakers

While theological writers have often been particularly concerned with *distributional* questions (how is the global cake to be divided up?), mainstream economists have tended to emphasize the relative *efficiency* of resource use under different policies (how do we get a bigger cake with less cost in resources?). For ecologically minded economists, however, both questions are important, as are issues about how to deal with uncertainty and political questions about who is to make the decisions. The latter will be postponed to later chapters; here the focus will be mainly on the planner in central or local government.

Fairness

We begin with the distributional question. We saw in chapter 4 that the world is a very unequal place and that many of those concerned about the environment are concerned too about a fairer distribution of resources. Chapter 3 noted that the economist's default philosophy of utilitarianism can be given quite a strong egalitarian slant using the argument that a dollar given to a poor person, who can use it to satisfy her basic needs, increases social welfare more than a dollar taken from a rich person will reduce it, since its loss will hardly be noticed.

Since utilitarianism, despite it attractions, is not universally accepted, in particular because it can be taken to imply that that the end justifies the means, it is worth asking whether there are any other arguments for fairness. The best known of these was developed by the late John Rawls, a Harvard philosopher who died in 2002.[1] Rawls was concerned that utilitarianism neglected what he saw as "inviolable" individual rights. To repair this omission, he based his own argument on a version of *social contract theory*, which asserts that by coming together to live in societies we implicitly agree to certain principles by which we will govern our mutual relationships. These principles, in Rawls's view, might justify the use of compulsion in

1. John Rawls, *A Theory of Justice* (Cambridge, MA: Harvard University Press, 1971).

redistributing income from richer to poorer but would also protect essential rights and liberties.

Rawls suggested that we try to envision ourselves making a choice between different sets of principles from behind a *veil of ignorance*. In such a situation, which he calls the *original position*, it is as if we were disembodied souls waiting to be born, motivated by rational self-interest, free to choose the principles that would govern the society into which we would be born *but ignorant of the position we ourselves would occupy once we got there*. Rawls believed that we would then choose a society in which the worst-off member would be better off than in any other form of society, since any one of us might be that worst-off member. Such a society would not be one of perfect equality because some measure of inequality, by acting as an incentive to effort and enterprise, might make all its members, including the worst off, better off than in a more equal society. But only to the extent that it did so would the inequality be justified (Rawls calls this the *difference principle*).

This argument has found support from some Christian theologians, as it encapsulates the Golden Rule by inviting us to consider how we would wish to be treated if we found ourselves in the position of the poorest members of society. Nonetheless, other Christians have objected, arguing that using rational self-interest as a motivation for decision making is "immoral" and reflects the overemphasis on the individual characteristic of liberalism (in the classic philosophical sense of the term).[2]

Economists have criticized Rawls from a different angle: they question whether it would be rational, in the original position, to choose the system that benefited the worst-off person the most. Rawls's approach uses the decision-making strategy known as the

2. For further discussion of the Christian response to Rawls, see Duncan B. Forrester, *Christian Justice and Public Policy* (Cambridge: Cambridge University Press, 1997), 113–39.

maximin (from *maximum minimorum*, the greatest of the least). Suppose you are offered a choice of two societies, Rawlsiana and Benthamania. In Rawlsiana, income for the worst-off person is $10 per year more than for the very worst-off person in Benthamania, but everyone else in Rawlsiana is $1,000 poorer than their counterpart in Benthamania. Would it be rational for you to choose to be born into the former society, as a strict application of the maximin strategy would imply? Using similar examples, John Harsanyi has argued that such extreme caution would be characteristic of irrational rather than rational behavior; many economists would probably accept his suggestion that rationality would lead us to choose, from behind the veil of ignorance, a society in which average utility was maximized.[3] We will revisit the maximin criterion when we consider decision making under uncertainty.

We also need to consider the principles that should govern fairness across the generations. In the last chapter we rather took it for granted that fairness requires our present generation to make good what we use up before we move out; otherwise, are we not cheating our children, as is commonly alleged? George Orwell once remarked that a test of anyone's morality, or lack of it, was whether that person cared about what happened to society after the person's death.[4] Under any ethical system, for the present generation to exhaust its resources in such a way as to plunge the next one into poverty would surely be reprehensible. But according to the more optimistic economists, we would not be doing this to future generations even if we were to use up some irreplaceable resources; overall, they may still enjoy a higher standard of living than we do. On this reading, to hold back on our own consumption of resources in order to leave more

3. John C. Harsanyi, *Essays on Ethics, Social Behavior and Scientific Explanation* (Dordrecht: D. Reidel, 1976).
4. D. J. Taylor, *Orwell: The Life* (London: Vintage, 2004), 122.

136

for them would be, in a travesty of Robin Hood, to take from the (relatively) poor to help the rich. Our view of this argument depends on whether we think that further income growth is possible, given the earth's resources and future developments in technology, and where we would situate ourselves along the spectrum from weak to strong versions of sustainability.

A further ethical question concerning future generations is precisely *how* to weight their interests against those of present generations. On this question, there has been some argument among economists going back to the 1920s. In 1928, Frank Ramsey argued from the standpoint of utilitarian ethics that we should give just the same weight to the welfare of a member of a future generation as we give to one of our own.[5] A similar point of view has been expressed by other writers, including A. C. Pigou and, most recently, Nicholas Stern, the author of a controversial report to the UK government on climate change.[6] This view has, however, been criticized as utopian by other writers, such as Dieter Helm, who attacks it as not reflecting the actual preferences of ordinary people (as opposed to some academic economists).[7] While we may feel altruistic impulses toward others, the strength of these impulses is a decreasing function of the perceived closeness of the others to ourselves, whether we consider closeness in terms of space, time, or consanguinity.

Helm's view seems highly plausible as a factual statement of how we respond to family, friends, and strangers. Arguably, it is also less principled than the "impartial" approach he rejects. In particular, if we adopt a Christian perspective, according to which we have to

5. F. P. Ramsey, "A Mathematical Theory of Saving," *Economic Journal* 38 (December 1928): 543–59.

6. A. C. Pigou, *The Economics of Welfare*, 4th ed. (London: Macmillan, 1946), 25; Nicholas Stern, *The Economics of Climate Change: The Stern Review* (Cambridge: Cambridge University Press, 2007), 35.

7. Dieter Helm, *The Carbon Crunch: How We're Getting Climate Change Wrong—and How to Fix It* (New Haven: Yale University Press), 62–67.

love our neighbor as ourselves, even if the neighbor is a foreigner or someone with whom our only connection is a common humanity, there seems no reason to give less weight to that person's interests than to our own. Why should the fact that the "someone" may not be born yet, or even for a thousand years, make any difference to us?[8] Yet casual observation suggests that most Christians do not in fact succeed in loving their neighbors as themselves, and in any case a democratic government cannot commit itself to utopian principles that appeal to only a minority of the electorate. Helm is right to argue that decisions about how to cope with global warming have to recognize how people actually do behave. Policies have to be implemented in the inherently flawed global political system, a point to which we return in chapter 7.

While it may be true that people in their role as citizens of the world often lack the altruism of the Stern report or indeed of strictly applied Christian ethics, this does not mean they are entirely selfish. And as Helm also points out, aspects of the environmental crisis are already upon us; we need to grapple with these problems not simply for the benefit of unborn generations in the distant future but because they could well affect the lives of children who are already born.

Later in this chapter we will return to techniques for implementing more egalitarian policies in relation to the interests of future generations as well as those of the less well-off in the present generation.

---

8. See also Donald A. Hay, "Responding to Climate Change: How Should We Discount the Future?" in *Creation in Crisis: Christian Perspectives on Sustainability*, ed. Robert S. White (London: SPCK, 2009), 53–66.

Efficiency

Just as there is a strong case for saying that economists should broaden their concerns to include social justice, so too it may be argued that theologians and moralists should take efficiency seriously. This is especially true in the context of the environment. The problem is that scarce resources are being consumed as if they were plentifully abundant, instead of being carefully husbanded and used as efficiently as possible. Efficiency, no less than justice, is clearly a moral question: it is immoral to waste scarce resources.

Why, then, is efficiency often linked with the adjective "soulless" in popular discourse?[9] I think this is because the term refers not so much to a desirable goal in itself as to a means of pursuing goals, not all of which may be themselves desirable: some regimes have been all too efficient in pursuing evil. But when allied with a worthy goal, such as that of environmental protection, efficiency itself becomes a moral requirement.

Some who might be willing to admit this rather obvious point may, however, balk at the one that follows. If we accept efficiency as desirable in the pursuit of environmental goals, we must also be prepared to use the tools of efficiency. Prominent among these is the market mechanism.

Efficiency, Markets, and the Environment

In support of the use of markets as an efficiency tool, I would refer you to the discussion in chapter 3 in which market prices were said to offer two important desiderata: information and incentives. We saw that for this to work well, market prices must truly measure

---

9. To check this assertion, in August 2013 I used the search engine Bing to look for the phrase "soulless efficiency." I was offered 145,000 examples.

all relevant costs and benefits. Additionally, many environmental problems are characterized by the partial or complete absence of market prices for benefits conferred or costs imposed by the use of resources. All this would suggest two possible courses of action for policymakers. One possibility is to impute "shadow" prices where no actual market prices already exist (or where they do not exist for *all* relevant benefits and costs or exist but are in some way distorted). The second possibility is to facilitate the creation or modify the operation of markets where these do not already function adequately. The first course of action provides better information for policy decisions and is the subject of the latter part of this chapter dealing with cost-benefit analysis; the second is a way of providing better incentives and will be considered in chapter 6.

Here, however, I wish to return to an issue of principle touched on briefly in chapter 3: the criticism that to apply market prices to environmental goods and services is to treat them as commodities when they are somehow more than that. The implication of this is that certain classes of goods or assets are to be treated as "sacred"—that is, they should be set apart from common use and not be profaned by being bought and sold or having even a purely notional price assigned to them. One such class would include environmental resources; others would include human life and perhaps human body parts.

Few if any economists would argue that all goods should be for sale—the right to a fair trial, for instance, should not be bought or sold. But many of us have some difficulty with the categorization of environmental goods as necessarily outside the market's domain. To see why, consider the following list of natural resource inputs a firm might use in the process of production:

- Raw materials
- Energy inputs
- Water
- Amenity resources
- Waste disposal services

This differs a little from the treatment of resources in figure 3.2. Instead of viewing waste disposal as an "output of bads," it is taken to be an activity that uses up environmental services: in this case, the services of providing a sink for industrial by-products. Similarly, the list implies that amenity services are sometimes used up as part of the production process, as for example when the construction of a road or factory destroys or degrades a previously more peaceful or scenically attractive area.

While some people may wish to abolish the use of the market altogether, this is an extreme position, and many who would not go so far are nonetheless uneasy about making market evaluations of environmental goods. Yet as inspection of the list above shows, much of the environment is already commodified: copper, iron, and other minerals used in production all have a price, as do energy resources such as coal, oil, and gas; similarly, firms are generally expected to pay for the water they use in production. These resources are part of the natural environment that it is acceptable to treat as commodities. But the last two items on the list seem to be the ones that create problems. An attractive country scene is also part of the environment. Why not treat it as a commodity too? And why not charge to use the environment for waste disposal?

The economist's view, as explained in chapter 3, is that these areas of the environment have often been left outside the market's domain not because they were considered too sacred to be subject to market disciplines but because of the difficulty—the prohibitive transaction costs—of creating markets in their use. But this has been to their disadvantage inasmuch as markets provide some protection (admittedly, not always sufficient) against overexploitation. Their use does have a cost, and it is important to discover what this cost is (and who pays it) and to compare it with the benefit derived from using them (and who receives that benefit). There *is* an ethical issue here: not that we have taken from the environment but that we have not paid for what we have taken. In disobedience to the eighth commandment, we have in effect stolen it, whether from others in our own generation or from future generations. If we were made to pay, or if we even made a serious attempt to estimate the cost of what we were destroying, we might take much less.

This is not to imply that we can make plausible market valuations of all environmental resources, as we shall see later in this chapter, or that there are no other considerations to be addressed in policy decisions. As will become clear from chapter 6, the market is not the only or always the best mechanism for restricting overuse. But it is one important tool among several, and we need all the useful tools we can devise if we are to deal effectively with the threats to our natural environment.

Coping with Uncertainty

Do not boast about tomorrow, for you do not know what a day may bring forth.

—Prov. 27:1

Policymakers have to steer a course through the fog of uncertainty, and if the rest of us want to influence the direction they are taking us, we too must struggle with this aspect of decision making.

Much discussion of this issue by economists begins with an important distinction made by Frank Knight in 1921: the distinction between *risk* and *uncertainty*.[10] We use the term *risk* to refer to situations where we do not know the outcome of any single action but do know the *frequency* with which particular outcomes will result when that action is repeated. Where there is uncertainty, however, we lack such information about frequency.

By way of a simple example, suppose you put fifty black and fifty white balls into a bag and shake it up thoroughly. You then put your hand in the bag, without looking, and withdraw a single ball. What color will it be? Obviously, it has an equal chance of being either black or white. Suppose you repeat the action one hundred times, replacing the ball each time. While on each occasion you will still not know which color to expect, it would be plausible to assume that by the end of the experiment roughly fifty of each color will have been drawn out. We would say that there was a 0.5 probability, of a black ball, and, likewise, a 0.5 probability of a white ball. If we had put in three black balls for each white one, then the probability of a black ball being drawn on any one occasion would be 0.75; for a white one, obviously, it would be 0.25.

Two industries in particular—gambling and insurance—are based on the exploitation of probability measurements. In the case of gambling, setting up situations like the one mentioned, perhaps using slot machines or roulette wheels, can be a major source of profit to the owners of the equipment. For insurance, information on frequencies results not from constructing a particular set of probabilities as part of a game but on finding out how often particular events occur through empirical investigation of real-world situations. Thus, for insurance against burglary a company will investigate how often in the course

10. Frank H. Knight, *Risk, Uncertainty and Profit* (Boston: Houghton Mifflin Company, 1921).

of a year houses in a given class of neighborhood, and protected by particular types of security equipment, are broken into and will charge insurance premiums that reflect the frequency of such events.

In the case of uncertainty, however, there is no widely accepted basis for assigning such probability numbers. Some decision makers may nevertheless have a feeling about whether a particular outcome is more likely than not or very much more likely than not, and they may even be prepared to express such a feeling in quantitative terms. For example, if they think the outcome is extremely likely, they may attach a subjective probability of 0.95, or nineteen in twenty, to that outcome, as was done in the IPCC report we considered in chapter 4. This may partly reflect their past experience of such situations, which nonexperts do not share. It could also be a consequence of their own natural pessimism or optimism rather than of any features inherent in the situation itself. Either way, it lacks objectivity because it has no basis in evidence or logical argument that would be equally convincing to anyone else who had the situation explained to them, regardless of their own past experience or where they were located on the pessimism–optimism spectrum. On the other hand, if several people with relevant experience come up with the same subjective probability estimates, this may encourage the rest of us to take the estimates seriously.

Where risk is involved, we can work out the *expected value* of our decisions. Suppose we were thinking of setting up an ice cream stall at a local resort, and past experience has indicated that we would net $20,000 over a warm summer season but only $10,000 in a rainy summer. Further, we know from Meteorological Office records that there is a 60 percent chance of a good summer and a 40 percent chance of a bad one. The expected value (EV) of the project would be calculated as follows:

$$EV = \$20,000 \times 0.6 + \$10,000 \times 0.4 = \$16,000$$

This could then be compared with the EVs of alternative projects we might undertake.[11]

Would we necessarily choose the project with the highest EV? This would depend on our attitude to risk-taking. For example, a project that offered an equal chance of either a $100,000 gain or a $60,000 loss would have an expected value of $20,000. But would you prefer it to the option above, with a lower EV of only $16,000? Perhaps not, since the option above has a downside outcome that still provides a modest gain, whereas the second option could easily leave you seriously out of pocket if the venture was not successful.

Much may depend on the proportion of your resources at stake. If you are a rich person with lots of projects, the losses on one will balance the gains on another; you will record gains of $100,000 as often as losses of $60,000, so on average you will indeed make $20,000. But if you have few resources and face a one-off choice where the downside outcome could lead to bankruptcy with no chance to stay in the game until you recoup your losses, you may wish to be much more cautious.

Economists tend to assume that most people are somewhat risk averse. The notion of *diminishing marginal utility* implies that a gain of $10 will not increase our utility by as much as a loss of $10 will reduce it. Thus a bet that gave us an equal chance of either outcome would have an expected *value* of zero but would have a lower expected *utility* than the certain alternative of refusing the bet and remaining at our present level of wealth; thus, we would not take the bet. This makes it difficult to explain the gambling industry, in which people necessarily choose to accept bets with a negative expected

---

11. You will notice that "expected value" is, paradoxically, an amount that in general we *don't* expect to make from any single decision. Rather, it is an average we expect to emerge after a number of similar trials.

money value; the odds are always stacked against the gambler by the entrepreneur who provides the gambling opportunity and would soon go out of business if unable to take a cut of the proceeds. The insurance industry also offers people contracts with negative expected money values since the premium has to cover both expected payouts and the costs of running the insurance company. But when people purchase insurance, they are paying to avoid risk, whereas gamblers are paying to take it on. The fact that some people purchase house or car insurance and also buy lottery tickets is a problem for the mainstream theory of rational economic behavior.

Many environmental issues are very complex, as we have already seen. Typically, we lack the probability information needed to calculate expected values. In such situations of uncertainty rather than risk, how should we make decisions? We have already seen one possible answer when considering the Rawlsian theory of justice. The maximin strategy invites us to rank the options that face us according to the worst possible outcome associated with each option, then to choose the "least worst" option. But, as we also saw, this strategy has been criticized, particularly for ignoring other aspects of the choices we make. In effect, it is as if we were estimating expected values for each option but, in the absence of any objective probability information, chose to assign a probability of 100 percent to the worst outcome for each alternative and 0 percent to all the other possible outcomes for that alternative. Is this really a sensible way to make decisions?

This discussion bears on a principle often recommended in environmental decision making: the *precautionary principle.* While there are various conflicting interpretations of this principle, in very general terms it implies that courses of action with uncertain but possibly harmful outcomes should only be adopted with caution.[12] But how much caution? The principle, as just expressed, can seem empty of practical content. Yet if we try to tighten it, for example by insisting that we can proceed with a policy only if those who propose it can offer a 100 percent guarantee there will be no harmful effects, we are in danger of losing what may be substantial benefits from the policy for reasons based on excessive nervousness about (perhaps quite minor) disadvantages.

Now, the maximin rule might be taken to imply a particularly extreme version of the precautionary principle. However, there may be circumstances in which it would nevertheless be appropriate. In the second edition of *A Theory of Justice*, Rawls responded to those who, like Harsanyi, had criticized his use of the strategy.[13] He accepted that maximin was by no means always a good strategy but suggested three general situations in which it might apply. The first, as indeed we are currently assuming, would be a situation of uncertainty rather than measurable risk. The second would be a situation in which decision makers might gain from choosing a strategy other than maximin but care little about any such gains—as might be the case if the payoff were at best only marginally above the worst-case payoff from the other strategy. The third would be a situation in which choosing an alternative strategy to maximin could result in potentially disastrous downside consequences.

Rawls, it will be recalled, is not recommending maximin in the context of environmental decision making but rather as part of his theory of justice. But for our present purposes, the question is how well his revised version of maximin transfers from the context of justice to that of applying the precautionary principle to the environment. Some writers, including the moral philosopher Stephen

---

12. For a brief critical survey of views, see Stephen M. Gardiner, "A Core Precautionary Principle," *Journal of Political Philosophy* 14, no. 1 (2006): 33–60.

13. John Rawls, *A Theory of Justice*, rev. ed. (Cambridge, MA: Harvard University Press, 1999), 133–34. Rawls notes that his argument here is based on earlier work by Fellner; see William Fellner, *Probability and Profit* (Homewood, IL: R. D. Irwin, 1965), 140–42.

Gardiner and the ecological economist John Aldred, have argued that it is well suited for this task and that it gives useful guidance for applying the precautionary principle, particularly in the context of such large-scale environmental issues as climate change.[14]

Climate change, Gardiner argues, involves "uncertainty" rather than measurable risk; it would be impossible to assign probabilities to the effects of climate change because of their complexity. This would satisfy Rawls's first condition, and Gardiner's claim here seems plausible in light of the discussion in chapter 4. So too does his claim that Rawls's third condition is met: there is a downside possibility of catastrophic consequences from climate change. Perhaps more controversially, he also suggests that Rawls's second condition—that gains above the maximin offered by other strategies are unimportant—is fulfilled. The argument here seems to be that the cost of preventing climate change is not so very large that the strategy of restraint looks seriously unattractive compared with the strategy of "business as usual." It is unlikely this would be acceptable to skeptics. Their view is that the resources being devoted to switching away from fossil fuels are imposing a very substantial burden on the world economy; in effect, the benefits from mitigation of global warming may well be less than, and unlikely at best to be much more than, the costs.[15]

Aldred argues that the issue is not really one of comparing costs and benefits in terms of the contribution of different policies to the growth of national income.[16] He sees the possible losses from the prospect of significant global warming as "qualitatively distinct" from

---

14. Gardiner, "Core Precautionary Principle," 55; John Aldred, "Climate Change Uncertainty, Irreversibility and the Precautionary Principle," *Cambridge Journal of Economics* 36, no. 5 (September 2012): 1051–72.

15. See, for example, Nigel Lawson, *An Appeal to Reason: A Cool Look at Global Warming* (London: Duckworth, 2009), 65–81.

16. Aldred, "Climate Change Uncertainty," 1061.

the costs in reduced GDP growth necessary to avoid those losses. As other writers have done, he compares the effects of catastrophic global warming with those of events such as the great wars of the twentieth century. These had a surprisingly small negative effect on long-term global growth rates. But the immensity of the suffering they caused is incommensurable with any such changes.

Suppose that unchecked global warming did indeed lead, whether through sea-level increases or through extensive land erosion and desertification, to the widespread destruction of habitats and of the communities, including human communities, they had supported. Further suppose, as seems likely, that this would cause great hardship through malnutrition or outright starvation, the enforced disappearance of traditional ways of life, and severe social conflict arising from mass migration. Posterity would not be impressed by the willingness of present generations to trade the possibility of such worst-case changes against reductions in GDP growth rates that would be seen, in hindsight, as almost irrelevant in comparison. In this sense a revised Rawlsian maximin rule is perhaps justified.

In the remainder of this chapter, however, we will turn from such tricky decisions on system-wide problems with highly uncertain outcomes to decisions involving smaller-scale consequences with more measurable probabilities. As we shall see, some awkward ethical issues arise even in this context.

Project Appraisal and the Ethics of Cost-Benefit Analysis

Should Donald Trump have been allowed to build a golf course and hotel complex on the east coast of Scotland, creating income and employment opportunities, if the development caused damage to an environmentally fragile area, as protesters claimed? Should firms be allowed to quarry scarce types of gravel if doing so would destroy a beautiful view? Should energy companies be allowed to erect wind turbines in order to lessen dependence on fossil fuels if the wind farms would threaten the nesting sites of rare birds?

All such questions involve trade-offs between desirable objectives. Clearly, we need some method of making decisions about which projects are worthwhile in spite of their disadvantages and which should be rejected. Decisions about which projects to accept and which to reject are of course being made all the time in the private business sector, which has devised various appraisal techniques. For reasons outlined in chapter 3, what is most financially profitable for private companies is not always best for the wider society, and this is particularly true when the decisions have major implications for the natural environment. Nonetheless, it will be helpful to begin by examining what private business regards as the best practice method of project appraisal; we can then look at how such techniques could be modified or supplemented in order to incorporate broader social objectives and concerns.

Project Appraisal in the Private Sector

To get an idea of the principles at work, consider the following very simple and rather contrived example. Imagine that Stikigloo Inc. is considering installing new plant to produce an even stronger adhesive; market research suggests it could be sold at a higher price than the existing product, though it will also require inputs of more costly raw materials. From past experience, the price advantage gained is expected to diminish steadily through competition from other firms and will be no greater than the extra material cost after five years, by which time the plant will also have become obsolete. How will the company decide whether the investment in the new plant is worthwhile?

The obvious first step is to set out the changes in costs and returns in a spreadsheet. Suppose the figures are as follows (where the letter *m* implies "million"):

	Today	End of year 1	End of year 2	End of year 3	End of year 4	End of year 5
Cost of new plant	$10m					
Extra materials cost		$2m	$2m	$2m	$2m	$2m
Extra revenues		$7.5m	$6m	$4.5m	$3m	$2m

On first sight, it might seem that the project would indeed be modestly profitable. The cost items total $20m, but the extra revenues over the whole period come to $23m—an apparent profit of $3m. But matters are not quite so simple; we have to account for the rate of interest.

Suppose the firm has to borrow money to undertake this project at an interest rate of 10 percent per year, the whole debt to be paid back at the end of five years. After one year it will owe not $10m but $11m. After a second year, this debt will have accumulated by a further 10 per cent; since 10 percent of $11m is $1.1m, the total debt will have amounted to $12.1m by that date, and so on.

The usual way to handle the interest cost is not to "compound forward," as we have just done, but to "discount back" so that all costs and returns appear as if they were arising today and can be directly compared.

To see how this works, put yourself in the position of a lender. If I asked to borrow $10 from you, promising to pay it back after one year, would you regard that as a fair deal? Even if you considered me to be a completely reliable debtor, you know you would lose money if you agreed; your money could be sitting in a savings account earning interest for that year—on our present assumptions, $1.00 of interest. So how much, then, would it be sensible to lend me today in return for the certain promise of $10 after one year? The answer, to the nearest cent, turns out to be $9.09.[17] The alternative to lending me this latter sum would be to leave it in the savings account; at 10 percent interest, it would then accumulate to just $10 in a year's time.

Following this logic, to make all the numbers in the column headed "End of year 1" comparable to those in the column headed "Today," we need to multiply them by a *discount factor* of 0.909. We will then have the *present value* (PV) of these future sums of money. Thus, the extra materials costs will have a PV of $1.818m, and the extra revenues will have a PV of $6.8175m. In each case, these are the sums that would have to be invested today at 10 percent return in order to equal the figures in the year 1 column.

What about the other years in our example? Our results so far show that when the compound factor is 1.1, the discount factor is 0.909. This latter number is simply the *reciprocal* of 1.1, which is given by 1/1.1 to three decimal places.[18] We also saw when compounding forward that $10m in two years' time will amount to $12.1m; we could say that the two-year compound factor, then, is 1.21. Taking the reciprocal, we get 1/1.21, which approximates to 0.826: this, then, is the discount factor for two years when the rate of interest is 10 percent. As an exercise, you might like to calculate the PVs of the figures in the year 2 column.[19]

Fortunately, we don't have to work out compound and discount factors from first principles as I have done here. All this was done

17. This is because $9.09 plus 10 percent of $9.09 equals $9.09 plus $0.909 equals $9.999, which rounds up to $10.
18. If you're not familiar with the term, the reciprocal of any number is simply what you get if you divide that number into 1. Thus 2 has a reciprocal of 1/2 or 0.5, 3 of 1/3 or 0.333, and so on.
19. The cost figure of $2m now gives a PV of $1.652m, and the $6m revenue figure becomes $4.956m.

for us long ago by accountants who constructed tables for a whole range of interest rates and years. Today, we simply enter the numbers into spreadsheet software, such as Excel, with costs given a negative sign and revenues a positive one, and call up the appropriate formulas. We would first have the program subtract costs from returns in each year of the project, thus getting a net cash flow over the project's life, and then discount the amounts in each year by the appropriate factor. Adding the positive amounts together and subtracting the negative ones would give us the *net present value* (NPV) for the project. If we apply this procedure to the figures given in our example, we find that the NPV, while still positive, is much less than $3m—in fact, it is only about $864,000. If the rate of interest had been a little higher than 15 percent, which is about the rate at which the project breaks even (known in the trade as the *internal rate of return*, or IRR), the project would not have been worthwhile at all.

We may express the private decision rule, then, as follows.

Calculate NPV, where:

NPV = Sum of [(Revenue for each year − Cost for each year) x discount factor for that year].

If NPV is greater than zero, accept the project.

From Private to Social Decisions

The rule just described is intended to help private companies to maximize their profits. So how do we get from decisions about private profitability to decisions about social desirability, given the problems we considered in chapter 3? The environmental economist's argument is that we should adopt the same logical structure for our decision rule, but modify the information we feed into it. Thus, we relabel the variables in the private rule to get *net social benefit* (NSB) as follows:

NSB = Sum of [(SB for each year – SC for each year) x sdf for that year]

In this formula, SB is a measure of the social benefit arising in a given year of the project's life, SC is the corresponding social cost, and sdf is the social discount factor, derived from the interest rate considered appropriate to use when appraising public sector projects. This last, as we shall see, may not be the same as the commercial rate. Relabeling, of course, is the easy bit. How do we decide what figures to fit into these boxes? What principles are at work here?

Two core value judgments underpin this kind of *cost-benefit analysis* (CBA), according to the late David Pearce, one of its foremost practitioners.[20] First, the figures used in estimating costs and benefits should *reflect individual preferences*; this is based on the principle of consumer sovereignty examined in chapter 3. Second, these preferences should be *weighted* in some particular way. In practice, the first of these principles is often taken to mean "preferences as they are expressed by individuals through the ways they are prepared to spend their money," while the second is commonly interpreted as "each dollar is to have the same weight, regardless of whether it belongs to a rich or a poor person." Pearce acknowledged that both these value judgments may be challenged and that CBA may be modified to take such challenges into account; these issues will be discussed later, but meanwhile I will continue to explain what might be called the "default" version of CBA.

The first of these principles implies that in estimating social benefit of any project we are trying to find private individuals' *willingness to pay* (WTP) for the outcomes arising from that project. Similarly,

20. David W. Pearce, *Cost-Benefit Analysis*, 2nd ed. (London: Macmillan, 1983), 4–9.

in estimating social cost the task is to measure WTP for the output which we could have had if we had put the resources required for that project to their next best alternative use: economists often refer to this latter amount as the project's "opportunity" cost. WTP is a way of putting a money value on the net addition to total utility that will result from the project, by subtracting the second total from the first.

As we saw in chapter 3, use of WTP as a guide for those making social policy raises the issue of *compensation criteria*—in particular, the Kaldor-Hicks criterion. To recapitulate, the Kaldor-Hicks criterion states that we should accept those policies for which the gainers *could afford* to compensate the losers and still have something left over—*even if no such compensation were to be paid in practice*. Clearly, this condition would be satisfied if the social benefits, measured by WTP, were to exceed the social costs, after discounting. But remember that the criterion treats all dollars alike and thus implicitly assumes that the expenditure of a dollar by a rich person has the same effect on social welfare as a dollar spent by a poor person.

Leaving that aside for the present, where do our WTP figures come from? We may not be able to use the prices actually paid in the marketplace for the outputs from and inputs to the project, either because no such prices are actually paid or because the existing market prices do not properly reflect social benefits and costs arising from the project. The reasons why this may happen were explained in chapter 3 in the discussion of externalities and public goods, but it may be helpful to give an example by way of reminder.

Suppose, for example, that in a region of high unemployment a government agency decides to embark on a program of local road improvements. What actual cash flows would arise from this project, and how would these compare with the flows of social costs and benefits?

Consider the costs first. Some costs will indeed appear in cash flows for the project: these will include the cost of materials used for the road surfaces, the hire of machinery, and the wages received by the construction workers (we assume that they will be paid union rates). The payments for the materials and equipment, which would all have alternative uses somewhere else in the economy, may well approximate to social opportunity costs (unless there are serious distortions elsewhere). But are the wages paid also the true social costs of the labor used? If the workers would have been employed in other activities, their wages should indeed be included in the social costs. But we are assuming that the region is one of high unemployment; many of the workers may have been unable to find any alternative use for their services and may have been willing to give up their enforced leisure for a much lower wage than the wage being offered by the government. So this component of the cash flow may overstate the social cost.

There may also be other social costs that do not appear in the agency's financial cash flow statement at all. Environmentalists might argue that the road improvements will give rise to extra pollution costs by encouraging more journeys than would otherwise have been undertaken and thus increasing vehicle emissions. A proper CBA should try to find some way of taking these into account.

What if the improvements involved not only upgrading but also new road construction in the open countryside in order to bypass town centers currently congested by through traffic? Such proposals often attract hostility from conservationists because they destroy wildlife habitats. If this is the case and we could find some measure of what people would be willing to pay to save it, then the value of the wildlife habitat destroyed should also be counted as a cost.

Turning to the benefits side, recall that these roads are local networks, not major trunk routes, so no tolls would be charged on them; in economists' language, the *transaction costs* of imposing direct user charges (setting up the toll stations and hiring personnel to operate them) would be too high. There may be no financial cash flow on the "revenue" side of the account, But the improvements will still yield benefits by increasing traffic speed and reducing journey time. Since the journey-time benefits will not be charged directly to the beneficiaries, we have to find some way of "imputing" them in order to fill up the social benefits (SB) box in our formula. Moreover, it is likely that accidents will also be reduced and lives saved. These, again, could be highly important benefits, but how do we incorporate them in our imputed cash flow?

Finally, there is the question of the discount factor. In our example of a private investment decision, the company was assumed to use the rate at which it could borrow money for the long term. So in calculating discount factors, should government agencies simply use the rate of interest at which they themselves can borrow?

From the early days of CBA, economists have generally been critical of the use of the long-term government borrowing rate to derive social discount factors. Governments through their central banks use interest rates to help control variables in the economy as a whole; for example, they may increase rates to discourage inflationary borrowing or lower them to encourage economic activity in a slump. Such short-term monetary policy considerations affect the whole structure of interest rates and may cause the government borrowing rate to diverge from its socially optimal level as a determinant of long-term investment decisions. But this leads us to a further problem: what considerations, then, *ought* to determine the social rate of discount? We will explore this question shortly as part of a more general discussion of *shadow pricing*. But before we do, it may be helpful to examine the broad principles of CBA in the light of the theological views discussed in chapter 2.

First, what about the more radical theological approaches? CBA at least tries to take account of some of the criticisms of mainstream economics: it does not neglect or sideline externalities, for example, but gives them a central place in decision making. But this alone, while acknowledged by some as a step in the right direction, does not go far enough—not nearly far enough—to deflect all criticism. At the end of our discussion of radical theologians in chapter 2, I listed a number of the social criticisms that seemed to be part of a consensus for this group. If you refer to this list you will see several that are particularly relevant to our road improvements example.

The most fundamental of these, perhaps, is the criticism of the utilitarian philosophy that underlies the CBA technique. Also, the value judgment that individual preferences should count in the estimates of benefits and costs is criticized by those who prefer a communitarian approach to decision making, at least where environmental issues are concerned: "citizen sovereignty" rather than "consumer sovereignty."[21] There would also be concern that a WTP criterion would lead to decisions favoring those with more money. Those who disapprove of markets on principle will not be happy that much of the approach is based on attempts to obtain surrogate market values where no actual markets exist. In particular, they would dislike the notion that the impact on wildlife of new road building may be measured by some kind of imputed cost that can be added to other costs in a financial calculation. To a convinced environmentalist, this would seem like putting a price on sin (an issue to be examined more fully in chapter 6). No less hair-raising would be the idea that lives saved from such improvements could be valued in terms of financial benefits.

---

21. See Celia Deane-Drummond, *Eco-Theology* (London: Darton, Longman and Todd, 2008), 17–19. This comment follows from her criticism of the imputation of monetary values in the evaluation of environmental outcomes.

Some of these criticisms of CBA can probably be taken on board by economists, who certainly do not regard the technique as perfect and have given much thought to how it could be improved or supplemented by other methods. But some reveal fundamental differences in value judgments between economists, however ecologically sensitive, and radical theologians. In the rest of this chapter, as we look at examples of the various techniques in more detail, we will try to see which criticisms may be resolvable and in which matters the two sides will simply have to agree to differ.

For the sake of completeness, however, we should first ask how far the more conservative theologians—supporters of the Cornwall Alliance, for example—would be willing to accept the CBA approach. Although I have so far come across no instances where there has been explicit discussion of this issue by such groups, I think it likely there would be some reluctance to embrace it. Those who espouse neoliberal economic theories, as we have seen, tend to disapprove of government attempts to override market outcomes. Economists of this school worry that CBA may become a mechanism allowing governments to justify spending taxpayers' money on commercially unprofitable projects; the claim that there are beneficial externalities associated with such projects and the attempts to find sophisticated ways of measuring them are viewed with suspicion. Readers may decide for themselves whether such suspicions are justified in the case of the procedures we now consider.

Shadow Pricing and Environmental Values

There are two broad approaches to estimating shadow or surrogate prices for environmental benefits or costs.[22] The first of these, the

---

22. This section, and indeed much of the rest of the chapter, is concerned with techniques that have now generated a very substantial literature, much of it aimed at practitioners of environmental

expressed preference (or *stated preference*) approach is simple in concept, though not to carry out in practice. Here, we ask members of households likely to be affected by the project how they would value the environmental goods (or "bads") arising from it. The second approach is through *revealed preference*. Here the analyst observes actual behavior in some market related to the project so as to deduce how the project itself would be valued. These techniques will become clearer as we consider some examples.

In the scholarly literature, it is customary to distinguish different types of values that might arise from environmental assets.[23] First, there is *use value*. This may be *direct*, as when woodland is cut for timber or a sea inlet used for fish farming; it may also be *indirect*, as when the woodland or inlet are developed for recreation. But there is also *option use value*, in which people would be willing to pay to preserve the availability of an asset they have not yet used, and may indeed never use, but think it possible they might be able to use someday. If they would be willing to pay to keep this possibility open, that amount would measure their option use value. But what if they have absolutely no intention of visiting the asset themselves (perhaps pollen from vegetation would give them hay fever or an asthma attack) but would like their children (fortunately allergy-free) to be able to do so? In this case, they would perhaps be willing to pay for *bequest value*, to keep the option open for future generations (which, for altruists, may of course include other people's descendants as well as their own).

---

project appraisal. Since the present text is intended for a nonpractitioner market, I have tried to give only a simplified summary that concentrates on issues of principle, at least insofar as the latter can be divorced from more technical matters.

23. The discussion here follows the treatment in R. Kerry Turner, David Pearce, and Ian Bateman, *Environmental Economics: An Elementary Introduction* (New York: Harvester Wheatsheaf, 1994), ch. 8. This source also gives a user-friendly explanation of many of the other issues covered in the present work, for those who wish to study the economics in greater depth.

All of these are a form of use value. But there is also a *nonuse* value. Suppose a variety of monkey were discovered in a forest area of the Congo, unique to that area. Difficulties of access mean that very few people are for the foreseeable future likely to go there or to see the creature. Would you be prepared nevertheless to pay to preserve the habitat? If so, you are paying for *existence value*, a value that often reflects a concern for biodiversity.

The techniques of CBA are designed to convert these values into money equivalents, to find the *total economic value* by adding them all together.

Expressed Preference

We begin by looking at the most comprehensive approach through expressed preference. The technique used here is known as the *contingent valuation method* (CVM). In the context of our road improvements example, the social cost of destroying a woodland to construct the bypass could be estimated by asking locals how much they would pay to preserve this environmental asset from destruction. It would not be necessary to ask every household in the locality; statistical methods would allow the analysts to get a close measure of the views of the all households from a representative sample that had been properly structured to include differences in income, educational background, family composition, and any other factors thought likely to affect responses. The average amounts stated by those in the sample could then be multiplied up to give an estimate of the total WTP for the relevant population.

There are some well-known problems with this procedure. The most obvious have to do with the trustworthiness of the responses. When approached by researchers with clipboards and questionnaires, people may be tempted to give wild or ill-considered answers just to get rid of them. There are techniques, such as "bidding games," to mitigate this problem by focusing the attention of the respondent. In such a game respondents would be asked how much they would be willing to pay to preserve the asset, perhaps starting at a relatively high amount they would not pay and reducing the amount until they agreed (or until zero was reached). There are also more sophisticated variants designed to minimize bias in responses.[24]

Another interesting problem with the CVM is that answers tend to vary systematically depending on whether questions are expressed in the form "how much would you be willing to pay to obtain an environmental asset?" or in the form "how much would you be willing to accept in compensation for the loss of an asset?" Generally, "willingness to pay" (WTP) amounts are less than "willingness to accept" (WTA) amounts. *Loss aversion theory*, based on a psychologically subtler model of behavior than the economist's usual concept of rational choice, provides one possible explanation.[25] This theory claims that people particularly dislike losing something they consider themselves to possess already, something part of their existing "endowment" of goods (hence the term *endowment effect* for this phenomenon). They will expect more compensation for an endowment loss than they will be prepared to pay for an addition to this endowment.[26]

In practice, where several different types of value are present, the CVM may only be able to provide an overall figure for total

24. For details, see Anil Markandya, Patrice Harou, Lorenzo Giovanni Bellù, and Vito Cistulli, *Environmental Economics for Sustainable Growth: A Handbook for Practitioners* (Northampton, MA: Edward Elgar, 2002), 423–35.

25. A readable summary of the behavioral models is given by one of the founders of that approach in Daniel Kahneman, *Thinking, Fast and Slow* (London: Penguin, 2012).

26. This is not the only explanation, and a rather technical case may be made to justify the WTP/WTA divergence in terms of rational choice theory. On the other hand, the endowment effect seems well supported by the evidence.

economic value. However, despite the difficulties associated with the CVM, it does have the advantage that it may be widely applied, not just to provide estimates for local situations in which people are directly affected by changes in their immediate environment but also to give estimates for existence values relating to situations on the other side of the world.

Revealed Preference

The methods related to revealed preferences are often more limited in scope and application than the CVM, but they are derived from what people actually do rather than from what they say they would do in a hypothetical situation. In the environmental context, there are two revealed preference methods often used to obtain measures of cost or benefit: the *hedonic pricing method* (HPM) and the *travel cost method* (TCM). In both cases, the basis of the method is quite simple. Although there is no direct user charge for an environmental asset itself, market prices will still reflect the decisions people make in order to enjoy it. In the case of the HPM, these decisions are made in the property market; the TCM is based on expenditures incurred in order to reach the area where the asset is located.

Suppose you decide to buy a house in or near an area of outstanding natural beauty. You will probably have to pay a price for the house above what you would have to pay for an identical house in an area with no such advantages. This premium, then, is a market measure of WTP for the environmental asset.

In practice, as usual, the actual measurement of the premium is no simple task. The problem is that house prices reflect a large number of characteristics. Thus, even two houses built by the same builder, to the same specifications but in different areas, will not in fact be otherwise identical. The one in the less environmentally attractive area may still have some advantages the other lacks: for example, it may be closer to a good shopping area, to better schools and hospitals, or to convenient transport facilities. In any case, most houses are not physically identical; they differ in the number of rooms, size of rooms, energy efficiency, exposure of main living areas to sunlight, and so on. Any of these factors could offset or add to the environmental premium. To unscramble the individual effects of each of these factors on house prices—and thus to obtain the net effect of location near an environmentally attractive area—requires large amounts of data analyzed using sophisticated statistical techniques.

Many of the studies undertaken using the HPM have measured not the benefit of positive features such as proximity to areas of natural beauty but the costs of negative ones, such as pollution or aircraft noise. However, one study from the United Kingdom carried out in the early 1990s showed that proximity to open water could increase the price of a house by 5 percent.[27]

The TCM is perhaps the best-established technique for measuring WTP for recreational or wilderness areas and thus the benefits these confer on those who visit them. A sample of visitors to the site are confronted by a clipboard-carrying researcher who takes them through a series of questions about where they have come from, how much they spent on gasoline to get there, and how often they visit in the course of a year. To prevent seasonal factors from biasing the results, this would normally be done at different periods of the year. In some studies, income details are obtained, as richer people can afford to pay more and the object is to measure the demand for the site in relation to price alone, without the income factor. Some studies also take account of the time spent on the journey, since time cost is part of the total cost. The annual value of the site can be

27. Cited in Turner, Pearce, and Bateman, *Environmental Economics*, 120. The study was carried out by G. D. Garrod and K. G. Willis from the University of Newcastle on Tyne.

estimated by taking the responses from the sample of visitors and multiplying based on the total number of visitors to the site in the course of the year.

Again, while the broad principle is clear, the implementation of the method often has to resolve difficulties. For example, how do we estimate time costs? There are various techniques used in transport studies, which often show a higher value of time for the better-off (a rich person can earn more in an hour than a poor person). But some question the validity of treating journey time as a cost because for many (though not all) the drive is itself a source of satisfaction rather than a cost. Also, how much of the travel cost do we assign to any one site when visitors come from a great distance, perhaps even abroad, and include a whole series of local sites in their holiday package?

Clearly, no one method is perfect. Compared with the CVM, both the TCM and HPM provide more "objective" information about user value but can tell us nothing about existence value or option value, both of which imply that those who value the site do not actually visit it. However, it is interesting (and, to the environmental economist, comforting) to note that in cases where the different methods have been applied in similar situations, they do seem to yield broadly similar results.[28]

There is a further general point I will make about these different approaches and will repeat elsewhere. The techniques of CBA are *not* intended to yield a single definitive figure that would allow policymakers to give a clear and resounding answer to what is to be done about any environmental project. There will be a range of net social benefit estimates, generally depending on the decisions made regarding how (and whether) to value time cost in TCM, whether to

---

28. See the discussion in David W. Pearce and R. Kerry Turner, *Economics of Natural Resources and the Environment* (New York: Harvester Wheatsheaf, 1990), 152–53.

use WTP or WTA in a CVM study, and so on. The technique can help to clarify issues, but it will not give the last word.

Shadow Pricing of Nonenvironmental Resources: Labor

So far, we have been considering costs and benefits associated with particular environmental goods and services. We now turn to other inputs to environmental projects, looking first at the workforce and then, in the next section, at the cost of capital.

In areas of high unemployment, as we saw earlier, projects may be able to draw on workers in some employment categories without having to attract them from alternative employment elsewhere. It is tempting to conclude that the opportunity cost of such workers is zero, even if they have to be paid a wage determined by union rates or minimum wage legislation. But this would ignore the cost of leisure foregone. This may be quite low; indeed, many workers may find the experience of unemployment so depressing they would be willing to work for a pittance if not prevented by unions or legislation. Many, in fact, may be doing unpaid work, providing childcare for other members of the household, growing food in their gardens, or engaging in voluntary social service in their local communities. All such activities have positive values, and a movement back into paid employment therefore has a genuine opportunity cost. Even if this were not so, leisure itself has value, especially when compared with the kind of job opportunities environmental projects may have to offer. Unemployment disproportionately affects unskilled workers and those whose skills are no longer required because of technological change; as a result, it is likely that such workers will be employed on environmental projects in roles requiring more tedious or unattractive kinds of work effort. Thus, the "shadow wage" should arguably be above zero, but perhaps less than the wage the previously unemployed people are actually being paid. This is another of those cases in which CBA requires a series of estimates to test the sensitivity of the net social benefit outcome to the particular judgments used about the true social cost of labor.

The Social Rate of Discount

We now consider the cost of capital, which in this context refers to the rate of discount used in the CBA formula. This is a very important part of the formula, perhaps especially for environmental projects, because of its potential effects on costs and benefits arising in the more distant future.

A table of discount factors will tell you that at an annual interest rate 2.5 percent, the present value of one dollar received or paid out after fifty years will be only twenty-nine cents. If we double the interest rate to 5 percent, the PV falls away even more rapidly, to less than nine cents. If we double the time horizon, to one hundred years, the 2.5 percent rate will reduce the present value of a dollar to eight cents, and the 5 percent rate will reduce it to less than one cent. So the rate we choose can make a lot of difference to the *attractiveness* of a long-term project.

Historically, many Christian thinkers have viewed the levying of interest charges with great suspicion, given the prohibition on "usury" in the book of Leviticus (Lev. 25:35-36); Islamic theologians still oppose the practice. Yet the interest rate serves an important economic function. Neoclassical theory gives two reasons for interest: one psychological, the other technological.

The psychological reason is termed *time preference*: people in general prefer present over future consumption, perhaps from impatience ("I want it now"), and will demand compensation, in the form of interest, for postponement of satisfaction. The technological reason concerns the productivity of investment. Resources we do not need to consume today can be invested to yield greater returns in the future. For example, I might spend half a million dollars reequipping my factory so that next year, and for the foreseeable future, I get an extra $50,000 each year. If someone else borrows the money from me, I lose this opportunity for as long as the other person does not pay back the loan; I face an opportunity cost of capital of 10 percent and will presumably expect to get this back from the borrower.

Time preference explains our reluctance to postpone consumption; the productivity of capital gives us a motive for doing so. In a free market, on neoclassical theory, competition among lenders and borrowers would give rise to a market rate of interest bringing the rate of time preference into equality with the rate of return on capital. In practice, this does not happen; there are many imperfections in the capital market, not least taxes on income from capital that drive a wedge between time preference and capital productivity. So should we base our social rate of discount on the time preference rate or on a rate that reflects the opportunity cost of capital?

A complication is that, as we saw earlier, time preference has been criticized as both irrational and unethical. A. C. Pigou regarded it as a consequence of a "defective telescopic faculty."[29] On the ethical side, our numerical example shows that even a modest discount rate will give returns to future generations a very low and ultimately negligible weight in today's calculations; hence, some argue we should use a zero rate of time preference for public decisions.

Yet if we accept that individual preferences are to count in our decision criteria, we cannot ignore this preference, even if we do not altogether approve of it. We may, however, argue that, in their

29. Pigou, *Economics of Welfare*, 25.

capacity as citizens, people are prepared to accept that government, acting on their behalf, should take the interests of future generations into account in its investment decisions. This could be modeled as a prisoner's dilemma: acting as individuals we may have no significant effect on social outcomes, but we are willing to permit the state to override individual preferences (including our own) in the interests of the greater good. In view of this, some writers have suggested that government use a social time preference rate that, though still above zero, would be below the private one. This still leaves the question of whether a time preference or an opportunity cost of investment rate should be used.

Others have argued that no one interest rate is appropriate and that government should apply a more complicated decision rule that treats investment from taxes as coming from consumption, regards government borrowing as crowding out private investment, and uses both time preference and opportunity cost rates in the calculation.[30] A simpler and more transparent approach is to use a range of discount rates to test for the sensitivity of the outcome to this variable.

Valuing Life

One of the most controversial areas of CBA, and perhaps of all economics, is the valuation of human life. For good reason: in the past, economists have often given ill-considered answers to the question of what a human life is worth. For example, they have worked out how much the potential victim of an accident or illness would have contributed to the national income had this event not

---

30. This approach originates with Stephen Marglin. See Marglin, "The Social Rate of Discount and the Optimal Rate of Saving," *Quarterly Journal of Economics* 77 (February 1963): 95–111; Marglin, "The Opportunity Costs of Public Investment," *Quarterly Journal of Economics* 77 (May 1963): 274–89; and Pearce, *Cost Benefit Analysis*, 46–58.

occurred. The PV of this future income stream was then taken as the benefit of saving the life or the cost of losing it. But this calculation gives most weight to the lives of high earners, and no weight to the lives of the retired. It is also bad welfare economics from a neoclassical viewpoint. The neoclassical value judgment to which we keep returning emphasizes individual preferences, and the value people place on their own lives is not to be confused with the value of their livelihoods.

Of course, if you were asked to state how much you would accept in compensation for the certainty that you would be exposed to a fatal dose of radiation tomorrow morning, you would be unlikely to name a figure that could meaningfully be entered in a CBA. But in practice, this is not the sort of choice you have to make. A more relevant question is what you would accept in compensation for a small increase in the risk of death.[31] This is the kind of decision most of us make several times a week. If you decide to travel by private car rather than by train, you increase your chances of a fatal accident in return for a minor gain in convenience. Many people make decisions about eating, smoking, and drinking that show a willingness to swap a higher risk of premature death for a small boost in satisfaction. And the examples go on.

Fine, but how do we get from here to putting a value on life? As for other kinds of environmental benefits, this may be done using expressed preference or revealed preference approaches. Expressed preference studies, for example, might use a questionnaire in which respondents are asked how much they would pay for safer methods of travel, with safety being defined in terms of risk of death.[32] Revealed preference methods often focus on the workplace. Occupations with

31. Thus the literature is generally at pains to distinguish valuation of a statistical life, which is what the method described seeks to estimate, from the value of life of a particular individual.
32. M. W. Jones-Lee, M. Hammerton, and P. R. Phillips, "The Value of Safety: Results of a National Sample Survey," *Economic Journal* 95 (March 1985): 49–72.

a higher death rate generally offer a wage premium to reflect this greater risk. Of course, wages differ for all sorts of reasons, including skill differences, so it is important to control for these by using statistical analysis to isolate the specific risk effect.

Suppose, then, there are two groups of ten thousand workers each. In occupation A, there are no hazardous effects worthy of consideration, so no workers suffer death from employment in the course of a year. In occupation B, however, one worker on average will die in the course of a year from occupational injury. Further suppose that to compensate for this risk, workers in B expect an additional thousand dollars per year. The annual wage bill for B will then be $10 million more than for A; this will be how the workers in the industry *implicitly* value the loss of a life.

In the expressed preference approach, individuals are encouraged to think about probabilities, but in the revealed preference approach they often apply for a job without consulting fatal accident tables. Does this necessarily invalidate the method? Supporters of the method may argue that most people nevertheless have at least some qualitative idea of the relative risks associated with different occupations and expect to be rewarded accordingly.

The Environmental Protection Agency (EPA) in the United States has drawn on a range of studies (twenty-one using the wage-premium approach and five using the expressed preference method) to obtain a single figure for this valuation. Most of the studies were published in the 1980s or 1990s and have been adjusted to take account of inflation. The current rate used for the *value of a statistical life* (VSL) is based on an estimate of $7.4 million, measured according to the purchasing power of the US dollar in 2006; this is then updated for subsequent years to allow for inflation.[33]

Cass Sunstein, who is sympathetic to the use of CBA in risk analysis, nevertheless criticizes the use of a single-figure VSL for all purposes.[34] The rationale for the underlying method is, as we have seen, that "individual preferences are to count," and in practice individual preferences in this area are quite diverse. As Sunstein points out, estimates vary depending on the nature of the risks and the personal characteristics of those on whose choices the estimates are based. On the first of these issues, many people would prefer a sudden death in an accident, or as a result of a heart attack, to a more lingering one from cancer: the EPA accepts that there is a "cancer differential," which may have to be taken into account when its guidelines on CBA are revised, as is currently in process.[35] On a per-mile basis, airline travel is safer than automobile travel, but people are more nervous of the former and indeed will pay more for increased air safety than for highway improvements.[36] On the second, it appears that, as with any estimate based on willingness to pay, the wealth or poverty of individuals is likely to affect results. Rich people will pay more than poorer people for a reduction in the risk of death. This is particularly marked when we make international comparisons. Sunstein quotes evidence from a widely respected study by Viscusi and Aldy giving VSL estimates for Taiwan of less than $1 million compared with almost $20 million for the United Kingdom (both estimates in US dollars as of the year 2000) .[37]

For some, the notion that CBA calculates lower values for the lives of poor people than for the lives of rich people will confirm all their worst suspicions about the heartlessness of economists, their

---

33. See National Center for Environmental Economics, "Frequently Asked Questions on Mortality Risk Evaluation," United States Environmental Protection Agency, last updated September 8, 2014, http://yosemite.epa.gov/ee/epa/eed.nsf/webpages/mortalityriskvaluation.html.

34. Cass R. Sunstein, *Laws of Fear: Beyond the Precautionary Principle* (Cambridge: Cambridge University Press, 2005), 129–74. This provides an excellent summary of the crucial issues.

35. National Center, "Frequently Asked Questions."

36. Sunstein, *Laws of Fear*, 140.

37. Ibid., 145, table 6.3; W. Kip Viscusi and Joseph E. Aldy, "The Value of a Statistical Life: A Critical Review of Market Estimates throughout the World," *Journal of Risk and Uncertainty* 27 (2003): 5–76.

sycophancy toward the rich and powerful, or their disdain for the poor and unsuccessful. But remember that the economists are not stating their own personal beliefs about the relative value of people's lives; they are simply reporting how the individual people themselves value a reduction in their own risk of death, given the constraints on their choices.

Suppose the government of a poor country is considering licensing a plant for the treatment of hazardous waste and has to decide what health and safety regulations to impose on the company. A CBA will balance the costs of regulations against the valuation of lives saved. In a rich country, we would expect the regulations to be much more stringent because of the higher VSL. Should policymakers in the poorer country, taking the view that their fellow citizens are just as valuable as those of any other country, insist on using a rich-country VSL in this calculation? If they do so, they may find that an otherwise viable plant no longer seems worthwhile. But perhaps the workers, in return for taking on a risk of death exceeding that acceptable in a rich country, would have been able to earn a wage that provided themselves and their families with better nutrition, access to health care, or education for their children to raise them out of poverty? How much has their government's imposition of a rich-country attitude to risk really helped them? Might it even be that in the absence of the plant the risk of premature death to themselves or to family members would be greater because there are no alternative ways of avoiding the life-threatening effects of poverty?[38]

---

38. This argument is not to be taken as implying that local health and safety regulations in poorer countries should be abolished or that multinationals or local firms that ignore them should escape the penalties for doing so (though corruption may facilitate this). Governments do need to make decisions about how much regulation to have and then enshrine these in laws that are strictly enforced. But there is a trade-off between safety standards and other desirable and important objectives.

The root of the problem, of course, is the extreme inequality that characterizes our world, both within societies and between them. Project appraisal methods alone cannot cure this inequality. Some writers, however, have suggested ways such methods may help to reduce it.

CBA and Income Distribution

We have seen that WTP is an unsatisfactory measure of welfare because it weights the poor person's dollar equally with that of the rich when an extra dollar will likely contribute much more to the welfare of the former. To take this into account, some economists have suggested that CBA calculations should have a built-in weighting system that encourages the selection of projects favoring the less well-off.

One simple way of doing this would be as follows. First, calculate the average income in the relevant community (the group whose members pay the costs and gain the major benefits of the project). Then divide the community into groups (in practice, probably rather broadly defined) depending on their own actual incomes. Work out a weighting factor for each group by dividing average income by the income of the group, then multiply the benefits or costs accruing to group members by these weights.

For example, suppose the average income for the community was $40,000 and the poorest group had an average income of only $20,000. Their weight would then be 2. Any costs or benefits that accrued to this low-income group would be multiplied by 2 in the cost-benefit calculation. Thus, a project that favored this group would have an increased chance of being selected. But if the project gave rise to costs that were mainly borne by the poorest group, these would also be given a double weight, which would make it difficult for such projects to gain acceptance. Such effects would be reinforced by the downgrading of projects that favored the rich. A group with twice the average income, $80,000, would have their benefits and costs weighted by a factor of 0.5. As a result, projects for which the gains were mainly received by the rich would have these gains downsized; similarly, costs paid by the rich would be given a lower weight in the calculation.

This and similar proposals give CBA a clear "bias to the poor." E. J. Mishan has pointed out that, even so, the calculation would not always prevent projects from making the rich richer and the poor poorer; this would depend on the magnitude of the relative advantages accruing to the two groups. David Pearce, however, has noted that a CBA incorporating distributional weights is not intended *purely* as a mechanism for redistribution; it tries rather to integrate *both* efficiency and equity considerations.[39]

Use and Limitations of CBA

I return to the point made earlier: CBA does not provide a magic formula that gives infallible answers to difficult questions of social choice. It does not offer the last word in answer to the question of what is to be done. But it may provide one of the first words by serving as a helpful initial input to policy discussions. By laying out the pros and cons of a proposal in a systematic way, quantifying them where possible and making clear the judgments on which the calculations are based, it can help to clarify thought.

Arguably, the methods discussed here are best applied to projects that are fairly narrowly defined in scope. A proposal to protect an area of wetlands from commercial exploitation would lend itself more to

39. For further discussion, see Pearce, *Cost-Benefit Analysis*, 59–72.

analysis by means of these techniques than, say, policies to remove or impose a ban on genetically modified crops or to allow or prevent a rise in global average surface temperatures above 3 degrees Celsius. Such proposals will involve far-reaching consequences very difficult even to enumerate, still less to evaluate. Sometimes economists do try to predict costs and benefits in these cases, too.[40] One may be impressed by the ingenuity and panache with which these exercises are undertaken while at the same time wondering the wisdom of placing much faith in the results.

40. A comprehensive review of attempts to estimate the costs and benefits of climate change is given in Richard S. J. Tol, "The Economic Effects of Climate Change," *Journal of Economic Perspectives* 23, no. 2 (Spring 2009): 29–51. While the studies reviewed generally show relatively small overall adverse impacts of a few percent on global GDP, these effects are sometimes much worse for the poorest countries in the world, particularly in Africa (see 31, table 1).

6

Ethical Environmental Polices

The previous chapter was about how to remedy the failure of the market, left to itself, to provide decision makers with satisfactory *information* about the environment. The present chapter is concerned with policies to remedy the market's failure to provide adequate *incentives* to persuade private decision makers, whether in companies or in households, to use environmental resources in a socially desirable way.

Do We Need State Regulation?

In much traditional welfare economics, the remedy for market failure is assumed to be intervention by the state. The role of the state in environmental matters is indeed very important, and much of this chapter will assess the techniques of government intervention. However, this is not the only alternative to free markets, and I begin by examining two other approaches: the development of greater *corporate social responsibility* within private firms, on the one hand, and, on the other, the emergence of collective forms of organization, or *common pool resource regimes*, that do not directly involve the state. These proposed remedies typically concern different areas of economic activity. Corporate social responsibility is generally discussed in the context of medium to large enterprises, often in modern industries, whereas common pool resource systems are usually found in more traditional sectors such as forestry, animal husbandry, or fisheries.

Is Corporate Social Responsibility Sufficient?

During the 1990s, there was increasing discussion of broadening the objectives of private businesses beyond the maximization of profit. Businesses have been urged to switch their focus from the narrow interests of shareholders to the broader requirements of *stakeholders*, including employees, consumers, and citizens with environmental concerns. *Triple bottom line accounting*, a phrase first coined by John Elkington, founder of a UK consultancy called SustainAbility, is one popular strategy for taking these interests into account. Instead of producing only an annual financial statement on profits, Elkington argued, businesses should produce two further statements on "people" and "planet"; the first of these would show how the company had pursued its social obligations, and the second how it had affected the environment.[1]

Such concerns may be subsumed under the general heading of corporate social responsibility (CSR). A 2011 EU document defined this concept as "the responsibility of enterprises for their impacts on

1. John Elkington, *Cannibals with Forks: Triple Bottom Line of 21st Century Business* (Monkato: Capstone, 1997).

society" and explained that the enterprises "should have in place a process to integrate social, environmental, ethical human rights and consumer concerns into their business operations and core strategy in close collaboration with their stakeholders."[2]

As soon as we try to extend the objectives of private companies as widely as this, we run into a dilemma—a prisoner's dilemma, to be precise. Companies have always been subject to the law in pursuit of their traditional goal of profits. But the CSR agenda does not just consist of exhortations to obey the law; it expects companies to go beyond this and take account of social goals that, though desirable, are not actually mandated by the legal system.

So where does prisoner's dilemma come in? Suppose the CEO of a chemicals firm, one of a number in a broadly competitive industry, is being lobbied by a member of her family, who is also a member of Greenpeace, to introduce more stringent emissions standards than are strictly required by law. The CEO may sympathize with the arguments for such standards and accept that if everyone introduced them society would be better off, but if she introduces costly improvements to the firm's waste disposal systems when her competitors do not, her firm may lose the competitive struggle to drive costs and prices down. Its very existence may be threatened, or a more ruthless competitor may make a successful takeover bid for the firm and replace the CEO with a manager who understands the imperatives of the single bottom line. Refer once more to figure 3.3; rewrite the strategies as "introduce tougher standards" and "do not introduce such standards," and we have the familiar dilemma.

For such reasons, some economists would argue that, if we are really concerned about environmental standards, the most sensible

2. "Corporate Social Responsibility (CSR)," European Commission, Enterprise and Industry, http://ec.europa.eu/enterprise/policies/sustainable-business/corporate-social-responsibility/index_en.htm.

approach is to ensure that our environmental goals are backed by law rather than placing unreasonable expectations on company executives.

Some critics are skeptical about the CSR discourse found in the speeches and writings of executives of firms engaged in environmentally threatening activities. The critics may note, for example, that oil companies are particularly eager to flaunt their environmental credentials and suspect that this is no more than a smokescreen behind which the companies engage in business as usual.[3] The more cynical may argue that this is not always a bad thing, at least in those instances in which the environmental standards demanded by activist organizations are set unnecessarily high such that there would be a net social cost from implementing them.

There may also be benefits from persuading firms to commit to CSR codes of behavior. Managers who want to behave ethically and obey the spirit as well as the letter of the law can then appeal to the code as justification for their actions. The code may also nudge companies in the direction of behavior that is not only socially responsible but also in the long run may help them save costs, whether in the form of legal fees or damage to their reputation. But it cannot be a substitute for well-designed and properly policed legal restrictions on antisocial behavior.

3. Thus both Lord Browne of British Petroleum and Sir Mark Moody-Stuart of Shell were particularly prominent advocates of "green" business practices in the late 1990s; see David Henderson, *Misguided Virtue: False Notions of Corporate Responsibility* (London: Institute of Economic Affairs, 2001), 58–81. Yet both companies have continued to be the subject of severe criticism for their environmental impact: Shell most notably perhaps for oil spillage in the Niger Delta, and BP most recently for the Deepwater Horizon oil spill in the Gulf of Mexico.

Collective Action and Common Pool Resources

Turning to the case of common pool resources (CPRs), it may at first sight seem that areas such as forestry and fishing are the very ones to which the prisoner's dilemma applies with particular force: those allegedly affected by what Garrett Hardin called, in a famous article in *Science*, "the tragedy of the commons."[4] Hardin argued that under feudalism, in which the peasants in each village were entitled access to common land for their livestock, there would be overgrazing, as each peasant would be driven inexorably to maximize his own use of the resource, fearing that others would if he did not. But Hardin has been criticized for confusing "open access" with "common access." In the first case, anyone at all may use the resource freely; in the second, access is restricted to members of a particular group, and there are rules about how this right is to be exercised. In fact, the medieval common fell into the latter category and was not overused by those with access to it.[5]

How, then, may institutions be successfully structured to avoid the prisoner's dilemma and ensure that common pool resources are not degraded? In recent years, it has become apparent that there are many situations in which a national governmental authority is neither the only nor necessarily the best institution for ensuring appropriate collective action. Much of the work demonstrating this was overseen or stimulated by Elinor Ostrom, who, although a political scientist, was named Nobel laureate in economics in 2009, not long before her death in 2012.

Ostrom was critical of the view, typical among neoclassical welfare economists, that where the market was manifestly inadequate to deal with collective choice problems in the use of environmental

4. Garrett Hardin, "The Tragedy of the Commons," *Science* 162 (December 1968): 1243–48.
5. Michael Common and Sigrid Stagl, *Ecological Economics: An Introduction* (Cambridge: Cambridge University Press, 2005), 339.

resources, only the state could offer a remedy. She argued that models such as the prisoner's dilemma assumed constraints on individuals that, while undoubtedly present in some collective action situations, are not present in all. Thus, in the original version of the prisoner's dilemma, one important feature is that the two prisoners are kept in separate cells and are unable to communicate with each other. A second feature is that the game is only played once; each prisoner will have to live for a long time with the consequences of a single decision. But if people in a group are able to communicate with each other, they may agree on rules for collective behavior, and if they are in an ongoing relationship in which the game is played many times, they may then be able to "punish" those who break the rules. One way of doing this, for example, is through the tit-for-tat strategy. Under this strategy, I begin by cooperating, and in all subsequent plays of the game I copy your actions. If you cheat in the first round, I will cheat in the second; if you subsequently decide to cooperate, I will cooperate thereafter; and so on. Both communicating and monitoring subsequent behavior are easier when groups are relatively small.

Ostrom's empirical work revealed many instances in which institutions for collective action had evolved in ways that worked better than either the market or the state. On the basis of these case studies, she identified eight *design principles* common to the successful and long-lasting CPR regimes on which evidence had been collected.[6] Subsequent work, summarized by Cox, Arnold, and Tomás, has provided substantial confirmation for Ostrom's principles while modifying and elaborating some details, in effect increasing them from eight to eleven principles through subdivision.[7]

---

6. Elinor Ostrom, *Governing the Commons: The Evolution of Institutions for Collective Action* (Cambridge: Cambridge University Press, 1990).

A number of the principles were found to have particularly strong support. These included a *boundary condition*, which clearly defined the community of those entitled to use the resource system, ensuring that the system was not open access. Rules about who gets what needed be in harmony with both the conditions on the ground and with local customs and ideologies; where government agencies tried to override these customs, the success of the system could be threatened. Members of the community also had to be persuaded that the return from their own participation in the system matched the effort they put into it. Of further importance was policing of the rules; when members of the community monitored the rules, or at least oversaw the monitors, the sustainability of the system was favored.

Cox, Arnold, and Tomás are skeptical about whether the design principles that work for relatively small groups can be applied with equal success to larger ones. Ostrom, too, insists that there is no panacea: "We have found that government, private and community-based mechanisms all work in some settings. People want to make me argue that community systems of governance are always the best: I will not walk into that trap."[8] It does appear, though, that opportunities for face-to-face communication between members of a CPR group have greatly facilitated its success. This has been confirmed by laboratory experiments in which student volunteers found themselves in social situations designed to test game-theory models involving common pool resources.[9] When similar

7. Michael Cox, Gwen Arnold, and Sergio Villamayor Tomás, "A Review of Design Principles for Community-Based Natural Resource Management," *Ecology and Society* 15, no. 4 (2010): 38, http://www.ecologyandsociety.org/vol15/iss4/art38/

8. Elinor Ostrom, with contributions by Christina Chang, Mark Pennington, and Vlad Tarko, *The Future of the Commons: Beyond Market Failure and Government Regulation* (London: Institute of Economic Affairs, 2012), 70.

9. Elinor Ostrom, "Beyond Markets and States: Polycentric Governance of Complex Economic Systems," *American Economic Review* 100 (June 2010): 1–33. This source is a revised version of

experiments were carried out with villagers in Colombia who were personally engaged in forestry or fishing, the results tended to agree with those obtained for the students in the lab. Interestingly, in other experiments, when an outside agency limited the villagers' use of resources, monitoring their compliance with occasional external inspections, the degree of cooperation diminished.

The importance of face-to-face communication in the CPR studies reinforces the view that alternative mechanisms may be necessary to resolve large-scale, more impersonal environmental situations such as climate change or atmospheric pollution in cities. In smaller groups, people get to know who can be trusted and find ways of penalizing those who are untrustworthy. More formal systems, whether involving the market, the state, or a combination of the two, may be necessary for the larger-scale dilemmas. Nonetheless, the work by Ostrom and her colleagues has greatly increased our understanding of the complexity of collective choice and of the possibilities for devising institutions to deal with its problems. In particular, the emphasis in Ostrom's work on the ability of local communities to develop both long-lived and ecologically sustainable forms of resource exploitation supports the claims of some writers, such as Vandana Shiva, concerning the environmental superiority of such societies over more developed ones (see chapter 2). The notion that such communities are best run by women, however, does not appear in the CPR literature reviewed here.

There remains the problem of how to deal with larger-scale environmental issues, those issues requiring the development of market or state mechanisms. To such systems we now turn.

Ostrom's Nobel Lecture of December 8, 2009. See especially 14–17 on the experimental testing of the models.

Alternative Policy Instruments

I begin with a brief description of the range of policy instruments[10] developed for the control of pollution, broadly interpreted, and for the achievement of sustainability. Subsequent sections of the chapter will give the neoclassical environmental economist's appraisal of the design of these instruments and also note the criticisms made of the neoclassical approach to these issues. There will follow a consideration of international aspects of environmental policy, which will conclude with an appraisal of the policies currently being followed by national governments and international organizations in their response to key global environmental issues.

Command and Control Systems

For those who consider the state should simply replace the market with an administrative mechanism in areas where the market fails in its task of resource allocation, the *command and control* (CAC) system seems the obvious approach, and historically this has been the most popular method. Under CAC, regulation is achieved by the establishment of mandatory *standards* that set a maximum acceptable level of pollution. The "control" aspect is achieved by inspection and enforcement, by court action if necessary. Acceptable levels may be defined either in terms of the quality of the environment that receives the waste disposal (*ambient standards*) or in terms of the level of emissions at the point of exit from the source of the waste (*emissions standards*). In the first case, inspectors might check pollution levels downstream from a plant releasing chemicals into a river; in the

---

10. For a fuller treatment, see David W. Pearce and R. Kerry Hunter, *Economics of Natural Resources and the Environment* (Hemel Hempstead: Harvester Wheatsheaf, 1990), 102–119; Common and Stagl, *Ecological Economics,* 402–441.

second case, they would check the volume of pollutant at the outlet. A CAC approach might also include specifications on the types and quality of inputs to a production process (for example, on the type of coal acceptable in power stations or on the species of livestock allowed to be converted into sausages in a processed food plant) or on the technology to be used in the process.

Market-Based Instruments: Taxes and Subsidies

An alternative to the administrative approach of CAC is the use of market-based measures. The objective here is not to outlaw pollution above a certain level but to discourage it. The most obvious form of discouragement is a tax based on the volume of effluent from a process or on the level of use of a pollution-intensive input. Thus, a carbon tax on the release of carbon dioxide or methane to the atmosphere is a market-based response to global warming that is often suggested. Increasing the price of making carbon emissions is intended to deter their creation.

Subsidies are the mirror image of taxes. Here, governments reduce the cost, and hence encourage the use, of activities considered more desirable. Thus, if some methods of supplying energy are considered cleaner or more sustainable than others, governments could subsidize the cleaner ones rather than taxing the more harmful ones. This should make users switch to the former and reduce reliance on the latter.

Market-Based Instruments: Market Creation, or "Cap and Trade"

An alternative method of making emissions more expensive is to issue a limited quantity of "permits to pollute" and create a market in which those who really need to emit the pollutant could purchase those permits. Again, the ultimate aim is to make emissions more expensive and thus discourage firms from producing them. As the Stern report points out, this approach may be regarded as a CAC-market "hybrid." The global permissible level of pollution, or "cap," is set by the regulator; the market finds the price of the permits through trade on the "carbon credits exchange."[11]

Evaluating Policy Instruments: Neoclassical Arguments

Is the difference between the CAC and the market-based instrument (MBI) systems really all that important? After all, if a company decides to ignore the CAC standards and gets caught, it will have to pay a fine for pollution, just as it would have to pay an effluent charge under the MBI system. In fact, however, the mechanisms differ in some important respects. Economists tend to favor MBI approaches and recommend CAC only in situations where MBI approaches are not viable. Critics of the economist's worldview are more suspicious of the market, as we have seen in earlier chapters. I begin, however, by explaining the merits of MBIs, as economists see them.

Criteria for Policy Evaluation

At the beginning of chapter 5 we considered in general terms the principles that should guide policymakers. We saw that among these principles economists have traditionally emphasized efficiency, and perhaps especially for this reason they favor the use of the market. However, they are prepared to acknowledge that other issues, such as equity and uncertainty, may require other approaches.

---

11. Nicholas Stern, *The Economics of Climate Change: The Stern Review* (Cambridge: Cambridge University Press, 2007), 353.

The efficiency criterion itself raises a cluster of issues. For present purposes, we can consider three in particular. First, will the policy under consideration help achieve an "optimal" allocation of resources, implying an optimal level of pollution, given our present production technologies? Economists would refer to this as achieving *static allocative efficiency*. Noneconomists may wish to know what is meant by "optimal pollution." Shouldn't the optimal level of pollution be zero? A moment's reflection will suggest that this cannot be the case. Just by being alive and engaging in normal bodily functions we are emitting pollutants. To grasp the notion of optimal pollution, look again at the section in chapter 3 headed "Internalizing Externalities" and the example of the polluted river. Recall that the problem was not that the pollution occurred but that it was not taken into account by the private firm. If it had been, its cost would have added to the private cost and would thus have reduced the firm's output by increasing the price of the product, but it would not have reduced the output to zero. The product would still have a social value, which could be balanced against all costs, both private and external.[12] Once the external costs had been internalized, output of the product would be socially optimal, and thus the pollution associated with that output would also be at its optimal level.

The second kind of efficiency question is whether the policy will create incentives for desirable change: will it encourage the discovery and implementation, over time, of more environmentally friendly

---

12. More precisely, the output of the factory should be set at the point where the *marginal social cost* equals the *marginal social benefit* from the product. The marginal social cost is the addition to total social costs, including external costs, resulting from the production of one more unit of the product; the marginal social benefit is the additional amount people would be willing to pay for that unit (in the example in chapter 3, this would be the price of the unit). It would not be optimal to produce more than this, as the extra cost (including external cost) of another unit would then exceed the extra gain. But it would also be inefficient to produce less, as this would imply that some additional production would be valued more highly than the alternative uses of the resources consumed in producing it (including environmental ones).

technologies? And the third is about the resources used in the process of designing and enforcing the policy itself. Can we implement the policy without incurring excessive *transaction costs*—the costs, that is, of reaching agreement about what is to be done and of ensuring that this agreement is kept?

Suppose now that we apply these criteria to the CAC approach. A common form of this policy specifies that emissions of a pollutant should be kept below a designated level. For example, if water is used to get rid of chemical waste, the rule might say that waste water emissions should contain no more than X units of the hazardous chemical per liter. Suppose, too, that the damage caused by the emissions does not increase sharply after this point and that the cutoff level is therefore fairly arbitrary. Now consider two firms, A and B. Firm A is already below this level and indeed with only minor low-cost changes could reduce its level even further, to 0.25X per liter, but the regulation provides no incentive for further improvement. Firm B, however, which has older equipment, can only achieve a level of 1.1X unless it completely overhauls its production process; it simply cannot afford to do this in current economic conditions. The extra pollution damage caused by the additional emissions above the limit is not great, and if the firm were just being asked to pay for this, it could afford to do so, but the rigorous application of the administrative standard will force it out of business altogether.

This example implies that two of the efficiency requirements are not being met. The shutdown of Firm B will reduce the industry's output below what it should be, given the true social costs and benefits of keeping B in business: this fails the first test, that of static efficiency. The absence of any incentive for Firm A to improve its technology fails the second test.

By contrast, both these aspects of efficiency would be met by market incentives. Suppose a tax on effluent, or an emissions charge, were applied. This charge, by requiring Firm B to pay the full cost of its emissions, would reduce the firm's output to the socially efficient level without driving it completely out of business. At the same time, the policy would encourage Firm A to minimize its exposure to the tax by improving its own performance.

What about the other kind of MBI—the creation of a market in pollution permits? In practice, there are a number of ways this might work, but to get the general flavor of the argument, suppose each firm was given a permit to pollute up to X parts per thousand per hour but was allowed to buy a permit for more pollution. Firm A is already at this level, but Firm B would have to buy an extra permit to exceed this level. Firm A would then have a strong incentive to cut its level to 0.25X, which it could do cheaply; it would then save three permits every four hours, which it could sell on the permit exchange to firms like B. So this system would also satisfy the first two efficiency criteria.

Which system, though, would be most efficient in meeting the third criterion—keeping down transaction costs? All three systems would require monitoring to ensure that firms did not cheat, whether by exceeding the regulatory limit in the first instance, by trying to avoid tax through underreporting of emissions in the second, or by purchasing too few permits in the third. In this last case, resources would also be required to establish and operate the exchange, which could be an additional transaction cost. In the CAC case, there are usually substantial negotiating costs. These arise not only when the standards are being set but also when they are being implemented. They may for example involve bargaining over deadlines for compliance with the inspectorate's requirements or over vagueness in these requirements. For example, where the control is not on emission levels but on technology standards, companies may be required to use the "best practicable means," the "best available technology," the "best available control technology," or even the "best available technology not entailing excessive cost" to reduce emissions; precisely what these requirements might imply in a particular context may easily be a source of debate.

The scope for administrative discretion in such matters may lead to *regulatory capture* in which the relationship between regulator and regulated becomes too cozy; such issues will be further explored in chapter 7. While this problem is particularly obvious with CAC systems, MBIs are not immune to political lobbying either. An oft-quoted example concerns the initial implementation of the European Emissions Trading Scheme (EU ETS) introduced in 2005. Critics argue that to make the scheme more acceptable to business, the initial allowances, which were issued free rather than being auctioned, were too generous. However, the scheme has also run into difficulties for other reasons, most notably the severe economic downturn that affected the second phase of the scheme after 2008 by reducing the demand for allowances and hence the price of carbon.[13]

While economists still consider MBIs in general to have the theoretical edge over CACs, they acknowledge that there are situations in which CAC would be the simplest policy to implement. The Clean Air Act in the United Kingdom in 1956 relied mainly on this method, though subsidies were also offered to aid conversion to cleaner forms of fuel. It was easy for inspectors to tell whether a chimney was emitting "dark smoke" and therefore whether it was

---

13. See, for example, Ben Schiller, "Is It Time to Overhaul Europe's Carbon Trading Scheme?," *Yale Environment 360*, April 28, 2011, http://e360.yale.edu/feature/europes_co2_trading_scheme_is_it_time_for_a_major_overhaul/2396/. Violent fluctuations in the EU ETS carbon price, as well as the problems caused by industry lobbying, have persuaded many economists that the most effective way of increasing the carbon price is through a carbon tax. The price varied from around thirty euros per metric ton at the start of the scheme in 2005 to zero in late 2007, rising briefly to thirty again in early 2008 and falling below ten euros by early 2012. See Dieter Helm, *The Carbon Crunch: How We're Getting Climate Change Wrong—and How to Fix It* (New Haven: Yale University Press, 2012), 185.

liable for a standard fine; it would have been much harder to determine just how much harm each one of the millions of such chimneys was causing and to impose finely tuned effluent charges accordingly. Also, where there is a clearly defined threshold level, or tipping point, below which pollution has minimal effects but above which it becomes a serious problem, there may again be a case for CAC. And there are other arguments for the approach, as we shall see when we come to consider issues of uncertainty.

First, however, what about equity? Pollution charges are often attacked on the argument that they are easily met by the rich but impose hardship on the poor. A common example is the use of fuel taxes to reduce energy use, whether for heating a home or running an automobile. Will a tax on domestic fuel lead to impoverished elderly people dying of hypothermia? Might an increase in gasoline taxes make it more difficult for poor people in rural areas to get to work, go shopping, or visit the doctor? To these criticisms there are a number of answers.

It may not make much difference from the point of view of the less well-off whether we use CAC or MBI to reduce energy consumption. True, the latter method will affect prices directly, but CAC will also tend to push prices upward. Precisely how will depend on the control method used. The regulations may require the use of cleaner but generally more expensive fuel inputs, in which case prices will increase. Or there may be a decision to restrict supply, issue ration coupons in the interest of fairness, and keep prices down by price control, as was done in many countries during wartime. There would be no guarantee that the available fuel would go to its most important uses, as the signaling function of price would have been abolished. Those whose rations gave them more fuel than they needed would squander it, leaving others who needed it more without enough to meet those needs. In practice, a flourishing black market would then develop, as sure as night follows day. Users who wanted or needed to supplement their rations would have to pay extortionate black-market prices; poorer groups would be unable to do so.

In any case, there are ways of preventing low-income people from suffering the effects of environmental taxes while still using such taxes to restructure prices in line with true social costs. Suppose low-income groups would suffer a cut in real income of one thousand dollars every winter if fuel taxes pushed prices up to the extent considered necessary to avoid global warming and excess pollution. This could be offset by means of a cash transfer of one thousand dollars to the income groups affected. Fuel tax revenue from all the other taxpayers who did not qualify for the transfer would be available to pay for this, with plenty left over. Of course, some of the recipients might choose to spend some of this allowance not on heating but on other items—beer, perhaps.[14] This would be their choice, which should be respected if we accept the value judgment that individual preferences are to count.

The very poorest are not always those most affected by fuel price increases. In particular, members of this group are less likely than others to possess an automobile, so a rise in gasoline prices will affect them less. Use of a fuel tax to subsidize public transport might indeed benefit both the worst-off groups and the environment.

In brief, then, there seems to be no reason why MBIs will necessarily be particularly disadvantageous to those with low incomes, as long as they are used as part of a policy package designed to protect the less well-off.

---

14. Economic theory, indeed, would predict that the whole thousand dollars would not be spent on heating, as the increase in the relative price of energy vis-à-vis other goods would encourage consumers to substitute other goods for energy in their spending patterns.

There remains the question of uncertainty. Uncertainty about the precise relationship between emissions and environmental damage makes implementing charges difficult. As a result, charges are most suitable for situations in which there is a lot of information about how damage increases with output (or with input of a particular substance). They are perhaps least suitable for those situations in which the danger of emissions is not precisely known but is considered so high as to make such emissions unacceptable above a very low level. They are also inappropriate for situations in which the failure to use the very safest technologies could give rise to a catastrophic event, such as a nuclear meltdown or a major oil spill, where the damage and costs may be very difficult to estimate before the event but could be very high. In these cases, the kind of trade-offs that are a feature of MBIs are simply not available; the only sensible approach seems to be a strict regulatory regime accompanied by severe and even criminal penalties if the regulations are breached.

Ethical Criticisms of the Market-Based Approach

There are broader criticisms of MBIs, however, that do not just consider their technical unsuitability in particular situations but oppose them in principle. This will come as no surprise to readers of chapter 2, or indeed of chapter 5, in which I examined the view that cost-benefit analysts, by trying to impute money values to all kinds of inputs and outputs, are seeking to extend commodification too far beyond the market's proper domain.

Permits as Indulgences?

If you call a dog's tail a leg, how many legs will a dog have? Four. Calling a tail a leg doesn't make it a leg.

—attributed to Abraham Lincoln

Earlier I asked whether it was a matter of indifference whether polluters were asked to pay a charge for emissions or a fine for exceeding a regulatory limit, and I suggested that the two approaches did have important but different implications for efficiency. Antimarket critics also see an important distinction here, but one based on ethics, not efficiency. Whatever the efficiency arguments for charges, these critics believe that regulations and fines are the more ethical way of dealing with pollution.

As we saw in chapter 3, one the best-known critics of the extension of the market into new policy areas is Michael Sandel. On the specific issue of fines versus charges for pollution, he argues that pollution is a moral issue; companies who poison the air or water, like vacationers who litter the countryside with beer cans, are guilty of antisocial behavior. The appropriate policy response is to outlaw such behavior and impose a fine as a punishment for crime—an action that carries not just a cost but a moral stigma in a way that a "green tax," or for that matter an obligation to buy a permit on a carbon exchange, would not.[15]

Sandel notes that some critics who take this view compare the trade in permits to the sale of indulgences, a major scandal in the Catholic Church. In the early sixteenth century, the Dominican friar Johann Tetzel sold indulgences to raise money for the rebuilding of Saint Peter's Basilica in Rome; his actions helped spark the Lutheran reformation. In using the term, the critics are drawing on a forceful

---

15. Michael Sandel, *What Money Can't Buy: The Moral Limits of Markets* (London: Allen Lane, 2012), 72–79.

and emotive symbol, one that may resonate, in particular, with those from a theological background. So it is worth taking a little time to consider whether the analogy is a fair one.

A fully developed version of the argument is found in a 1994 paper by Robert Goodin of the Australian National University; his article was included in a recent well-reviewed collection of "essential readings" on climate ethics.[16] While both Goodin and Sandel admit the analogy is not perfect, Goodin justifies it by noting the similarities between the theological criticisms of the sale of indulgences and the environmentalist criticisms of the marketization of the right to pollute. He argues that the sale of indulgences was wrong because the pope and his agents were selling what was not theirs to sell (God's grace); further, they were selling something that could not be bought (here Goodin references thesis 27 of Luther's 1517 *Disputatio pro Declaratione Virtutis Indulgentiarum* in which Luther attacks the slogan attributed to Tetzel: "As soon as the coin in the cashbox rings, the soul from purgatory springs"). Moreover, the suggestion that cash payment could somehow atone for wrongdoing encouraged people not to take sin seriously enough (as thesis 40 points out). It appeared, in Goodin's phrase, to "render wrongs right," or at least to imply that sinning was acceptable as long as you made a cash payment in recompense. This removed a key part of the process of contrition: the sincere intention to amend one's life, to go and sin no more. Further, by making forgiveness conditional on payment, its distribution among the faithful would depend unfairly on ability to pay rather than true repentance.

These seem convincing grounds for criticizing the sale of indulgences by the sixteenth-century Catholic Church. The question

16. Robert E. Goodin, "Selling Environmental Indulgences," *Kyklos* 47 (1994): 573–96; reprinted in *Climate Ethics: Essential Readings*, ed. Stephen Gardiner, Simon Caney, Dale Jamieson, and Henry Shue (New York: Oxford University Press, 2010), 231–46. References are to this latter source.

is how far Goodin succeeds in applying the same arguments to the sale of pollution permits or, indeed, to the use of any other MBIs—to any policy that, rather than treating pollution as a crime, allows some pollution as long as the polluter is asked to pay for the right to pollute. I do not consider him entirely successful in making these arguments, for reasons I will explain once I have outlined his case.

Goodin begins with the claim that governments who sell such permits are "selling what is not theirs to sell." We saw in chapter 2 that some writers (especially feminists) take a religious view of nature, perhaps personified as the Mother Goddess; is it she, then, who alone could forgive attacks on her person? Goodin refers to this view but makes clear that his argument does not depend on any such mystical personification; instead, he invokes the concept of stewardship toward the nonhuman world and toward future generations. It would be wrong of stewards to allow others to "destroy irrevocably" (his phrase) what was their duty to preserve.

Turning to his second proposition, Goodin argues that environmental goods, like God's grace, are not appropriate to sell. Here, he seems to be expressing a distaste for the use of pecuniary motivation in an environmental context. He gives an example in which the cutting down of a rain forest might, as a last resort, be justified if this were the only way to provide for the inhabitants, but he argues it would be wrong to auction licenses to cut it down to the highest bidder. Here, and at other points in his argument, his opposition to auctioning entitlements to pollute seems partly for reasons of justice, as the ability to bid is very unevenly distributed. But he also raises the issue Galbraith put forward in *The Affluent Society* that private affluence may be difficult to enjoy in conditions of public squalor. Finally, he puts forward a "crowding out" argument: if we appeal to people to protect the environment as a matter of duty, they may do so, but pecuniary incentive may reduce this voluntary motivation.[17] Luther's argument that payment for indulgences reduces the perceived heinousness of sin is reflected in Goodin's claim that allowing people to pay for pollution reduces their sense of its moral reprehensibility whereas criminalizing them for pollution would reinforce this sense.

In the final section of his paper Goodin contrasts two versions of the economic (or, as he prefers to describe it, "economistic") argument for market-based incentives ("indulgences for environmental despoliation").[18] The more modest approach uses incentives as a means of persuading people to match their demands on the environment to what policymakers (hopefully through some democratic process) have decided the environment can bear. The more ambitious approach uses MBIs to determine what the level of pollution should be. Goodin is opposed to both approaches but claims that the information required to implement the more ambitious version is not generally available to policymakers, who are obliged as a matter of pragmatism to content themselves with the more limited version. Goodin himself shows some hints of pragmatism by acknowledging that since complete criminalization of all pollution may not be politically acceptable, some use of MBIs to limit pollution may be better than no policy at all.

In coming to grips with Goodin's argument, we first have to be clear on what he means by "environmental pollution." In the final section of his paper he considers as his preferred alternative to the "polluter pays principle" the requirement that "polluters desist from

17. The crowding-out argument against the extension of market principles is strongly featured by Sandel in a variety of contexts. For example, there is the case of the playgroup that tried to improve the punctuality of parents coming to collect their children by charging them for lateness. This made lateness worse because the parents then considered themselves entitled to take advantage of the extra time they had, in effect, paid for. See Sandel, *What Money Can't Buy*, 64–65.
18. The addition of the letters "ic" to other people's disciplinary titles seems to be a genteel academic way of administering a slap on the wrist to those considered to have overstepped the bounds of their proper sphere. Another common example is "scientistic."

polluting altogether." But we saw when considering the notion of optimal pollution that this is simply a physical impossibility: we are all, unavoidably, polluters. Elsewhere in his argument, in the introduction, Goodin does acknowledge that not all emissions are "wrong" because not all cause "environmental despoliation"; some, he explains, "actually do no harm." Suppose there *is* some despoliation from an economic activity, however, but it is outweighed by the good the activity produces: is this still to be regarded as wrong? Goodin is clear that it is wrong and that in such a case we are "operating in the realm of 'tragedy': even if we have done 'the right thing on balance' we will nonetheless have committed a wrong."

Pollution, then, in the "sinful" sense, is taken to mean any activity that causes any damage to "nature," however worthy the cause—and, presumably, however minor the damage, though Goodin does not say this in so many words. But he is surely committed to this view by his insistence on encompassing pollution in the theological category of sin rather than the economic (economistic?) category of costs. For sin, of course, is not to be trivialized merely because its material effects are trivial.

A second problem is to determine precisely where to draw the boundaries of the "nature" it is allegedly sinful to damage in any way. This point was already made in chapter 5 when considering the "commodification" criticism in the context of CBA. There, I suggested that virtually all economic activity does some damage to the natural environment but that concern over marketization seemed aimed mainly at the despoliation of those aspects of the environment in which private property rights had not previously been established because of the high transaction costs of establishing them. These aspects include, in particular, "sink" resources and "amenity" resources. It is not clear why this rather technical criterion should be used to distinguish the sacred from the secular, or the permitted from the forbidden. But some grounds for distinction are required if we are to criminalize activities that "despoil" nature; *all* economic activity uses at least some resources torn from nature's bosom, but we cannot criminalize it all.

Some of Goodin's more specific criticisms of MBIs, I believe, are wide of the mark, and the remainder can be justified without recourse to the "indulgences" metaphor. Take the criticism that governments are "selling what is not theirs to sell," which he links to the concept of stewardship—the notion, in particular, that as stewards of environmental assets governments are failing in their duty if they allow these assets to be irrevocably destroyed for a fee. The valid point here really has to do with the notion of sustainability. If we take even a moderately strong view of this concept, then there will indeed be a range of diverse environmental assets for which no substitutes are available and which it is considered very important to protect either for their own sake or for future generations of humans, depending on how we interpret the duty of stewardship. Examples might include coral reefs, the white rhinoceros, and the Antarctic ice shelf, among a host of others. In such cases, it would be criminal to sell off permits to exploit these resources *beyond the point where they risked being irrevocably destroyed.* Where resources are replaceable, however, and the revenues from the sale of licenses may be used to help replace them, it is not clear that this policy infringes the duties of stewardship in any way.[19]

Goodin is of course correct to argue that the ability to pay is very unevenly distributed. In the case of green taxes, this may be

---

19. Readers may wonder whether all green taxes really go to repair environmental damage. Might they not be absorbed in the general revenues of government and perhaps used for other purposes? But it is not always a good idea to insist that particular tax revenues be used for a related purpose (they may be needed for other urgent social objectives). The main thing is to ensure that government accepts an obligation to prevent and repair environmental damage in the long run and uses taxes, where appropriate, as one method of achieving this.

taken into account through targeted income transfers, and we further saw that restricting supply through administrative fiat, rather than taxes, will also raise the prices paid by everyone, rich or poor. When licenses for resource exploitation are auctioned to the highest bidder, the object is to ensure that they are used as efficiently as possible, which seems a worthwhile goal. But Goodin may be right about the undesirability of auctioning the right to cut down a rain forest, and here indeed the government may be selling off something it does not possess; however, this does not imply that market incentives are not relevant. The best solution may be to accept that the right of exploitation should be clearly vested in the indigenous communities, who should then be paid *not* to harvest the timber unsustainably, both in their own interest and in that of the international community.

The crowding-out argument is valid in the sense that there are many situations in which overuse of market incentives can replace "high-trust" relationships with "low-trust" ones. High-trust relationships (as in the case of voluntary blood donation, for example) are often associated with altruistic behavior, which is morally praiseworthy. They also reduce monitoring costs, which is efficient. But market mechanisms are not the only low-trust social devices. Passing laws and enforcing them with fines or even imprisonment will do at least as much to drive out mutual trust. With MBIs, we pursue society's goals because we are bribed to do so; with CAC, we pursue them because we will be criminalized if we do not. Why should the stick produce more moral behavior than the carrot?

In summary, the use of the indulgences metaphor does nothing to help us decide how best to reduce the abuse of the environment. I suspect it is being brought into play not as an analytical tool but as a rhetorical one: it involves the use (or misuse) of emotive language to persuade us to abandon market mechanisms because the user has an aversion to the market, or perhaps to the very idea of having to make trade-offs between environmental and other goods. But the term is, in fact, a category error: calling an emission charge an indulgence does not make it an indulgence. Rather, it is a payment of compensation to society for the cost imposed on others (present or future) by the appropriation of a scarce resource. If compensation were not paid, there would indeed be a sin: the sin of theft. If adequate compensation *cannot* be paid, as when the environmental asset is important and genuinely irreplaceable, then legal restrictions or an outright ban are appropriate, and, as we saw earlier in the chapter, there are a number of situations where CAC is the correct policy instrument. But these arise from a case-by-case examination of each situation and not from a blanket ban on MBIs based on the misuse of a theological concept.

Environmental Policies in Practice

In this final section of the chapter, I consider some important environmental issues in light of the general principles laid out earlier. These issues are important enough to involve not just national policy decisions but also, in some cases, international attempts to coordinate policies. We begin, however, with a national (or perhaps regional) success story: the control of sulfur dioxide pollution in the United States. We then turn to international environment policies, not all of which have been so successful.

Control of Sulfur Dioxide Pollution

Acid rain is the term used, somewhat inaccurately, to describe pollution caused by acidic substances (the oxides of nitrogen and sulfur).[20] While in some circumstances this pollutant may indeed fall as rain (in effect, as dilute nitric or sulfuric acid), it can also be deposited as dry particles (nitrates or sulfates). The principal source of acidic deposition in the United States has been sulfur dioxide (SO2) from coal-fired power stations. Acidic deposition degrades the environment in a variety of ways. It poisons lakes and rivers, killing fish and other aquatic life and damaging ecosystems. It is implicated in the death of forests, particularly at high altitudes, both by causing damage to leaves and by replacing soil nutrients with toxins. It destroys building surfaces and automobile paint, and it reduces visibility. Inhalation of acidic particles can cause health problems through effects on lung tissue.

This form of pollution may be carried by the winds hundreds of miles from its original source. In consequence, it crosses state boundaries in the United States and national boundaries in Europe. Although the problem of acid deposition has been more acute in Europe than in the United States, the US Environmental Protection Agency pioneered the creation of SO2 credits as a policy solution. Under the previous CAC system, local authorities were seeking to minimize pollution by requiring the companies responsible to use higher chimney stacks. This reduced pollution falling locally but increased the amount falling in more distant areas.[21] Also, we saw earlier that the CAC system involves a great deal of negotiation between regulators and the companies concerned. In the SO2 case, existing (and often heavily polluting) companies had been able to obtain relatively lenient restrictions while the more severe restrictions were reserved for new companies; this gave incumbents an advantage over newcomers, thus reducing competition while also reducing the incentive for the incumbents to clean up their act.[22]

20. For details, see "Acid Rain," US Environmental Protection Agency, http://www.epa.gov/acidrain/index.html.
21. Tom Tietenberg, *Environmental and Natural Resource Economics*, 6th ed. (Boston: Addison Wesley, 2003), 392–93.

The Acid Rain Program was created under Title IV of the Clean Air Act Amendments of 1990. The program created a cap-and-trade system, with the objective of reducing SO2 emissions to half the 1980 level, in two phases: the first targeted the most pollution-generating units over the period from 1995 to 1999, and the second phase, from 2000 onward, tightened the cap and extended it to all units. Unit owners were given permits or "allowances" to emit SO2, each for one ton, and their distribution was based on historical emissions rates (a process sometimes known as grandfathering). Rather than being auctioned, as economists would generally recommend, the great majority of allowances were given free to ensure the passage of the legislation, though there was a small annual auction of permits withheld from distribution (about 3 percent of the total).

Analysis of the early years of the program by Schmalensee and his colleagues shows that the emissions limits were overachieved during this period.[23] Owners of units, aware that tougher rules would apply in the future, may have been trying to "bank" some of their permits for future use by quickly implementing more efficient production methods, such as introducing "scrubbers" to desulfurize emission exiting the unit and switching to low-sulfur coal. But did the use of tradable permits achieve these reductions at a lower cost than a CAC system would have? The problem, as so often in economics, is that we are trying to compare what actually happened with a counterfactual situation that might have happened had the policy been different. The authors in this case assume that the alternative policy would have required the reduced levels by issuing the same allowances but

---

22. This detail and those that follow are taken mainly from Richard Schmalensee, Paul L. Joskow, A. Denny Ellerman, Juan Pablo Montero, and Elizabeth M. Bailey, "An Interim Evaluation of Sulfur Dioxide Emissions Trading," *Journal of Economic Perspectives* 12, no. 3 (Summer 1998): 53–68; and in the same issue from Robert N. Stavins, "What Can We Learn from the Grand Policy Experiment? Lessons from SO2 Allowances Trading," 69–88.

23. Schmalensee et al., "Interim Evaluation," 56–59.

without allowing the trading of permits; they estimate that actual costs were about one quarter to one third less than would have been the case with the alternative.[24]

The scheme was successful because each unit was continuously monitored to ensure that emissions did not exceed allowances. Although this procedure was not cheap, it did not negate the cost advantages of the permit system. But as Schmalensee and his coauthors note, the task of monitoring and enforcing a tradable emissions scheme poses more problems where such a scheme crosses international boundaries. It is not clear, therefore, that the success of the US scheme for sulfur dioxide emissions would carry over to any global scheme for the control of carbon emissions. In addition, although the scheme did succeed in reducing SO2 emissions in the United States, even larger reductions were achieved in Europe by means of a CAC mechanism. Over the period from 1980 to 2001, US emissions in the electricity supply industry fell by a little less than 40 percent; in the fifteen countries which at that time comprised the EU, the corresponding fall was greater than 70 percent.[25]

The Prisoner's Dilemma in a Global Context

The prisoner's dilemma is present in many areas of environmental degradation that require international cooperation. The atmosphere is an "open access" resource that any country may use as a sink for waste gases, but there is rivalry in consumption; each country's emissions limit the scope for others to use it in this way without adverse global consequences. Fisheries, at least in the oceans outside

24. Ibid., 64.
25. Milten Ltd., the Danish National Research Institute and the Centre for Clean Air Policy, *Assessment of the Effectiveness of European Air Quality and Measures, Case study 1: Comparison of the EU and US Approaches Towards Acidification, Eutrophication and Ground Level Ozone*, 4 October 2004, 9, Table 3.

international boundaries, are open access to the fleets of all nations and vulnerable to overuse. The oceans are also characterized by biodiversity; other such habitats, such as rain forests, are legally the property of the states in whose territory they are located or of those to whom the states license these rights. But while the forests themselves may be technically "excludable" assets, the benefits biodiversity brings are not. First, for many people throughout the world there are existence or option benefits from biodiversity, as defined in chapter 5. Second, the forests are home to many organisms that have proved useful for medical research and may well be home to many more than have yet been discovered; the results of such research, once made public, will again be nonexcludable. If the forests are converted to timber, these opportunities will be lost forever. They are opportunities that may be enjoyed by everyone without rivalry in consumption.

In such international prisoner's dilemma problems, the actors may be nation-states rather than private individuals, but the strategies are much the same, as is the structure of payoffs. In the case of climate stability, the strategies would be "restrict emissions" versus "do not restrict emissions"; for fisheries, "do not overfish" versus "maximize take"; for biodiversity, "protect habitats" versus "do not protect."

We saw earlier that the prisoner's dilemma does not always lead to the worst outcome, especially when games are repeated; there are strategies, notably tit-for-tat, that may build trust over time, with sanctions deployed for those who depart from the collectively optimal strategy. Ostrom's work confirms this, particularly for small communities exploiting natural resources. But will such strategies work for national governments negotiating with each other? If we take international diplomacy as the "metagame" in which sovereign states are engaged, then clearly there are opportunities for trust to develop. This, however, does not always happen. Within a state, there is a fallback position; government can step in and compel socially desirable behavior through regulation or encourage it through taxation or subsidy. But there is no "world state" to do this when individual countries cannot reach a genuinely binding and effective agreement. In the cases that follow, we will see examples of both success and failure in collective action on the environment.

Success with Chlorofluorocarbons

We begin with the success story.[26] In the 1970s, scientists began to realize that the emission of chlorofluorocarbons (CFCs) into the atmosphere was threatening the stratospheric ozone layer. At the time, CFCs were widely used as refrigerants. The ozone layer affords protection from ultraviolet radiation from the sun; in the absence of such protection, skin cancers would inevitably increase. By the mid-1980s, it had become apparent that large "holes" were appearing in the layer above Antarctica.

By that time, a number of countries, including the United States, were already making unilateral attempts to limit the use of CFCs. In 1977, the UN Environment Program had convened an international conference that triggered negotiations leading to the 1985 Vienna Convention for the Protection of the Ozone Layer. The evidence from Antarctica encouraged further international cooperation, in the form of the Montreal Protocol, signed in 1987; this set a 1999 target for reduction of CFC consumption by as much as half the 1986 level in some cases. By 1990, revisions to the protocol had extended the range of gases affected, and the target became a complete ban on

---

26. See Scott Barrett, "Montreal versus Kyoto: International Cooperation and the Global Environment," in *Global Public Goods: International Cooperation in the 21st Century*, ed. Inge Kaul, Isabelle Grunberg, and Marc A. Stern, published for the United Nations Development Programme (Oxford: Oxford University Press, 1999), 192–219.

use. Compensatory payments ("side payments" in the jargon of game theory) were also agreed by the industrial countries to encourage less developed countries to comply with the protocol. By 1998, participation had extended to 165 countries, and there had been further tightening of the procedures for implementation as well as reductions in the time scale initially proposed.[27]

The Montreal Protocol has rightly been regarded as a model of its kind, an unusually impressive example of international cooperation. So how did it overcome the problems of collective action as exemplified by the prisoner's dilemma?

As Barrett notes, CFC substitutes were fairly readily available; the costs of substitution, though not zero, were expected to be (and in fact have been) low in relation to the anticipated benefits.[28] The latter included the avoidance of cancer deaths through the preservation of the ozone layer; these were estimated using the value of statistical lives saved, as described in chapter 5. In the early years, even unilateral action by large industrial countries made sense in cost-benefit terms; however, to avoid the possibility that other countries, as they developed, would increase their production of CFCs, it was desirable to have an international agreement to get them on board.

Besides, the prisoner's dilemma is not the only game in town; some argue that the ozone layer problem is better modeled by a different one, known as the *assurance game*.[29] Here we need to change the structure of the payoffs in the matrix as done in figure 6.1. The accompanying story line is as follows: Our representative country America, like each country playing this game, knows that the best

27. Ibid., 194–96.
28. Ibid., 200–202.
29. See Judith Mehta and Rathin Roy, "The Collective Action Problem," in *Making the International: Economic Interdependence and the Political Order*, ed. Simon Bromley, Maureen Mackintosh, William Brown, and Marc Wuyts (London: Pluto Press in association with the Open University, 2004), 415–54.

result for them would be that everyone, *including themselves*, ban CFCs. This contrasts with the prisoner's dilemma payoff, in which an individual player would receive a still better result if everyone else bore the costs of the ban but that player alone did not. In the assurance game, this outcome is given only as second best. Third best for America is if nobody bans CFCs, and worst is if America alone bans CFCs. So what, in practice, will happen? In the assurance game, the final result is not as obvious as in the prisoner's dilemma because there is no single dominant strategy. It will be better for the American government to institute a ban if other countries also introduce a ban; however, if others do not ban CFCs, America will be better off not to ban them either. Every country faces exactly the same dilemma. The two outcomes just specified are given in bold. They are in each case the best any individual country can do, given the strategies pursued by every other country; in the language of game theory, such outcomes are known as *Nash equilibriums*.

		Other countries' strategies	
		Ban CFCs	Don't ban CFCs
America's strategies	Ban CFCs	**Best**	Worst
	Don't ban CFCs	Second best	**Third best**

Figure 6.1 Assurance Game

How might we justify the structure of this matrix? In a case in which the bulk of CFCs was being produced by a relatively few industrialized countries, as was indeed the situation in the early days of international negotiations on CFCs, each country could expect that its own adherence would make some worthwhile, rather than negligible, difference to the outcome (such a negligible outcome was the case with our "clean air" example in chapter 3). Making a crucial difference would benefit the country itself as well as others, especially if the cost of participation were relatively small. As we saw, replacing CFCs was a relatively low-cost adjustment in relation to the benefits from repairing the ozone layer. However, each country might feel that if it were the only one to contribute, the impact on the ozone layer might not reach the necessary threshold to remove the cancer threat, in which case there would be no benefit to justify the cost.

This might explain how the payoffs came to be as shown in the matrix. But there are two equilibriums here, at "best" and "third best." How do we get to the optimum outcome rather than being stuck with the inferior one? The clue is in the name: assurance. Hesitant players must be given some grounds for confidence that if they take action, others will as well. This may require some players to start taking action before formal agreement has been achieved; as we have seen, in the ozone layer case this did happen, as the United States and some others were reducing CFCs from the mid-1970s onward. The offer of side payments can further help to cement a cooperative outcome. The payments obviously change the payoffs from cooperation in a positive way for those receiving them, but they also provide assurance that other countries are committed to the common goal.

Climate Change Policy: Not a Success Story

By contrast with the case of the ozone layer, international attempts to deal with the problem of climate change have been much less successful. Initially, they began in a similar way: governments became concerned at the evidence produced by scientists and signed an agreement promising to do something about the problem. In this case, the initial deal was the UN Framework Convention on Climate Change, signed at the UN Conference on Environment and Development, popularly known as the Earth Summit, held in Rio de Janeiro in 1992. The first signatory was President George H. W. Bush, and soon afterward, following Senate approval, the United States became the first industrial country to ratify the convention.[30] Developed economies, but not the less developed ones, agreed to reduce greenhouse gas emissions to 1990 levels by 2000. However, it became increasingly clear that the industrial countries would not succeed in keeping to the agreement. Following further reports by the Intergovernmental Panel on Climate Change (see chapter 4), it was decided that the restrictions had to be tightened, and a new conference was arranged for the Japanese city of Kyoto in 1997.

At Kyoto, the developing countries continued to refuse to cut their emissions on the grounds that most of the greenhouse gases in the atmosphere had been put there by the developed countries. The developed countries, however, did agree to reduce emissions to 6 to 8 percent below 1990 levels, by 2012 at the latest. This time, however, the United States did not ratify the treaty; it was clear to successive administrations, Democratic and Republican, that in the absence of a comprehensive agreement including large and rapidly industrializing economies such as China, the Senate would have voted it down. The fear was that the additional costs required to switch from carbon-based energy to other forms would penalize US industry, already suffering from severe competition from the emerging nations, particularly China.[31]

Barrett has pointed out that an important difference between the problem of climate change and that of the ozone layer is the relation

---

30. For background, see Daniel Yergin, *The Quest: Energy, Security and the Remaking of the Modern World* (London: Allen Lane, 2011), 453–70.

31. Ibid., 487.

of costs to benefits.[32] The cut in CFCs could be achieved at low cost and yielded large benefits. By contrast, the costs of switching away from fossil fuels to untried renewable energy sources were expected to be large. There was also debate about the benefits of a switch, which of course depend on the *damage function* that relates environmental harm to the rise in temperature; as we saw in chapter 4, estimates of the magnitude and timing of the harm effects are uncertain. At the time of the Kyoto negotiations, there had been a series of economic studies of the possible benefits from abatement. At one extreme, studies by William Nordhaus suggested that the benefits would likely be small; at the other, a study by William Cline estimated they would be much larger.[33] As Barrett notes, different assumptions about the rate of discount to be used in the present value calculations are a major reason for the difference between the two results. In Cline's case, the rate of discount was 2 percent, whereas Nordhaus used 4 to 5 percent. You will recall from chapter 5 that the rate of discount is of great importance when costs arise in the near future and benefits arise in the distant future.[34]

Whereas the Montreal negotiations could be modeled as an assurance game, the prisoner's dilemma seems more appropriate for Kyoto. Indeed, from the point of view of the United States, the sucker's payoff was virtually guaranteed by the provision allowing China and other large and rapidly industrializing countries to "cheat" without any sanctions.

---

32. Barrett, "Montreal versus Kyoto," 202–6.
33. William D. Nordhaus, "To Slow or Not to Slow: The Economics of the Greenhouse Effect," *Economic Journal* 101 (1991): 920–37; and Nordhaus, *Managing the Global Commons* (Cambridge, MA: MIT Press, 1994). William R. Cline, *The Economics of Global Warming* (Washington, DC: Institute for International Economics, 1992).
34. More recent studies, alas, have done little to reduce the range of estimates. Stephen Smith, *Environmental Economics: A Very Short Introduction* (Oxford: Oxford University Press, 2011), 109, notes that recent estimates of the social cost of carbon range between $30 per metric ton (Nordhaus, again) to $312 per metric ton (Stern). These differences reflect differences in both discount rates and the treatment of uncertainty.

Why, then, did the European Union accept the Kyoto agreement despite its obvious flaws? Daniel Yergin suggests that the task of cutting emissions below the 1990 levels was actually much easier for the European countries than for the United States.[35] The reunification of Germany, for example, meant that some very dirty coal-fired power plants in East Germany, which had pushed up European emissions before 1990, were now being phased out anyway. In Britain, coal-fired power stations were in the process of being replaced by North Sea natural gas. Green parties also hold more influence in many parts of Europe, where proportional representation is common, than in the United States; in Germany, for example, they were partners with the Social Democrats in a red-green national coalition government at the time of the Kyoto negotiations.

By 2008, China had become the largest single source of carbon dioxide emissions, with 23 percent of the global total; the United States had 19 percent and the EU 13 percent.[36] Despite a lack of support from other parts of the world, the EU continued to pursue the Kyoto target. The onset of the recession following the financial crisis that year made this easier by reducing energy demand. However, the Fukushima nuclear disaster in Japan in 2011 was a setback. In response to this, the German government, which had decided to extend the life of its nuclear plants, reversed this decision and closed the eight oldest ones immediately; the remainder are to be phased out by 2022. Since the preferred option of renewable energy will take time to put in place, it has been more difficult for Germany to fulfill its energy needs without importation (perhaps from France's energy industry, which itself relies heavily on nuclear power). There are no doubt lessons to be learned from the Fukushima experience,

---

35. Yergin, *Quest*, 483.
36. "Global Greenhouse Gas Emissions Data," US Environmental Protection Agency, last updated September 9, 2013, http://www.epa.gov/climatechange/ghgemissions/global.html. The EU figure excludes Latvia, Lithuania, and Estonia.

in particular not to build a nuclear power station in an earthquake zone and especially not to build one on the coastline of the country that invented the word *tsunami*. Neither of these lessons applies to Germany, and the government's reaction seems lacking in economic rationality.

Dieter Helm, a UK energy economist, has argued persuasively that the same criticism could be generalized to European policy toward greenhouse gases.[37] Despite the clear indications that the kind of agreement that worked well in Montreal failed in Kyoto, the EU has sought to replicate the strategy of obtaining international agreement on mandatory quantitative cuts in emissions. As a consequence, the original failure has been repeated at conferences in Copenhagen in 2009 and Durban in 2011.

Helm's criticisms of the Kyoto approach echo those of some commentators in the "skeptical" camp, such as the Danish environmentalist Bjorn Lomborg and Nigel Lawson, who served as Britain's chancellor of the exchequer and earlier as secretary of state for energy.[38] Helm also dismisses some of the more extreme statements from environmentalists that have not been well supported by scientific evidence.[39] Yet it is quite clear that he is seriously concerned about global warming. While suggesting that average surface temperature increases limited to around 1 degree Celsius would not be too worrying (and possibly would be beneficial in some regions), he accepts that increases of 3 degrees or more are likely and

37. Helm, *Carbon Crunch*.
38. Bjorn Lomborg, *Cool It: The Skeptical Environmentalist's Guide to Global Warming*, 2nd ed. (New York: Vintage, 2010), 21–23. Nigel Lawson, *An Appeal to Reason: A Cool Look at Global Warming*, 2nd ed. (London: Duckworth Overlook, 2009), 54–64. Both Lomborg and (perhaps to a lesser extent) Lawson do accept that global warming is taking place and that it is probably caused by human agency, though they are critical of what they consider to be overconfident predictions and alarmist responses. See Lomborg, *Cool It*, 21–23; Lawson, *Appeal to Reason*, 22.
39. See Helm, *Carbon Crunch*, 17–20.

would be "bad enough to merit action," but not the sort of action that has dominated policy so far.[40]

Toward a Better Strategy

What is needed, according to Helm, is a strategy that tackles growing sources of emissions in the newly industrializing countries, such as China and India, where energy is heavily based on coal, the dirtiest fuel of all in terms of both greenhouse gases and, as we saw earlier, sulfur dioxide. Such a strategy needs to focus not on production but on consumption of carbon—more precisely, on its embodiment in the goods we consume. Further, the strategy should make use of the most effective policy instruments.

Seen in this light, current policies can be criticized on several grounds. First, they tend to focus on energy production. This allows both Europeans and Americans to congratulate themselves on having cut emissions by switching from coal-based sources to gas-based energy sources (which are less carbon intensive) or even to renewables like wind and solar power. In the United States, for example, the Yale Climate Media Forum notes that carbon dioxide emissions have been falling from 2008 to 2013; further, this decline is not only due to the recession during the earlier part of that period but also reflects the switch to natural gas, greater fuel and energy efficiency, less carbon-intensive transportation, and increased use of wind power.[41] But in the meantime, both Europe and the United States continue to import ever-increasing quantities of goods from China, which makes heavy use of coal-fired power stations. In 2010,

40. Ibid., 24.
41. Zeke Hausfather, "What's Behind the 'Good News' Declines in U.S. CO2 Emissions?" *Yale Climate Connections*, May 29, 2013, http://www.yaleclimatemediaforum.org/2013/05/whats-behind-the-good-news-declines-in-u-s-co2-emissions/.

China's share of electricity produced from "coal and peat" was about 38 percent of the total world production of electricity from this source; the corresponding figure from the United States was 23 percent.[42] In 2013, China was building coal-fired power plants at a rate equivalent to one per week.[43]

Recent studies have sought to determine the amount of emissions created by consumption in particular regions and countries. This is not as easy as for production, but it is possible to make such estimates using the technique of multiregional input–output analysis. One such study, by Steven Davis and Ken Caldeira of the Carnegie Institution of Washington, uses data on carbon dioxide emissions from 2004 (the most recent available for the study). At that time, about one fifth of the emissions produced in China (22.5 percent) were created as a consequence of the energy requirements for the production of exports from Chinese industries, principally to the developed nations. In some large European economies, including France and the United Kingdom, over 30 percent of total emissions from consumption were "imported," in the sense that they had been released not in these countries themselves, but in the process of making the consumption goods in the countries of export; the corresponding figure in the United States, which has a proportionally smaller trading sector, was 10.8 percent.[44] These are net figures, after allowing for emissions from production of goods exported by the western countries concerned.

Clearly, if we are seeking to identify who is ultimately responsible for increasing emissions from China, we have to take account of

42. International Energy Agency, *Key World Energy Statistics* (Paris: OECD/IEA, 2012), 25.
43. "The Challenge," China/US Energy Efficiency Alliance, http://chinauseealliance.org/background/the-challenge.
44. Steven J. Davis and Ken Caldeira, "Consumption-Based Accounting of CO2 Emissions," *Proceedings of the National Academy of Sciences of the United States of America* 107, no. 12 (March 8, 2010), doi:10.1073/pnas.09069174107, http://www.ncbi.nlm.nih.gov/pmc/articles/PMC2851800/.

the demand for Chinese goods by more developed countries; the same goes for emissions produced in the other emergent economies. Helm's solution to the problem is based on market incentives rather than on reviving the failed attempts to impose quantity ceilings. He suggests the imposition of a carbon tax on all production and also on imports.[45] Because the tax will hit imports from countries such as China and India, which still rely heavily on coal, it will provide these countries with a strong incentive to switch to alternative, low-carbon technologies if they wish to continue exporting to the US and European markets.

A further major advantage of the proposed carbon tax is that it would be more suited than current policies to cope with ongoing uncertainty about the speed and extent of global warming and the costs it will impose. These uncertainties cast serious doubt on the sort of systems-wide cost-benefit approaches that are used in the Stern report. They also call into question the rush by some governments to embrace particular technological fixes. At least in Europe, governments have been lobbied to support certain renewable technologies, such as wind power, by means of subsidies. There are two criticisms of this type of approach. The first is that subsidies for energy use pay people to consume more energy, and fewer nonenergy goods, than they would otherwise.[46] A carbon tax, by contrast, would deter unnecessary energy consumption by seeking to align prices with the true social costs of consuming energy. The second criticism arises from the economics of politics, which will be discussed more generally in chapter 7. The lobbying process does not necessarily (or indeed usually) lead to the most economically rational outcomes; by responding to pressure groups, the government can

45. Helm, *Carbon Crunch*, 175–94.
46. Jamie Whyte, *Quack Policy: Abusing Science in the Cause of Paternalism* (London: Institute of Economic Affairs, 2013), 69.

support technologies that are not the most effective. In the United Kingdom, for example, there has been a long history of governments, at great expense, backing "winners" that turned out to be losers. Helm sees the rush to provide government support for solar panels in northern European climates as a costly way of failing to solve the emissions problem; indeed, he is generally quite critical of the policy emphasis given to current renewables, including wind power and biomass.[47]

By contrast, a carbon tax will take a hands-off approach. It will encourage innovation to reduce the carbon intensity of productive processes, but it does not require civil servants to make decisions about which technologies are most likely to pay off; this can be left to competition in the marketplace among entrepreneurs, each of whom has a strong interest in getting the answer right. Even though we do not know exactly what the carbon price should be, the very fact that the tax has been imposed will create desirable incentives.[48] Helm anticipates that it will encourage existing moves away from coal as an energy source and toward gas, which as we saw in chapter 4 is a cleaner fuel with significantly lower greenhouse gas emissions. We also saw that unconventional methods, such as the production of shale gases by fracking, create their own environmental threats, and these will have to be subject to control through whichever mechanisms (CAC or MBI) prove most effective in particular cases. Moreover, the shift toward gas can only be a transitional policy because it will still add to the stock of greenhouses gases in the atmosphere, though at a slower rate. To ensure that we do not become locked into a gas technology, the carbon price will have to increase, which over time

---

47. Ibid., 75–99. See also chapter 4 above.
48. Based on a review of studies of the effects of climate change, Richard Tol suggested in 2009 that a carbon tax rate of between $25 and $50 per metric ton might be appropriate. See Richard S. J. Tol, "The Economic Effects of Climate Change," *Journal of Economic Perspectives* 23, no. 2 (Spring 2009): 46.

will encourage further innovation in renewables, developing more efficient ones than at present.

Conclusion

This chapter has been concerned with the best ways to resolve the collective action problems fundamental to the explanation of environmental damage. Perhaps the most useful general principle to emerge is Eleanor Ostrom's comment that in seeking to resolve collective action problems, no single approach will deliver the goods in all situations.

Some theologians, as we have seen, are instinctively more attracted to particular types of solution than to others. To the more radical "plague on both your houses" commentators, hostile to both the market and the state as mechanisms for resource allocation, decentralizing environmental decision making to local communities may seem the most attractive option. Ostrom's own work shows that sometimes indeed it is, but there are also situations in which it is not. The more conservative will prefer solutions that involve free trade in well-defined environmental property rights; again, this will sometimes work well, but transaction costs often rule such solutions out. Those who attack the commodification of the environment are, it seems to me, no less guilty than their free market opponents of allowing the demands of ideological purity to override the imperative to find workable and effective solutions to serious problems. This task may be difficult, but it is not insuperable as long as we are prepared to be ruthless in choosing the most appropriate tools for each task, whether they come from the toolbox compartment labeled "market," "state" or "community."

7

Christian Environmental Activism

Opportunities and Dangers

We have seen that there are urgent, serious, and worsening problems that have arisen from human interaction with the environment. There are also ways of dealing with these problems, but these solutions are not yet being adopted on a sufficient scale.

What, then, are the implications of all this for Christians who have a concern for the environment? For some, the implications will be confined to personal behavior, and many books advise us about how to measure our environmental footprints or how to reduce them.[1] While such books have their value, this book is not one of them, for reasons explained below. Rather, I am concerned with the role of Christians as political activists in a democratic society. Therefore, we will look at some economists' theories about how such societies respond to pressure groups. Encouragingly, as we will see, these

---

1. See, for example, Charlotte Sleigh and Bryony Webb, *God's Green Book: Seven Bible Studies about the Environment* (London: SPCK, 2010).

theories suggest there is much scope for pressure group action, and Christians may be well placed to take advantage of this if they can overcome their striking tendency to disagree among themselves.

The Personal and the Political

Anyone who takes part in political action to impose better standards of behavior on society, which is of course what we are considering here in the environmental context, immediately becomes vulnerable to accusations of hypocrisy. It is reasonable, therefore, to expect that Christians who take a strong position on the environment act consistently with their stated beliefs. This may lead us to cut back on our own carbon footprint through avoiding extravagant consumption, wasteful use of energy, or unnecessary private car use where public transport is available. Should we refrain from all air travel, given its high level of carbon emissions? If you accept the logic of my rejection of the "indulgences" criticism in chapter 6, you may feel able to continue to travel by air, using one of the schemes that offset the carbon used up in this (or indeed any other) activity.

But the thrust of the argument in this book is that such acts of personal restraint will not really achieve the kind of reductions in ecological damage needed if the planet is to remain an attractive and hospitable environment for both humans and other species. The force of the prisoner's dilemma will simply be too strong for voluntary action to make enough difference, and in any case there are likely to be too few people for whom environmental problems are a sufficiently high priority. We need structural solutions: solutions that involve social arrangements to constrain individual agency so as to protect the environment.

Beware the Punctimonious Tendency

Dost thou think, because thou art virtuous, there shall be no more cakes and ale?

–William Shakespeare, Twelfth-Night, act II, scene 3

Other considerations suggest that the political approach to environmental restraint may actually be ethically preferable to the personal one. Many years ago I recall hearing a preacher, carried away in a flight of eloquence, criticizing the attitudes of the "punctimonious Pharisees." The adjective struck me at the time as a useful portmanteau coinage, combining the emphasis on scoring points over trivialities of the punctilious with the holier-than-thou piety of the sanctimonious. Unfortunately, it is a characteristic by no means confined to first-century Pharisees. Books that produce lists of acceptable and unacceptable actions in an attempt to make people feel guilty about the environment are, in effect, opening a whole new field of operations for modern members of the Punctimonious Tendency. They can create a sense of smugness among those who succeed in ticking off the points on the list, thus substituting the sin of pride for the sin of wastefulness.

An analogy may be helpful here. Acts of personal charity by the rich are certainly a moral requirement, and such actions may ease their consciences and make them feel good about themselves, but they are no substitute for the creation of a proper social security system, accessible to the needy as a matter of *right* rather than charitable whim and financed by compulsory taxation of the better off. Similarly, being made to pay to replace environmental resources we have consumed should not confer a sense of virtue on us any more than paying for a meal in a restaurant would. Replacing exhortations to individual restraint by a proper pricing system for scarce environmental resources will remove the need for the exhortations and the sense of moral superiority from responding to them. This will be a spiritually desirable outcome. But how are we to achieve it?

Economic Theories of Political Behavior

In 1767, Sir James Steuart stated the political economist's dilemma as follows: "In my enquiries, I have constantly in my eye, how man *may* be governed, and never how he *is* governed. How a righteous and intelligent statesman may restrain the liberty of individuals, in order to promote the common good; never how an ignorant and unrighteous statesman may destroy public liberty, for the sake of individuals."[2] Given the widespread corruption that characterized public life in Britain and elsewhere in the eighteenth century, this may suggest that Sir James was wasting his efforts. His approach, in fact, belongs to what is now known as the *mercantilist* school of economics, which envisaged a strong role for the state in economic affairs, despite its acknowledged flaws. Steuart's views were very soon overshadowed by the classical liberalism of Adam Smith and his followers; part of the force of Smith's arguments was that liberalism did not require the leopard to change his spots, or the "ignorant and unrighteous" statesman to become "righteous and intelligent." Instead, Smith showed how a policy of *laissez faire*—"leave well alone"—could promote a growth in prosperity. But Smith himself acknowledged that there were some benefits that could only be adequately provided by the state, and as already noted we now recognize that many aspects of environmental protection fall into this category.

So how do we ensure that the state does indeed "promote the common good" rather than merely serve as the instrument of

2. Sir James Steuart, *An Inquiry into the Principles of Political Oeconomy*, vol. 2 (Dublin: Printed for James William in Skinner Row, and Richard Moncreiff, in Caple Street, 1767), 523.

sectional interests? First, we need a theory of how governments actually function in liberal capitalist democracies in the twenty-first century. Actually, there is a huge literature on such matters, which tends to be drawn from both the left and the right of the political spectrum. Marxist writers are skeptical of the suggestion that the capitalist state can undertake the radical transformation required to deal with the failures of the market; ultimately, they believe, the purpose of the state is to preserve the system rather than to replace it with a better one. Liberal economists, for their part, believe that state intervention will often substitute political failure for market failure and may very well make matters worse. Both sides believe that powerful economic interest groups tend to dominate political decisions in what is supposedly a representative democracy.

Representative versus Direct Democracy

For the great majority of collective decisions in industrial societies, citizens do not get to decide policy by casting their own votes on each issue. Such a system of "direct" democracy is used occasionally, where referenda are held to allow individual voters to approve or reject clearly defined proposals. Much more often, voters elect representatives to make decisions on their behalf. If over time they do not like the way the representatives act, they may vote them out of office, but between elections the representatives have substantial discretion to interpret their mandate.

Some environmentalists dislike the gap this system creates between those who make policy and those in whose interests policy is supposedly being made. But it is difficult to see how a complex modern society could be run without some delegation of authority to representatives. Political issues often concern a vast range of highly complex and technical matters and unavoidably require a wholehearted commitment by those who have to make the decisions; it makes sense for the rest of us to choose representative bodies to specialize in these issues or at least to oversee the experts who understand particular aspects of them.

The enthusiasm of some in the green movement for decentralization and for small-scale, local decision making might appear to shift decisions, or their oversight, into the hands of those most immediately affected by policy. This is hard to fault, as long as the local decisions do not themselves have significant "external" implications for the wider community. Sometimes, for example, localism may degenerate into "NIMBYism"—not in my back yard. This can block developments in the national or even global interest. Such developments are not necessarily proposals by the usual suspects to set up oil wells, fracking sites, or nuclear installations. Nowadays, they often include projects to establish renewable technologies such as wind or solar power, which reduce reliance on carbon or nuclear energy but with some adverse impact on the local scenery or ecosystems.

The Economics of Democracy

So how, then, do representative democracies function? The groundbreaking work on the economic theory of democracy was undertaken in the 1950s by Antony Downs.[3] Downs believed that the assumptions of rational and self-interested behavior that neoclassical economic theory applied to the study of households and firms should also be applied to the behavior of participants in the political process. His seminal work on this topic still offers many intriguing if controversial insights, and it has encouraged the development of an

3. Antony Downs, *An Economic Theory of Democracy* (New York: Harper and Row, 1957).

important branch of applied economics, sometimes known as the "economics of politics" or "public choice theory." Here we can draw on this literature only very selectively to illuminate key areas of environmental policy.

The Role of Pressure Groups

As noted at the start of this chapter, one area of particular interest is the role pressure groups can play in influencing government decisions. The standard theory on this originates with Downs himself. Politicians, he believed, were influenced above all by the *vote motive*, analogous to the profit motive in business. Obviously, politicians cannot ignore votes any more than businesses can ignore profits; even if a politician really wants to make the world a better place, he or she needs the support of voters to provide the power to do so. But assuming rational self-interest, Downs argued that politicians do not, in fact, enter politics for idealistic reasons; it is simply a career choice like any other.

Political parties develop "ideologies" as a means of differentiating what they have to offer from the policies of other parties. Most voters are not very interested in politics. True, they want policies that will suit their own interests, which may well differ from those of other social groups, but as rational agents they are looking for shortcuts to minimize the costs of political involvement. They lack detailed information about many policy issues and about how policies will affect their own interests; however, they do not wish to make the effort to acquire such information. A party's general ideological stance allows the voter to choose the party with the ideology that seems most closely aligned with the voter's own interests without having to become too well informed about all the individual policies that party espouses.

So where do pressure groups come in? Their role is explained by the pervasive ignorance and uncertainty that characterizes social and political affairs. Uncertainty affects governments, who are seeking to develop a set of policies that will please as many voters (especially "floating" voters) as possible, and it also affects voters, as we have just seen, who may not know which policies will most benefit themselves.

Pressure groups find themselves in an intermediary role: on the one hand, they have to engage in consciousness-raising among voters to convince them that their interests are being crucially affected in ways of which they may have been unaware; on the other, they take advantage of the uncertainty of governments and seek to persuade them that the pressure group's preferred policies will be particularly attractive to voters. Such pressure group activity, of course, is costly; it uses up scarce resources of time and effort.

Downs puts forward the very important argument that, in the game of lobbying governments, the cards are stacked in favor of producer interests rather than those of consumers in general.[4] His own arguments are particularly related to such matters as tariff policy, but they certainly apply in an environmental context. Costs of exerting political influence are generally less, and often much less, for producers than for consumers, or more generally for the broad mass of citizens; at the same time, benefits for those who engage in lobbying are individually much greater than for individual citizens.

On the cost side, information is cheap for producers, who obviously have privileged access to knowledge about their own business denied to outsiders. Organizational costs of lobbying are also low. Producers are already members of business associations or trade unions, and while the interests of bosses and workers are often antipathetic, on issues that affect the survival or prosperity of the industry as a whole they may readily sink their differences in a

4. Ibid., 254–59.

common cause. Such associations also have command over substantial financial resources that may be used for lobbying purposes, often quite legally. They can afford to commission research on the effects of policy and to discard results that do not support their case. On the benefits side, the gains to be had from watering down legislation are often considerable; many millions of dollars in profits may be protected, many individual jobs saved.

By contrast, as far as consumers or citizens are concerned, the benefits from a policy may be substantial in the aggregate but will often be widely diffused among the population as a whole; thus, for any individual they may be perceived as quite small. As for the costs, there may be no significant preexisting citizen's organization, analogous to a producers' association or a trade union, with an interest in lobbying. "Citizen" lobbyists typically will have to operate on a shoestring budget compared with the vast resources on which businesses or even unions can draw. And it is likely they will also be at a serious informational disadvantage compared with producer lobbyists.

History abounds with examples of producer lobbies that have fought an effective rearguard action against health and safety or environmental legislation. Such actions do not necessarily prevent change completely because the underlying scientific evidence may eventually become too convincing to be ignored by lawmakers; however, they are likely to slow down political response and dilute the effectiveness of legislation. Perhaps the most famous case is the tobacco lobby's attempts to minimize the loss of profit from scientific findings that tobacco was a source of lung cancer (and a host of other health threats besides), whether through direct or secondary smoking. A 2007 study by the Union of Concerned Scientists drew attention to some strong similarities between the lobbying behavior of the tobacco firms and the activities of ExxonMobil, as the world's largest energy company, in casting doubt on scientific theories of global warming and influencing the US government's policies on this issue.[5]

At this point a brief digression, on an issue of principle, may be in order. We have to be careful here. Even if somebody clearly has a strong financial interest in putting forward an argument, it is not fair to assume that those who support this side must have been paid to do so or that they do not genuinely believe in the case they are making. Social psychologists are familiar with the concept of *cognitive dissonance*, the discomfort we feel when we realize that some of our beliefs are inconsistent with others.[6] For example, we may believe ourselves to be caring and responsible people; we then feel uncomfortable when we hear someone put forward an apparently plausible argument that implies we are actually using far more than our fair share of the world's resources or our lifestyle is damaging the life-support system on which our descendants will have to rely. To reduce our discomfort, we may decide to change our behavior. But there is an alternative: to change our belief in the plausibility of the argument and to seek other points of view that cast doubt on it. This is known as *confirmation bias*, and it may lead us to seek out only the information that supports our preferred belief and to reject any that would challenge it, until eventually we persuade ourselves of the weakness or falsity of the argument that had upset our comfortable assumptions.[7]

5. Union of Concerned Scientists, *Smoke, Mirrors and Hot Air: How ExxonMobil Uses Big Tobacco Tactics to Manufacture Uncertainty on Climate Science* (Cambridge, MA: Union of Concerned Scientists, 2007). See also James J. McCarthy, "Climate Science and Its Distortion and Denial by the Misinformation Industry," in *Creation in Crisis: Christian Perspectives on Sustainability,* ed. Robert S. White (London: SPCK, 2009), 34–52.
6. The theory was first developed in Leon Festinger, *The Theory of Cognitive Dissonance* (Stanford, CA: Stanford University Press, 1957).
7. The concept initially derived from research by Peter Wason. See P.C. Wason,"On the failure to eliminate hypotheses in a conceptual task," *Quarterly Journal of Experimental Psychology*, 12 (1960): 129-140.

Awareness of these regrettable human tendencies should render us suspicious of all arguments that seem designed to make us feel more at ease with ourselves and also of any that come from those with a clear financial stake in the issue. But there is another complication: a personal or corporate interest in criticizing an environmentalist claim does not demonstrate the falsity of the criticism. We are still left with the obligation to test all arguments for logical coherence and empirical consistency; as a useful discipline to counter our prejudices, whichever side they may favor, we ought actively to seek out evidence that casts doubt on our most cherished beliefs. Confirmation bias, after all, may also affect those who have committed themselves emotionally to a strong environmentalist position.

Returning to the main thread of the argument, we have so far been considering the role of three important groups—politicians, voters, and lobbyists—in policy making. The interactions of these groups, in a world of uncertainty, may distort policy away from the "optimal," at least from the point of view of economic analysis. But for policies to be implemented effectively, a fourth group may also be important. This group consists of *bureaucrats*: the government functionaries who carry out the instructions of politicians. How are they motivated, and what sort of distortions may result from their activities?

Bureaucrats and Budgets

William Niskanen's *Bureaucracy and Representative Government* is a major founding work in the economic theory of bureaucracy.[8] Niskanen took issue with earlier theories of bureaucracy, such as Max Weber's view that bureaucrats were motivated by the goal of rationally and efficiently carrying out the commands of those set in

8. W. A. Niskanen, *Bureaucracy and Representative Government* (Chicago: Aldine Atherton, 1971).

authority over them.[9] He argued instead that bureaucrats had their own motivations and some discretion in pursuing them. These might include income, power, reputation, or even on-the-job leisure. But Niskanen argued that, at the higher echelons at least, a good single proxy for bureaucratic goals would be the size of the budget available to the department they controlled. The manager of a larger budget would probably get higher pay, more prestige, and more power than the manager of a smaller one. Indeed, even an "altruistic" bureaucrat would be likely to seek a higher budgetary allocation. Altruists will want to believe their activities are in the public interest. The award of a bigger budget is a way of confirming this, as it was in the parable of the talents (Matt. 25:21): in effect, it may be considered as the recognition of a "good and faithful servant."

As we saw in the context of Downs's theory, uncertainty is an important determinant of the behavior of politicians and pressure groups; it is also important for bureaucrats. Politicians have less information about the true costs of implementing a desired policy than those charged with administering it; in negotiating budgets, they are therefore vulnerable to manipulation by those on whose advice they have to rely. Their position is somewhat analogous to that of the purchaser of a technologically sophisticated product in the marketplace who is worried about being deceived into paying too much by the supplier. In business, there are often alternative suppliers competing for customers, which helps to keep costs down; in public administration, by contrast, the department is often in a monopolistic position with more power to set the "price" for providing the set of policies requested by the politician. This *informational asymmetry* is an important source of the bureaucrat's power.

---

9. Max Weber, *Economy and Society*, 2 vols., ed. G. Roth and C. Wittich (Berkeley: University of California Press, 1978). This work was originally published posthumously in Germany in 1922.

As is true of Downs's work, Niskanen's theory has stimulated much interesting and sometimes controversial research into the way governments function in practice and how this might differ from the "optimal" behavior of government as assumed in neoclassical welfare theory. For our purposes, it is perhaps sufficient to note that these theories apply as much to agencies charged with implementing environmental policies as to any other branch of government. If they are valid, they suggest we be wary of "empire building" tendencies on the part of such agencies—a claim, indeed, often made by those who criticize demands for a more active government role in controlling pollution. As noted earlier, it would be unwise simply to dismiss such criticism, however much we may suspect the motives of those who make it.

The Theory of Regulatory Capture

Informational asymmetry, as we have just seen, helps explain the discretion afforded to bureaucrats in pursuing their own goals rather than those imposed on them by their supposed "masters," the elected politicians. But where regulatory agencies are concerned, as often happens in the context of environmental policy, there may well be other examples of asymmetrical information.

You may recall that this issue arose when we were looking at the transactions costs of command and control systems in chapter 5. We saw that, in practice, the regulatory body often has to negotiate with those whom it regulates when seeking to implement controls; this is inevitable, as the companies being regulated know much more about the relevant industrial processes than outsiders would. But this obviously makes the regulator vulnerable to being fed misinformation by the company concerned. Regulators who take too tough a line with companies in an attempt to overcome this problem may become mired in costly appeal proceedings against their decisions.

An obvious answer is for the agency to hire those with expertise in the industrial processes—to bribe the poacher to become a gamekeeper instead, so to speak. But this may cut two ways: companies may also hire former regulators to strengthen their own side in the negotiations. And the companies generally have deeper pockets than the agencies. This can give rise to an even more insidious phenomenon. Administrators may take employment with regulatory agencies as a form of personal career development, hoping to leave the agency in due course to join one of the companies. This may make them less willing while still at the agency to take a firm line with their potential future employers.

The neutralization of a regulatory process is known as *regulatory capture*, a concept developed by George Stigler, a Chicago economist and winner of the Nobel Prize for Economics.[10] The practice goes back to the nineteenth century, if not before. An oft-quoted example comes from the history of the first federal regulatory agency to be established in the United States, the Interstate Commerce Commission (ICC), which was set up to regulate rail freight rates. In 1893, Richard Olney, a lawyer who had worked for the railroads, was appointed by President Cleveland as the fortieth US attorney general. He was asked by a former employer whether he could do anything to get rid of the ICC. Olney's reply very clearly states the principle of regulatory capture: "The Commission . . . is, or can be made, of great use to the railroads. It satisfies the popular clamor for a government supervision of the railroads, at the same time that that supervision is almost entirely nominal. Further, the older such a commission gets to be, the more inclined it will be to take the business and railroad view

---

10. George Stigler, "The Theory of Economic Regulation," *Bell Journal of Economics and Management Science*, 2, no. 1 (Spring 1971): 3–21.

of things. . . . The part of wisdom is not to destroy the Commission, but to utilize it."[11]

The ICC has gone, but the phenomenon of regulatory capture has continued into the present century. We have been considering it as a limitation of bureaucratic oversight, but sometimes the politicians themselves have been accused of complicity in the emasculatory process, reflecting the power of business pressure groups. The 2009 article by Thomas Frank in the *Wall Street Journal* that quotes Olney's reply also lists a series of agencies, including the Environmental Protection Agency, that had effectively suffered this fate and points the finger of blame at the administration of George W. Bush. Similar claims have also been made by the Union of Concerned Scientists; in 2004 this group prepared a dossier in which they criticized the administration for, inter alia, seeking to alter the wording of an EPA report on global warming to introduce greater doubt concerning the human role in this process, suppressing a report on mercury poisoning, and interfering with the process of appointing experts to scientific agencies so as to privilege political or business acceptability over scientific expertise.[12] The administration's Office for Science and Technology, however, denied these claims.[13]

Limitations of the Public Choice Approach

While the theories we have been considering yield interesting hypotheses, like any other theoretical approach they have their limitations. Their application of the assumption of rational and self-

11. Quoted in Thomas Frank, "Obama and 'Regulatory Capture,'" *Wall Street Journal*, June 24, 2009, http://online.wsj.com/article/SB124580461065744913.html.

12. Union of Concerned Scientists, *Scientific Integrity in Policymaking: The Bush Administration's Misuse of Science* (Cambridge, MA: Union of Concerned Scientists, 2004).

13. Kirsten Philipkoski, "Scientists: Bush Distorts Science," *Wired Insider*, February 18, 2004, http://www.wired.com/medtech/health/news/2004/02/62339.

interested motivation to agents in the political sphere is a source of both strength and weakness: of strength because it is clear that such agents often do appear to act in this way, and of weakness because they sometimes do not. As an example of the latter, consider the most basic act in democratic politics: voting itself. In an even moderately sized electorate, the likelihood that any one person's vote will make a difference to the outcome of an election is vanishingly small. At the same time, there are costs in time and convenience associated with going to the polling station to cast one's ballot. Thus, on any rational cost-benefit calculation, the expected value of the act of voting must be negative. Yet millions of people whom the theory assumes to be rational and self-interested will vote. Indeed, in some countries new to democracy, people will queue for hours in the hot sun to get into the polling stations; in others, which are still struggling to achieve democracy, they will do so in spite of violence and intimidation. These aspects of behavior are difficult to accommodate within the theory.[14]

Some ecological economists have argued, in effect, that the theory is mistaken in its assumption that people are motivated to act as citizens in the political forum on the basis of the same axioms they employ when acting as consumers in the marketplace.[15] There is evidence from experimental economics that behavior is context dependent: as members of a social group, we take a more collective view of responsibility, transcending our own interests.[16] A middle-of-the-road position might be that people are prepared to make some sacrifices for others. In particular, they will be more willing to do

14. The act of voting can very easily be modeled as a prisoner's dilemma matrix: see John Struthers and Alistair Young, "Economics of Voting: Theories and Evidence," *Journal of Economic Studies* 16, no. 5 (1989): 1–42.
15. John Gowdy and Jon D. Erickson, "The Approach of Ecological Economics," *Cambridge Journal of Economics* 29, no. 2 (2005): 207–22.
16. Ibid., 214.

so if they feel that others in the same position as themselves are making such sacrifices too. To ensure this, they will sometimes vote for compulsory taxation or restrictive legislation to be imposed for some social goal. But they will resist being pushed too far in this direction.

Christians and Political Power

So what should we conclude about a possible role for Christian activists? In this final section of the book, I will first explain why I think, in light of pressure group theory, that church members may potentially be well placed to exert an influence on policy beyond their numbers. But this assumes that they are all pulling in the same direction; so far, they have not always been doing so, and differences of opinion likely will continue. Nonetheless, there may be some principles for action about which an effective coalition could be formed, and I will try, albeit tentatively, to list the main ones.

Churches and Pressure Groups

Political pressure by Christians of various denominations is a phenomenon of long standing. The first successful social movement of modern times, the campaign to abolish slavery, owed much to its evangelical supporters in both the United States and the United Kingdom. It is easy to see why Christians who take their faith seriously might want to influence policy in the direction of a more just society. The theory of pressure groups helps to explain why they might have some hopes of achieving such influence.

Consider again Downs's explanation of the relative power of pressure groups: the benefits of lobbying for the desired policy are substantial in relation to the costs. But how do these categories apply in the context of church-based pressure groups? In Downs's analysis, the benefits for producer groups are seen in terms of income, whether to bosses or workers. For church groups, this is not the goal; supporters of the antislavery movement did not generally stand to gain financially from abolition, and today supporters of movements to save endangered species or to impose a carbon tax will be unlikely to see their incomes rise if they are successful. For Christians, the gain is to be counted in terms of discharging the obligation of discipleship, to work for the good of the kingdom. For some, this can be an even more powerful motivation than income. For many of us, if we are honest, it probably is not, but it may still count for enough to rouse us to action.

What about the cost side? Individuals seeking change in a democracy are powerless unless they can find others to support them. But as church members, Christians already belong to a large preexisting network, committed to some common principles and beliefs about how people should behave toward each other. There are, of course, disagreements between denominations and within them, but there is also much in common that can be used as a basis for action. The existence of this network potentially reduces the costs of organization. Its active members already get together every Sunday (well, most of them, on most Sundays) to reflect on God's will for themselves and for the world; this provides opportunities for consciousness-raising, particularly if the pastor and office bearers are sympathetic to the cause. Even in increasingly "post-Christian" countries in the West, statements on politically controversial topics by prominent church leaders (the pope, the archbishop of Canterbury, or spokespeople for other major denominations) are still widely reported in the media, free of charge.

Problems involving global ecosystems, as we have seen, require a global response. Again, churches have the advantage of ready access to worldwide networks through contacts that date from missionary activity in an earlier era of globalization. Such contacts reduce the costs of information collection regarding the actual effects of environmental degradation by providing relevant feedback from some of the world's poorest and most fragile communities. They also facilitate resource transfers from relatively well-off churches in the West to support sustainable development in such communities. Church organizations with a focus on poverty issues in developing countries, such as Christian Aid in the United Kingdom or the Maryknoll Office for Global Concerns in the United States (to name but two of many), are now giving more and more emphasis to environmental questions as a necessary extension of this mission. While direct action to help local communities is important, the ability to tap into global support networks affords leverage for Christians who wish to bring pressure to bear on environmental policymakers, whether in developed or developing countries. In this context, knowledge of how environmental problems are affecting those most vulnerable gives credibility to the claims made in advocacy work.

Of course, there are numerous other organizations engaged in environmental advocacy without any church connection, such as Greenpeace, Friends of the Earth, and the World Wildlife Fund, to name only a few of the most prominent. This raises an intriguing question: should Christians set up their own environmentalist pressure groups, or should churches simply encourage their members to become involved in those that already exist and support them in that involvement?

There are advantages in both approaches. As we have just seen, for historical reasons the churches have much relevant experience to offer from their contacts with the communities most at risk from environmental pressures. Indeed, in those developing countries with weak or corrupt governments, local churches may be one of the very few organizations capable of mounting a vigorous but peaceful challenge to the depredations of extractive industries, loggers, or plantation owners. They have an important role to play in their own right, and their contacts in the better-off countries have a role in supporting them. On the other hand, green agencies that claim, and indeed wish, no church affiliation will often be doing what Christians consider the Lord's work nevertheless. The important thing is that the work gets done, not that any particular Christian group, or the church in general, should get credit for doing it. There is much to be said for Christians bearing witness to the social implications of the faith by working with non-Christians in a common cause; they might even learn something by doing so. Ultimately, individual church members must decide, in light of their circumstances and competencies, where best to direct their efforts.

There are, of course, pitfalls for Christians who get involved in political pressure groups, and this is true whether they do so as a church group or with a secular agency. Such groups may sometimes be tempted to take the view that the end justifies the means; this is perhaps most likely to arise when interpreting evidence and ensuring it is presented in the most favorable light. True, advocacy organizations are not under oath to tell the truth, the whole truth, and nothing but the truth. But it is not supposed to matter to Christians whether they are under oath or not (Matt. 5:37); the obligation to tell the truth, even when it is unwelcome, is an absolute one. This would be the case whether it was expedient to do so or not. But, in the long run, it will always be expedient. False claims are apt to come back and discredit those who make them; in earlier chapters we saw numerous examples in which carelessness with evidence on the part of environmentalists has had this consequence.

Problems for Christian Environmental Activism

Although membership in the Christian church gives potential organizational advantages to those moved to lobby for socially desirable causes such as environmental care, the recent history of Christian activism is at best a mixed one. The core problems are twofold. First, Christians have approached questions of political involvement from different and sometimes mutually hostile perspectives. Second, as we saw in chapters 1 and 2, the churches do not speak with one voice on the environment. In particular, while "mainstream" churches were inclined to support political action on the environment, attitudes among evangelicals were more mixed.

The first of these issues has been addressed by James Davison Hunter in his comprehensive critique of Christian political activity in the United States, *To Change the World*.[17] Hunter distinguishes three competing paradigms for Christian political engagement: the paradigm of those "defensive against" secularism, who are generally to be found on the Christian right; the paradigm of "relevance to" the secular world adopted by those on the Christian left; and the "purity from" paradigm favored by those whom he terms "neo-Anabaptists." But all, he argues, are flawed. The first two, each seeking to create its own version of a Christian society, fall into the temptation of Constantinianism: the pursuit of political domination to impose what are considered to be Christian values. The third defines itself against the broader society, in which it sees nothing of value; the solution is to retreat from it.[18]

In criticizing all three paradigms, Hunter draws on Nietzsche's concept of ressentiment: the bitter sense of grievance that reflects the belief, whether true or false, one has been deprived of one's

17. James Davison Hunter, *To Change the World: The Irony, Tragedy and Possibility of Christianity in the Late Modern World* (New York: Oxford University Press, 2010).
18. Ibid., 213–19.

entitlements by a hostile other. Each of the groups, Hunter claims, is characterized by just such a motivating belief, and its strength engenders hatred toward opponents and poisons the language of debate, as he easily demonstrates through a host of examples.

The present book is concerned with a more limited range of issues than those that exercise Hunter: not with culture in general but with the possibility of halting or reversing environmental damage. Hunter does not say a great deal about this particular topic, but he does note the growing movement among some evangelicals toward environmental concern.[19]

On this, some interesting work has recently been done by Nicholas Smith of University College, London, and Anthony Leiserowitz of the Yale Project on Climate Change Communication.[20] This research was based on a representative sample of more than two thousand American adults, 27 percent of whom identified themselves as evangelicals. As earlier studies, such as the Pew Center study cited in chapter 1, had shown, fewer evangelicals than nonevangelicals accepted that global warming was happening (61 percent compared with 78 percent), and fewer attributed it to "mostly human activities" (44 percent compared with 64 percent).[21] Yet, as these figures show and as we also saw in chapter 2, a substantial and perhaps growing minority of evangelicals believe that global warming is anthropogenic. Indeed, a high proportion of all evangelicals believe in taking at least some political action. This group must include some who are skeptical of the causes of global warming; for example, 90 percent of all evangelicals think the government should fund

19. Ibid., 139, 317n20.
20. N. Smith and A. Leiserowitz, "American Evangelicals and Global Warming," *Global Environmental Change* 23, no. 5 (2013): 1009–17, http://dx.doi.org/10.1016/j.gloenvcha.2013.04.001.
21. Ibid., table 1. Note that in both groups the proportion who accept the hypothesis that human activity has been causing global warming has increased, as compared with the Pew Center 2008 survey results reported in chapter 1.

renewable energy research, and 80 percent think tax rebates should be given to support energy-efficiency measures.[22] For each of the ten policy measures listed in the questionnaire, however, the proportion of evangelicals who support them is several percentage points less than for nonevangelicals.

Smith and Leiserowitz pay particular attention to the differences their results reveal *within* the evangelical camp. They argue plausibly that the differences among evangelicals over environmental issues have to be explained in terms other than theological ones, since often the theological views are rather similar on all sides of the debate. To explore this, they test a number of models drawn from theories of social behavior. These approaches include "affect theory," which seeks to explain attitudes toward risk in terms of the importance of emotional cues rather than rational calculation; "cultural theory," particularly concerning individualism versus egalitarianism; and "value-belief-norm" theory, which examines whether respondents are particularly motivated by perceived threats to their own welfare, to the welfare of others, or to threats to the biosphere. Within a particular theological orientation, individuals may still differ in their positioning with regard to these various characteristics. This, in turn, may explain their attitudes both to the risk of environmental catastrophe and to the policies that should be adopted in response. The study also measured the possible impact of socioeconomic variables such as ethnicity, gender, income, and political identification, inter alia. The strongest association it found was in terms of value orientation: that is, the higher evangelicals scored on measures of concern over threats to themselves, to other humans, or to the biosphere, the more highly they rated the risks and the

---

22. Ibid., fig. 2. The authors do not comment on why even some of those who do not believe in anthropogenic warming should support such policies; however, we may speculate that these particular measures are perhaps considered worthwhile simply to encourage useful innovations.

more willing they were to support political action. In addition, those evangelicals with a strong individualistic orientation appeared both more skeptical about global warming and less supportive of policy interventions.

Principles for Christian Environmentalists

As is clear, Christians are unlikely to agree to any single political program for environmental protection, and this to some extent must weaken the influence of the churches in bringing pressure to bear on those who hold power. Yet, if we take the mainstream churches together with the substantial minority of evangelicals concerned about "creation care," those who would support such pressure would greatly outnumber those who would oppose it. So for members of this large subgroup of Christians, perhaps it would be possible to establish some principles on which there would be general agreement. These might include the following features.

First, the solution to environmental problems cannot be left to free enterprise; a strong role for government will have to be accepted. This is because of the frequent divergence between private and social costs and benefits and because of the presence of the public goods problem in a number of environmental contexts, as was explained in chapter 3. Also, free enterprise is ill-suited to take account of the interests of future generations, who lack a presence in the marketplace.

Second, although the market cannot be left to itself, Christians should still be prepared to support policies that make use of market forces, where appropriate, rather than rejecting them on principle, as some of the more radical seem inclined to do (see chapters 2 and 6). The particular form of market intervention most likely to be effective is taxation (chapter 6); in the drive to prevent global warming, there is much to be said for introducing a carbon tax without delay, with a clause allowing for escalation as the need arises. It is unfortunate that this policy is also an unpopular one. The study by Smith and Leiserowitz revealed that only about a third of nonevangelicals and less than 30 percent of evangelicals were prepared to accept a modest gasoline tax increase. However, there was somewhat more support for the creation of a carbon market (just above 50 percent for nonevangelicals and just below 50 percent for evangelicals), which if done properly would have a similar effect in increasing the price of carbon.[23]

Third, and following from this, Christians should be pragmatic rather than utopian in their demands. In practical terms, this would likely mean accepting that it will take time to change to a noncarbon economy and that transitional arrangements might include shifting to natural gas (some of it produced by fracking) as a relatively low-carbon replacement for coal-fired power stations over the next two decades or so, as well as keeping nuclear stations operational during this period. When appraising alternative policies, Christian activists should be prepared to accept (but also to scrutinize) the use of cost-benefit analysis, subject to appropriate safeguards protecting the needs of the least well-off and the interests of future generations. They should not reject in principle the attempt to assign shadow prices to environmental assets or to health and safety outcomes, as long as these are considered simply as contributory evidence, not as providing the final word (chapter 5).

There are, of course, situations in which it is essential to take a strong stand against commercialization. "Neighbor care" should imply that the rights of traditional communities be protected, both because they are rights and also because such communities often (though not always) show a clearer understanding of sustainability

23. Ibid.

issues and how to respect them than outside agencies (whether market or state) do, as Ostrom's work has shown (see chapter 6). "Creation care" should imply a concern for biodiversity and the protection of wilderness areas.

Finally, though, does not the suggestion that Christians should involve themselves in the messy and potentially compromising business of pressure groups fall prey to accusations of Constantinianism? After all, the history of the church in politics provides many striking instances of Acton's dictum that "power tends to corrupt." Given our readiness to be corrupted, therefore, it is perhaps fortunate that in a democratic and secular society voters are unlikely to give us power just because we are the church. They may nevertheless, in the long run, respond to the power of arguments that are internally consistent, reflect values our fellow citizens acknowledge in their hearts to transcend sectional interests, and are soundly based on evidence. Such at least is the hope in which this book has been written.

Bibliography

Aldred, John. "Climate Change Uncertainty, Irreversibility and the Precautionary Principle." *Cambridge Journal of Economics* 36, no. 5 (September 2012): 1051–72.

Archer, David. *Global Warming: Understanding the Forecast.* Hoboken, NJ: Wiley, 2012.

Bachofen, Johann Jakob. *Das Mutterrecht.* Stuttgart: Verlag von Krais & Hoffman, 1861.

Barrett, Scott. "Montreal versus Kyoto: International Cooperation and the Global Environment." In *Global Public Goods: International Cooperation in the 21st Century*, edited by Inge Kaul, Isabelle Grunberg, and Marc A. Stern, published for the United Nations Development Programme. Oxford: Oxford University Press, 1999.

Bate, Roger. *Saving Our Streams.* London: Institute of Economic Affairs, 2001.

Bauckham, Richard. *Bible and Ecology: Rediscovering the Community of Creation.* London: Darton, Longman and Todd, 2010.

———. "Stewardship and Relationship." In Berry, *Care of Creation*, 99–106.

Bennett, H. S. *Life on the English Manor.* Cambridge: Cambridge University Press, 1937.

Bentham, Jeremy. *The Works of Jeremy Bentham, published under the superintendence of his executor, John Bowring.* Edinburgh: William Tate, 1843.

Berry, R. J., ed. *The Care of Creation: Focusing Concern and Action.* Downers Grove, IL: Inter-Varsity Press, 2000.

Berry, Wendell. *Sex, Economy, Freedom and Community.* New York: Pantheon, 1993.

Bookless, Dave. "Towards a Theology of Sustainability," in *When Enough Is Enough,* edited by R. J. Berry, 35–49. Nottingham: APOLLOS, 2007.

Bridle, Susan. "No Man's Land: An Interview with Mary Daly." *Enlightenment,* Fall–Winter 1999. http://www.scribd.com/doc/6146237/No-Mans-Land-Mary-Daly-Susan-Bridle.

Burke, Edmund, "Reflections on the Revolution in France" in Iain Hampshire-Monk, ed , *Edmund Burke: Revolutionary Writings,* ed. Iain Hampsher-Monk (Cambridge, UK: Cambridge University Press, 2014), 1-250..

Carlyle, Thomas. *Latterday Pamphlets No. 1: The Present Time.* Project Gutenberg, Ebook 1140, last updated November 30, 2012. http://www.gutenberg.org/ebooks/1140.

Carrington, Damian. "IPCC Officials Admit Mistake over Melting Himalayan Glaciers." *Guardian,* January 20, 2010. http://www.guardian.co.uk/environment/2010/jan/20/ipcc-himalayan-glaciers-mistake.

Cline, William R. *The Economics of Global Warming.* Washington, DC: Institute for International Economics, 1992.

Coase, Ronald H. "The Problem of Social Cost." *Journal of Law and Economics* 3 (October 1960): 1–44.

Coleman, D. C., and S. Pollard. "Introduction: The Industrial Revolution." In *A Survey of English Economic History,* edited by M. W. Thomas. London: Blackie and Son, 1957.

Common, Michael, and Sigrid Stagl. *Ecological Economics: An Introduction.* Cambridge: Cambridge University Press, 2005.

Cook, John, et al. "Quantifying the Consensus on Anthropogenic Global Warming in the Scientific Literature." *Environmental Research Letters* 8 (2013). doi:10.1088/1748–9326/8/2/024024.

Cox, Michael, Gwen Arnold, and Sergio Villamayor Tomás. "A Review of Design Principles for Community-Based Natural Resource Management." *Ecology and Society* 15, no. 4 (2010): 38–56. http://www.ecologyandsociety.org/vol15/iss4/art38/.

Daly, Herman E., and John B. Cobb Jr. *For the Common Good: Redirecting the Economy towards Community, the Environment and a Sustainable Future.* London: Green Print, 1990.

Daly, Mary. *Gyn/ecology.* Boston: Beacon, 1978.

Davis, Steven J., and Ken Caldeira. "Consumption-Based Accounting of CO2 Emissions." *Proceedings of the National Academy of Sciences of the United States of America* 107, no. 12 (March 8, 2010). doi:10.1073/pnas.09069174107. http://www.ncbi.nlm.nih.gov/pmc/articles/PMC2851800/.

Deane-Drummond, Celia. *Eco-Theology.* London: Darton, Longman and Todd, 2008.

Deane, Phyllis. *The First Industrial Revolution.* Cambridge: Cambridge University Press, 1965.

Delingpole, James. "Climategate: the Final Nail in the Coffin of 'Anthropogenic Global Warming.'" *Telegraph*, November 20, 2009. http://blogs.telegraph.co.uk/news/jamesdelingpole/100017393/climategate-the-final-nail-in-the-coffin-of-anthropocentric-global-warming/.

Dorling, Danny. *Population 10 Billion: The Coming Demographic Crisis and How to Survive It.* London: Constable, 2013.

Downs, Antony. *An Economic Theory of Democracy.* New York: Harper and Row, 1957.

Dresner, Simon. *The Principles of Sustainability.* 2nd ed. London: Earthscan, 2008.

Drèze, Jean, and Amartya Sen. *India: Development and Participation.* 2nd ed. Oxford: Oxford University Press, 2002.

Ehrlich, Paul. *The Population Bomb.* New York: Ballantine, 1968.

Ehrlich, Paul R., and Anne H. Ehrlich. *The Population Explosion.* New York: Simon and Schuster, 1991.

Elkington, John. *Cannibals with Forks: Triple Bottom Line of 21st Century Business.* Monkato: Capstone, 1997.

Eller, Cynthia. *The Myth of the Matriarchal Prehistory: Why an Invented Past Won't Give Women a Future.* Boston: Beacon, 2001.

Emmerich, Susan Drake. "The *Declaration* in Practice: Missionary Earth-Keeping." In Berry, *Care of Creation*, 147–54.

Engels, Frederick. *The Origin of the Family, Private Property and the State.* 4th ed. Translated by Ernest Untermann. Chicago: Charles H. Kerr, 1908. First published in 1891.

Eriksson, Ralf, and Jan Otto Anderson. *Elements of Ecological Economics.* London: Routledge, 2010.

European Commission, Enterprise and Industry. "Corporate Social Responsibility (CSR)." http://ec.europa.eu/enterprise/policies/sustainable-business/corporate-social-responsibility/index_en.htm.

European Environment Agency. *SC Opinion on Greenhouse Gas Accounting in Relation to Bioenergy,* 15 September 2011.

Fellner, William. *Probability and Profit.* Homewood, IL: R. D. Irwin, 1965.

Festinger, Leon. *The Theory of Cognitive Dissonance.* Stanford, CA: Stanford University Press, 1957.

FitzRoy, Felix R., and Elissaios Papyrakis. *An Introduction to Climate Change Economics and Policy.* London: Earthscan, 2010.

Fletcher, Joseph. *Situation Ethics: The New Morality.* London: SCM, 1966.

Forrester, Duncan B. *Christian Justice and Public Policy*. Cambridge: Cambridge University Press, 1997.

Frank, Thomas. "Obama and 'Regulatory Capture.'" *Wall Street Journal*, June 24, 2009. http://online.wsj.com/article/SB124580461065744913.html.

Galbraith, John K. *The Affluent Society*. 2nd ed. Boston: Houghton Mifflin, 1969.

———. *The New Industrial State*. 2nd ed. Boston: Houghton Mifflin, 1972.

Gardiner, Stephen M. "A Core Precautionary Principle." *Journal of Political Philosophy* 14, no. 1 (2006): 33–60.

Gaud, William S. "The Green Revolution: Accomplishments and Apprehensions." Address before the Society for International Development, Washington, DC, March 8, 1968. http://www.agbioworld.org/biotech-info/topics/borlaug/borlaug-green.html.

Gilles, Justin. "Climate Change Seen Posing Risks to Food Supplies." *New York Times*, November 1, 2013. http://www.nytimes.com/2013/11/02/science/earth/science-panel-warns-of-risks-to-food-supply-from-climate-change.html.

Goettner-Abendroth, Heide. "Modern Matriarchal Studies: Definitions, Scope and Topicality." Translated by Jutta Ried and Karen P. Smith. Societies of Peace, 2nd World Congress on Matriarchal Studies. http://www.second-congress-matriarchal-studies.com/goettnerabendroth.html.

Goodin, Robert E. "Selling Environmental Indulgences." *Kyklos* 47 (1994): 573–96. Reprinted in *Climate Ethics: Essential Readings*, edited by Stephen Gardiner, Simon Caney, Dale Jamieson, and Henry Shue (New York: Oxford University Press, 2010), 231–46.

Gorringe, Timothy J. "On Building an Ark: The Global Emergency and the Limits of Moral Exhortation." *Studies in Christian Ethics* 24, no. 1 (2011): 31.

Gowdy, John, and Jon D. Erickson. "The Approach of Ecological Economics." *Cambridge Journal of Economics* 29, no. 2 (2005): 207–22.

Greenpeace International. "The Trash Vortex." http://www.greenpeace.org/international/en/campaigns/oceans/pollution/trash-vortex/.

Grey, William. "Anthropocentrism and Deep Ecology." *Australasian Journal of Philosophy* 71, no. 4 (1993): 463–475.

Hardin, Garrett. "The Tragedy of the Commons." *Science* 162 (December 1968): 1243–48.

Harding, Sandra. *The Science Question in Feminism.* Ithaca, NY: Cornell University Press, 1986.

———. "Why Physics Is a Bad Model for Physics." In *The End of Science? Attack and Defense*, edited by Richard Q. Elvee. Lanham, MD: University Press of America, 1992.

Harrod, Roy. "The Scope and Method of Economics." *Economic Journal* 48 (1938): 383–412.

Harsanyi, John C. *Essays on Ethics, Social Behavior and Scientific Explanation.* Dordrecht: D. Reidel, 1976.

———. "Morality and the Theory of Rational Behavior." In Sen and Williams, *Utilitarianism and Beyond*, 39–62.

Hausfather, Zeke. "What's Behind the 'Good News' Declines in U.S. CO2 Emissions?" *Yale Climate Connections*, May 29, 2013. http://www.yaleclimatemediaforum.org/2013/05/whats-behind-the-good-news-declines-in-u-s-co2-emissions/.

Hawkins, Ed. "Recent Slowdown in Global Surface Temperature Rise." *Climate Lab Book*, National Centre for Atmospheric Science, July 25, 2013. http://www.climate-lab-book.ac.uk/2013/recent-slowdown/.

Hay, Donald A. "Responding to Climate Change: How Should We Discount the Future?" In *Creation in Crisis: Christian Perspectives on Sustainability*, edited by Robert S. White, 53–66. London: SPCK, 2009.

————. "Sustainable Economics." In *When Enough Is Enough: A Christian Framework for Environmental Sustainability*, ed. R. J. Berry. Nottingham: APOLLOS, 2007.

Helm, Dieter. *The Carbon Crunch: How We're Getting Climate Change Wrong—and How to Fix It*. New Haven: Yale University Press, 2012.

Henderson, David. *Misguided Virtue: False Notions of Corporate Responsibility*. London: Institute of Economic Affairs, 2001.

Henson, Robert. *The Rough Guide to Climate Change*. 3rd ed. London: Rough Guides, 2011.

Holman, Zoe. "Plastic Debris Reaches Southern Ocean." *Guardian*, September 27, 2012. http://www.guardian.co.uk/environment/2012/sep/27/plastic-debris-southern-ocean-pristine.

House of Commons, Select Committee on Science and Technology. *The Disclosure of Climate Data from the Climatic Research Unit at the University of East Anglia*, Eighth Report of Session 2009-10, March 31, 2010 (London: Stationery Office, 2010), 47.

Hunter, James Davison. *To Change the World: The Irony, Tragedy and Possibility of Christianity in the Late Modern World*. New York: Oxford University Press, 2010.

Hutcheson, Frances. *Inquiry into the Original of our Ideas of Beauty and Virtue Treatise II*. 2nd ed. London: Printed for J & J Knapton, 1729.

Intergovernmental Panel on Climate Change. "IPCC, 2013: Summary for Policy Makers." In *Climate Change 2013: the Physical Science Basis. Contribution of Working Group I to the Fifth Assessment Report of the Intergovernmental Panel on Climate Change*, ed. T. F. Stocker et al. Cambridge: Cambridge University Press, 2013.

————. *Third Assessment Report: Climate Change 2001, Summary for Policymakers*. Cambridge: Cambridge University Press for the IPCC, 2011. http://www.grida.no/climate/ipcc_tar/wg1/pdf/WG1_TAR-FRONT.pdf.

International Energy Agency. *Key World Energy Statistics.* Paris: OECD/IEA, 2012.

Jevons, W. S. *The Coal Question: An Inquiry Concerning the Progress of the Nation, and the Probable Exhaustion of Our Coal Mines.* London: Macmillan, 1865.

Jones-Lee, M. W., M. Hammerton, and P. R. Phillips. "The Value of Safety: Results of a National Sample Survey." *Economic Journal* 95 (March 1985): 49–72.

Kahneman, Daniel. *Thinking, Fast and Slow.* London: Penguin, 2012.

Kaldor, Nicholas. "Welfare Comparisons of Economics and Interpersonal Comparisons of Utility." *Economic Journal* 49 (1939): 549–52.

Kant, Immanuel. *Groundwork of the Metaphysic of Morals.* Translated by H. J. Paton. New York: Harper and Row, 1964.

Keller, Evelyn Fox. *Reflections on Gender and Science.* New Haven: Yale University Press, 1985.

Knight, Frank H. *Risk, Uncertainty and Profit.* Boston: Houghton Mifflin Company, 1921.

Kuhn, Steven. "Prisoner's Dilemma." In *The Stanford Encyclopedia of Philosophy*, edited by Edward N. Zalta. Fall 2014 edition. http://plato.stanford.edu/archives/fall2014/entries/prisoner-dilemma.

Lawn, Philip A. "A Theoretical Foundation to Support the Index of Sustainable Economic Welfare (ISEW), Genuine Progress Indicator (GPI), and Other Related Indexes." *Ecological Economics* 44, no. 1 (2003): 105–18.

Lawson, Nigel. *An Appeal to Reason: A Cool Look at Global Warming.* 2nd ed. London: Duckworth Overlook, 2009.

Layard, Richard. *Happiness: Lessons from a New Science.* 2nd ed. New York: Penguin, 2011.

Leadbeater, Charles. "Welcome to the Knowledge Economy." In *Tomorrow's Politics: The Third Way and Beyond*, edited by Ian Hargreaves and Ian Christie. London: Demos, 1998.

Lomborg, Bjorn. *Cool It: The Skeptical Environmentalist's Guide to Global Warming*. 2nd ed. New York: Vintage, 2010.

Lovelock, James. *Gaia: A New Look at Life on Earth*. Oxford: Oxford University Press, 1979.

Lukács, Georg. *History and Class Consciousness*. Translated by Rodney Livingstone. London: Merlin, 1971.

Malthus, Thomas Robert. *An Essay on the Principle of Population As It Affects the Future Improvement of Society with Remarks On the Speculations of Mr. Godwin, M. Condorcet and Other Writers*. London: Printed for J. Johnston in St Paul's Churchyard, 1798.

Mann, Michael E., Raymond S. Bradley, and Malcolm K. Hughes. "Northern Hemisphere Temperatures during the Past Millennium: Inferences, Uncertainties and Limitations." *Geophysical Research Letters* 26, no. 6 (1999): 759–62. doi: 10.1029/1999GL900070.

Marglin, Stephen. "The Opportunity Costs of Public Investment." *Quarterly Journal of Economics* 77 (May 1963): 274–89.

———. "The Social Rate of Discount and the Optimal Rate of Saving." *Quarterly Journal of Economics* 77 (February 1963): 95–111.

Markandya, Anil, Patrice Harou, Lorenzo Giovanni Bellù, and Vito Cistulli. *Environmental Economics for Sustainable Growth: A Handbook for Practitioners*. Northampton, MA: Edward Elgar, 2002.

Marx, Karl. *Capital*. Vol. 1, *A Critical Analysis of Capitalist Production*, edited by Frederick Engels. London: Lawrence and Wishart, 1974.

———. *Capital*. Vol. 3, *A Critique of Political Economy*. London: Lawrence and Wishart, 1972.

Marx, Karl, and Frederick Engels. *The German Ideology*. Edited and with introduction by C. J. Arthur. London: Lawrence and Wishart, 1974.

McCarthy, James J. "Climate Science and Its Distortion and Denial by the Misinformation Industry." In *Creation in Crisis: Christian Perspectives on Sustainability*, ed. Robert S. White, 34–52. London: SPCK, 2009.

McFague, Sallie. *The Body of God: An Ecological Theology*. Minneapolis: Fortress Press, 1993.

———. *A New Climate for Theology*. Minneapolis: Fortress Press, 2008.

McIntyre, Stephen, and Ross McKitrick. "Hockey Sticks, Principal Components, and Spurious Significance." *Geophysical Research Letters* 32, no. 3 (2005). doi: 10.1029/2004GL021750.

Mehta, Judith, and Rathin Roy. "The Collective Action Problem." In *Making the International: Economic Interdependence and the Political Order*, edited by Simon Bromley, Maureen Mackintosh, William Brown, and Marc Wuyts. London: Pluto Press in association with the Open University, 2004.

Merchant, Carolyn. *The Death of Nature: Women, Ecology and the Scientific Revolution*. San Francisco: Harper and Row, 1980.

Meteorological Office. *The Recent Pause in Warming, Paper 1: Observing Changes in the Climate System*. July 2013. http://www.metoffice.gov.uk/research/news/recent-pause-in-warming.

Michael Common and Sigrid Stagl. *Ecological Economics: An Introduction*. Cambridge: Cambridge University Press, 2005.

Mill, John S. *On Liberty*. 4th ed. London: Longman, Roberts and Green, 1869.

———. *Utilitarianism*. 7th ed. London: Longman, Green, 1879.

Morgan, Lewis H. *Ancient Society, or Researches in the Lines of Human Progress from Savagery through Barbarism to Civilization*. Chicago: Charles H. Kerr, 1877.

Naess, Arne. *Ecology, Community and Lifestyle: Outline of an Ecosophy*. Translated by David Rothenberg. Cambridge: Cambridge University Press, 1989.

———. "The Shallow and the Deep, Long Range Ecology Movements." *Inquiry* 16 (1973): 95–100.

National Center for Environmental Economics. "Frequently Asked Questions on Mortality Risk Evaluation." United States Environmental Protection Agency, last updated September 8, 2014. http://yosemite.epa.gov/ee/epa/eed.nsf/webpages/mortalityriskvaluation.html.

Niskanen, W. A. *Bureaucracy and Representative Government.* Chicago: Aldine Atherton, 1971.

Nordhaus, William D. *Managing the Global Commons.* Cambridge, MA: MIT Press, 1994.

———. "To Slow or Not to Slow: The Economics of the Greenhouse Effect." *Economic Journal* 101 (1991): 920–37.

Northcott, Michael S. "Anthropogenic Climate Change, Political Liberalism and the Communion of Saints." *Studies in Christian Ethics* 24, no. 1 (2011): 42.

———. *The Environment and Christian Ethics.* Cambridge: Cambridge University Press, 1996.

———. *A Moral Climate: The Ethics of Global Warming.* London: Darton, Longman and Todd, 2007.

———. *A Political Theology of Climate Change.* London: SPCK, 2014.

Oregon State University. "Garbage Patch' not Nearly as Big as Portrayed in the Media." *Oregon State University News and Research Communications,* January 4, 2011. http://oregonstate.edu/ua/ncs/archives/2011/jan/oceanic-%E2%80%9Cgarbage-patch%E2%80%9D-not-nearly-big-portrayed-media.

Ostrom, Elinor. "Beyond Markets and States: Polycentric Governance of Complex Economic Systems." *American Economic Review* 100 (June 2010): 1–33.

———. *Governing the Commons: The Evolution of Institutions for Collective Action.* Cambridge: Cambridge University Press, 1990.

Ostrom, Elinor, with contributions by Christina Chang, Mark Pennington, and Vlad Tarko. *The Future of the Commons: Beyond Market Failure and Government Regulation.* London: Institute of Economic Affairs, 2012.

Palmer, Lisa. "Preachable Moments: Evangelical Christians and Climate Change." Yale Climate Connections, June 28, 2012. http://www.yaleclimatemediaforum.org/2012/06/preachable-moments-evangelical-christians-and-climate-change/.

Pareto, Vilfredo. *Manual of Political Economy.* Translated by Ann M. Schweier. Edited by Ann S. Schweier and Alfred N. Page. New York: A. M. Kelley, 1971.

Pearce, David W. *Cost-Benefit Analysis.* 2nd ed. London: Macmillan, 1983.

Pearce, David W., and R. Kerry Turner, *Economics of Natural Resources and the Environment.* New York: Harvester Wheatsheaf, 1990.

Perry, Mark. "Julian Simon: Still More Right than Lucky in 2013." *Carpe Diem,* American Enterprise Institute, January 12, 2013. http://www.aei-ideas.org/2013/01/julian-simon-still-more-right-than-lucky-in-2013/.

Pew Research, Religion & Public Life Project, "Religious Groups' Views on Global Warming," April 16 2009.

Philipkoski, Kirsten. "Scientists: Bush Distorts Science." *Wired Insider,* February 18, 2004. http://www.wired.com/medtech/health/news/2004/02/62339.

Pigou, A. C. *The Economics of Welfare.* 4th ed. London: Macmillan, 1946.

Ramsey, F. P. "A Mathematical Theory of Saving." *Economic Journal* 38 (December 1928): 543–59.

Rand, Stephen. "Love Your Neighbor as Yourself." In Berry, *Care of Creation,* 140–46.

Rao, Vikram. *Shale Gas: The Promise and the Peril.* Research Triangle Park, NC: RTI International, 2012.

Ravallion, Martin, Shaohua Chen, and Prem Sangraula. "Dollar a Day Revisited." *World Bank Economic Review* 23, no. 2 (2009): 163–85.

Rawls, John. *A Theory of Justice*. Cambridge, MA: Harvard University Press, 1971.

Rawls, John. *A Theory of Justice*. Rev. ed. Cambridge, MA: Harvard University Press, 1999.

Royal Society. *Climate Change: A Summary of the Science*. London: Royal Society, 2010.

Ruether, Rosemary Radford. *Gaia and God: An Ecofeminist Theology of Earth Healing*. San Francisco: HarperCollins, 1992.

———. *Integrating Ecofeminism, Globalization and World Religions*. Lanham, MD: Rowman and Littlefield , 2005.

Sabin, Paul. *The Bet: Paul Ehrlich, Julian Simon and Our Gamble over Earth's Future*. New Haven: Yale University Press, 2013.

Sandel, Michael. *Reith Lectures 2009: A New Citizenship*. Transcript produced by the British Broadcasting Corporation. London: British Broadcasting Corporation, 2009.

Sandel, Michael. *What Money Can't Buy: The Moral Limits of Markets*. London: Allen Lane, 2012.

Schiller, Ben. "Is It Time to Overhaul Europe's Carbon Trading Scheme?" *Yale Environment 360*, April 28, 2011. http://e360.yale.edu/feature/europes_co2_trading_scheme_is_it_time_for_a_major_overhaul/2396/.

Schmalensee, Richard, Paul L. Joskow, A. Denny Ellerman, Juan Pablo Montero, and Elizabeth M. Bailey. "An Interim Evaluation of Sulfur Dioxide Emissions Trading." *Journal of Economic Perspectives* 12, no. 3 (Summer 1998): 53–68.

Sen, Amartya. *Development as Freedom*. New York: Knopf, 1999.

———. *The Idea of Justice*. London: Allen Lane, 2009.

———. "Utilitarianism and Welfarism." *Journal of Philosophy* 76, no. 9 (1979): 463–89.

Sen, Amartya, and Bernard Williams, eds. *Utilitarianism and Beyond*. London: Cambridge University Press, 1982.

Shiva, Vandana. *Staying Alive: Women, Ecology and Development*. London: Zed, 1989.

Shukman, David. "The Receding Threat from 'Peak Oil.'" *BBC News: Science and Environment*, July 15, 2013. http://www.bbc.co.uk/news/science-environment-23280894.

Singer, Peter. *Animal Liberation: A New Ethics for Our Treatment of Animals*. New York: New York Review, 1975.

Sleigh, Charlotte, and Bryony Webb. *God's Green Book: Seven Bible Studies about the Environment*. London: SPCK, 2010.

Smith, N., and A. Leiserowitz. "American Evangelicals and Global Warming." *Global Environmental Change* 23, no. 5 (2013): 1009–17. http://dx.doi.org/10.1016/j.gloenvcha.2013.04.001.

Smith, Stephen. *Environmental Economics: A Very Short Introduction*. Oxford: Oxford University Press, 2011.

Spash, Clive L. "The New Environmental Pragmatists, Pluralism and Sustainability." *Environmental Values* 18 (2009): 253-256.

Stavins, Robert N. "What Can We Learn from the Grand Policy Experiment? Lessons from SO2 Allowances Trading." *Journal of Economic Perspectives* 12, no. 3 (Summer 1998): 69–88.

Stern, Nicholas. *The Economics of Climate Change: The Stern Review*. Cambridge: Cambridge University Press, 2007.

Steuart, Sir James. *An Inquiry into the Principles of Political Oeconomy*. Vol. 2. Dublin: Printed for James William in Skinner Row, and Richard Moncreiff, in Caple Street, 1767.

Stigler, George. "The Theory of Economic Regulation." *Bell Journal of Economics and Management Science*, 2, no. 1 (Spring 1971): 3–21.

Struthers, John, and Alistair Young. "Economics of Voting: Theories and Evidence." *Journal of Economic Studies* 16, no. 5 (1989): 1–42.

Sunstein, Cass R. *Laws of Fear: Beyond the Precautionary Principle*. Cambridge: Cambridge University Press, 2005.

Taylor, D. J. *Orwell: The Life*. London: Vintage, 2004.

Tierney, John. "Betting on the Planet." *New York Times Magazine*, December 2, 1990. http://www.nytimes.com/1990/12/02/magazine/betting-on-the-planet.html.

Tietenberg, Tom. *Environmental and Natural Resource Economics*. 6th ed. Boston: Addison Wesley, 2003.

Titmuss, Richard. *The Gift Relationship: From Human Blood to Social Policy*. London: George Allen and Unwin, 1970.

Tol, Richard S. J. "The Economic Effects of Climate Change." *Journal of Economic Perspectives* 23, no. 2 (Spring 2009): 29–51.

Turner, R. Kerry, David Pearce, and Ian Bateman. *Environmental Economics: An Elementary Introduction*. New York: Harvester Wheatsheaf, 1994.

UN Department of Economic and Social Affairs. *International Decade for Action: 'Water for Life' 2005–2015*. http://www.un.org/waterforlifedecade/scarcity/shtml.

———. *World Population Prospects, the 2012 Revision*. New York: United Nations, 2013. http://esa.un.org/unpd/wpp/index.htm.

UN Food and Agriculture Organization, Water Development and Management Unit. "Hot Issues: Water Scarcity." 2013. http://www.fao.org/nr/water/issues/scarcity.html.

Union of Concerned Scientists. *Scientific Integrity in Policymaking: The Bush Administration's Misuse of Science*. Cambridge, MA: Union of Concerned Scientists, 2004.

———. *Smoke, Mirrors and Hot Air: How ExxonMobil Uses Big Tobacco Tactics to Manufacture Uncertainty on Climate Science*. Cambridge, MA: Union of Concerned Scientists, 2007.

US Environmental Protection Agency. "Global Greenhouse Gas Emissions Data." Last updated September 9, 2013. http://www.epa.gov/climatechange/ghgemissions/global.html.

US Global Climate Change Research Program. *Global Climate Change Impacts in the United States, 2009 Report.* New York: Cambridge University Press, 2009. http://www.globalchange.gov/usimpacts.

Veblen, Thorstein. *The Theory of the Leisure Class.* London: Macmillan, 1899.

Viscusi, W. Kip, and Joseph E. Aldy. "The Value of a Statistical Life: A Critical Review of Market Estimates throughout the World." *Journal of Risk and Uncertainty* 27 (2003): 5–76.

Weber, Max. *Economy and Society.* 2 vols. Edited by G. Roth and C. Wittich. Berkeley: University of California Press, 1978. This work was originally published posthumously in Germany in 1922.

White, Lynn, Jr. "The Historical Roots of Our Ecologic Crisis." *Science* 155 (March 10, 1967): 1203–7. Reprinted in *The Care of Creation: Focusing Concern and Action*, ed. R. J. Berry (Downers Grove, IL: Inter-Varsity Press, 2000), 31–42.

Whyte, Jamie. *Quack Policy: Abusing Science in the Cause of Paternalism.* London: Institute of Economic Affairs, 2013.

World Bank, and Food and Agriculture Organization of the United Nations. *The Sunken Billions: The Economic Justification for Fisheries Reform.* Washington, DC: World Bank, 2009.

Wright, Richard T. "The Declaration under Siege." In Berry, *Care of Creation*, 74–79.

Yergin, Daniel. *The Quest: Energy, Security and the Remaking of the Modern World.* London: Allen Lane, 2011.

Index of Names and Subjects